MEASURING MARKET RISK WITH VALUE AT RISK

WILEY SERIES IN FINANCIAL ENGINEERING

Risk Management and Analysis, Volume 1: Measuring and Modeling Financial Risk
Carol Alexander, Editor

Risk Management and Analysis, Volume 2: New Markets and Products
Carol Alexander, Editor

Implementing Value-at-Risk
Phillip Best

Derivatives Demystified: Using Structured Financial Products
John C. Braddock

Option Pricing Models
Les Clewlow and Chris Strickland

Derivatives for Decision Makers: Strategic Management Issues
George Crawford and Bidyut Sen

Currency Derivatives: Pricing Theory, Exotic Options, and Hedging Applications
David F. DeRosa

Options on Foreign Exchange, Revised Edition
David F. DeRosa

The Handbook of Equity Derivatives, Revised Edition
Jack Francis, William Toy, and J. Gregg Whittaker

Measuring Market Risk with Value at Risk
Pietro Penza and Vipul K. Bansal

Interest-Rate Option Models: Understanding, Analyzing, and Using Models for Exotic Interest-Rate Options
Ricardo Rebonato

Volatility and Correlation
Ricardo Rebonato

Derivatives Handbook: Risk Management and Control
Robert J. Schwartz and Clifford W. Smith, Jr.

Dynamic Hedging: Managing Vanilla and Exotic Options
Nassim Taleb

Credit Derivatives: A Guide to Instruments and Applications
Janet Tavakoli

Pricing Financial Instruments: The Finite Difference Method
Domingo Tavella and Curt Randall

MEASURING MARKET RISK WITH VALUE AT RISK

PIETRO PENZA
VIPUL K. BANSAL

John Wiley & Sons, Inc.

New York • Chichester • Weinheim • Brisbane • Singapore • Toronto

To our mothers
and
in memory of our fathers

The authors wish to offer their sincere thanks to Dr. John F. Marshall for his encouragement and guidance. He provided invaluable help, which made this publication possible. We would also like to thank our families for their unflagging support, love, and understanding.

Published by John Wiley & Sons, Inc.
Published simultaneously in Canada.

This publication is designed to provide accurate and authoritative information in regard to the subject matter covered. It is sold with the understanding that the publisher is not engaged in rendering professional services. If professional advice or other expert assistance is required, the services of a competent professional person should be sought.

Library of Congress Cataloging-in-Publication Data:

Penza, Pietro.
   Measuring market risk with value at risk / Pietro Penza, Vipul K. Bansal.
      p. cm. — (Wiley series in financial engineering)
   Includes bibliographical references and index.
   ISBN 0-471-39313-4 (cloth : alk. paper)
    1. Financial futures. 2. Risk management. I. Bansal, Vipul K. II. Title.
   III. Series.
   HG6024.3 .P46 2000
   332.1′2′0681—dc21   00-038207

Printed in the United States of America.

10 9 8 7 6 5 4 3 2 1

Foreword

All businesses are exposed to risks. These include market risks, credit risks, and a variety of operational risks. For many businesses, market risk is the dominant risk. Even for those businesses where another form of risk is the dominant risk, market risk is likely to loom large.

Early efforts to manage market risks were based largely on simple intuition. In an earlier era, when businesses were much less complex than they are today, this may have been adequate. But as the complexity and size of businesses have grown, measuring and managing market risks has demanded an ever-greater reliance on science—often coupled with the intuition that stems from experience.

The importance of risk measurement and risk management to the modern business enterprise should not be under appreciated. Over the past decade, a number of leading institutions have succumbed to market risk and others have been seriously damaged. Certain failures, because of their size, stand out. These include the well-publicized losses at Barings Bank, Daiwa Securities, California's Orange County, Sumitomo Bank, Long Term Capital Management, and the like. But, for every one of these headline grabbers, there are literally hundreds of smaller businesses that have failed due to market risk. Because of their smaller size, they pass away largely unnoticed by the financial press, but no less noticed by their owners, their employees, their creditors, their customers, and their vendors.

The globalization of the markets that has transformed world commerce over the past several decades has amplified most businesses' exposure to market risks for at least three reasons. First, to compete globally, a business must operate on a larger scale to drive down per unit costs. Second, global competition puts pressure on profit margins. To maintain or improve their return on equity, business enterprises will often increase their use of leverage. Third, the very act of entering the global marketplace exposes the enterprise to a set of market risks (i.e., exchange rate risks), that do not exist in a closed economy. While consumers are the principal beneficiaries of globalization, that very globalization presents a business and its stakeholders with a greater survival challenge. The larger scale of operation, the increasing use of leverage, and the need to deal in multiple currencies dramatically increase an enterprise's exposure to market risks. To meet this challenge, risk management methodologies have gotten ever more sophisticated, relying more on scientific approaches to risk measurement and management. This involves the development of better risk management tools—both theoretical and physical. The theoretical tools involve such things as financial theory, statistical theory, mathematical theory, and so forth. The physical tools involve instruments that can be used to manage market risks, particularly the derivative financial instruments such as futures, forwards, swaps, and options. These are the tools of the modern financial risk manager—a subset of a broader group of financial professionals that make up the financial engineering community.

I have spent my entire professional life as, simultaneously, both an academician and as a practicing financial engineer. As an academician, I wear two hats: researcher and teacher. As a researcher, I have tried to stay current with new theoretical developments. I have tried to distinguish between those ideas that had lasting value and those that were built on erroneous foundations or were otherwise just passing curiosities. All the while, I was trying to contribute to the former while avoiding the latter. As a teacher, I have tried to explain both to my students and my professional colleagues the theory and the practice of modern finance, with much of that effort devoted to derivatives and their applications. As a practicing financial engineer, I have structured financial transactions, evaluated trading regimes, run several trading operations, advised clients on risk management strategies, and so forth. In the course of all of this, I have watched with interest the development of value at risk (VaR) as a tool for both measuring and managing market risk and I have witnessed the rapid evolution of new VaR methodologies.

Over the past few years, a number of books on value at risk have appeared. Each of these attempted to convey the state of knowledge at the time. Some did it well, and some not so well. This book, *Measuring Market Risk with Value at Risk* by Vipul Bansal and Pietro Penza, has three advantages over earlier works on the subject. First, it takes a decidedly global approach—an essential ingredient for any comprehensive work on market risk. Second, it ties the scientifically grounded, yet intuitively appealing, VaR measure to earlier, more idiosyncratic, measures of market risk that are used in specific market environs (e.g., duration in fixed income). Finally, it encompasses all of the accepted approaches to calculating a VaR measure and presents them in a clearly explained fashion with supporting illustrations and completely worked out examples.

Measuring Market Risk with Value at Risk is an insightful and instructive work that resulted from a rare collaboration between a well-regarded academic and an experienced practitioner. These sorts of collaborations are ideal. They result in pedagogically sound works that also have practical importance. I have known and I have had the privilege of working with Dr. Bansal for about 11 years. In 1991, together with Robert Schwartz, we founded the International Association of Financial Engineers. It was largely from the membership of this organization that the elements of VaR arose. About the same time, Dr. Bansal and I authored one of the pioneering texts on financial engineering which, to our surprise and pleasure, is still in print today. I am convinced that *Measuring Market Risk with Value at Risk* will have at least as long a run and will make an equally important contribution.

JOHN F. MARSHALL, PhD
Principal, Marshall, Tucker & Associates, LLC

Contents

CHAPTER 4: A SIMPLE INTRODUCTION TO VALUE AT RISK   61

CHAPTER 5: MEASURING PRICES AND RETURNS   87

CHAPTER 6: STATISTICS FOR PRICES AND RETURNS   105

Global Banking Industry

The world of commercial banking is undergoing a deep transformation as a result of marketable instruments competing with loans and demand deposits. Because of this strong competition, commercial banks are struggling to make acceptable margins from their traditional business entering into investment banking.

Increasing competition has forced banks to search for more income at the expense of more risk. Banks that lent heavily to Asia in search of better returns than those available in Western markets are now being blamed for bad credit decisions. The Asian crisis has renewed interest on credit risk management casting doubts on the effectiveness of current credit regulations. Technological changes have also heightened competition by making it easier to imitate bank services. The traditional advantage of physical proximity to clients given by extended networks of branches has vanished. Banks have to compete with money market mutual funds for deposit business, commercial papers, and medium-term notes for bank loans.

As margins are squeezed, commercial banks in the United States and Europe have been forced to cut costs and branches while diversifying into pensions, insurance, asset management, and investment banking. In the United States, many banks call themselves financial service companies even in their reported financial statements. Diversification, however, has not always proved to be an effective strategy, and many banks have had to revert to a concentrated business. These examples illustrate how commercial banks are reinventing themselves, not just once but many times. All these changes are creating an identity crisis for old-fashioned bankers, leading to the key question, "What is a bank today?" The question is difficult, but evidence suggests that the concept of banking is being modified and the traditional barriers among financial service subindustries (retail banking, private banking, investment banking, asset management, insurance, etc.) are vanishing.

Illustrating what an entity does or serves for often is a useful way to define it. The identity crisis of banks—especially commercial banks—

stems from the deep and rapid changes in their traditional body of activities (particularly retail and corporate banking). On the other hand, investment banking, private banking, and *bancassurance* are the most profitable and fastest growing segments of the financial service industry. As banks undertake new activities, they also incur new risks. Since boundaries among subindustries are weakening, if not vanishing, banks—like all other financial service companies—must redefine themselves in terms of the products they offer and the customers they serve. The way banks pursue this redefinition is through a strategic repositioning in the financial service industry. All these factors represent a new challenge for commercial banks, provided this definition still has a unique meaning. Increased competition, diversification, new products, and new geographic markets mean that both the spectrum of risks and the risk profile for banks are dramatically changing. Not only have the risk parameters broadened, they have also changed: banks now face unfamiliar types of risk. In addition to the traditional credit risk, financial risk[1] has risen and is now playing a crucial role. Banks thus need integrated risk management techniques that can measure and manage market risk in a timely and effective manner. In this chapter, we briefly review the main trends that are affecting the global banking industry, underlining the effects of each of these changes on the risk profile of banks.

DEFINING A BANK

The scenario commercial banks face today differs greatly from that of the past. Diversification among subindustries is defining an environment where banks compete with other financial-service companies to provide mutually exclusive products and services to the same customers. Traditional branch banking is under the threat of new competitors and technological innovation, leading some analysts to wonder whether banks are dying.[2] Most likely what is dying is the old-fashioned concept of the bank and a new scenario is emerging.

Banks are changing as economic markets integrate, providing opportunities for diversification. Only 15 to 20 years ago, most Western banks generated 90% of revenue from interest income. Now this percentage has fallen to 60%, sometimes as low as 40%. New sources of income, such as fee-based income from investment services and derivatives,[3] are becoming increasingly relevant for the income statements of commercial banks. During the same period, the pattern of banking activities has changed through interactions with the developing security markets. The well-known phenomenon of disintermediation that has taken place in all Western countries since the 1970s has progressively reduced the monopoly of banks over the collection of savings from customers. This has created much tougher competition among financial service companies and has forced banks to find new and diversified sources of income.

The traditional core business of commercial banks has been retail and corporate banking. As retail and corporate banking become less and less profitable, banks are diversifying into new businesses to stop the decline of profits. Investment banking, for example, is estimated to be worth US$14 million, with an annual growth rate of about 14% up to 2010. Derivative-based earnings for larger commercial banks now account for about 15 to 20% of the total earnings.[4] The drawback is that volatility of earnings has dramatically increased. The management of these new types of risk—typically, market risk and credit risk on traded assets—requires competence and expertise. Hence, the risk profile of commercial banks is changing as a consequence of diversification.

Capital markets are playing a key role in defining the bank of the twenty-first century, but they are also making banks riskier. In fact, with a few exceptions, AAA ratings for banks have disappeared and consequently the importance of market risk management is being emphasized. Future competition will not be played in the classic retail banking industry that, at least in continental Europe (but not in the United Kingdom), is only slightly profitable. Global competition will take place in asset management and investment banking. Not casually, huge U.S. investment banks are merging among themselves and with asset management firms. Alliances and takeovers are occurring also on a transatlantic basis, confirming the global characters of these two subindustries (the most related to global capital markets). The following trends are affecting the banking industry and most likely will shape the competition in the next several years:

- The market share for financial services that banks hold is declining, while securities firms, mutual funds, and finance companies are getting a growing share of available customers. In the United States, the share of total assets held by banks and other depository institutions relative to all financial intermediaries fell from 56% in 1982 to 42% in 1991, and this downward tendency is likely to continue.[5] Banks will face growing competition from financial service companies and nonbank firms.
- Disintermediation is making traditional banking less and less necessary, leading to consolidation. The natural shrinkage of the market share held by commercial banks started this process in the past decade, but it has dramatically accelerated in the past few years because of global competition.

- To remain competitive, commercial banks will have to exploit new sources of income:
    Offering new services (selling mutual funds or insurance policies).
    Charging customers with noninterest fees.
    Offering new services through the phone and the web.
    Entering into joint ventures with independent companies.
    Entering new geographic markets yielding higher returns.
- Banks will need more expertise to manage new sources of risk. Market risk management models must become an integral part of a bank's risk management culture.

THE FALL OF RETAIL BANKING[6]

Retail banking, the most traditional business of commercial banks, is where margins are being progressively squeezed by new competitors. Until the beginning of the 1990s, nearly every country had a domestic retail banking sector that was separate from its neighbors and was dominated by a handful of established banks.[7] The core asset of banks were extensive branch networks, each branch being equal to all the others, with a manager, front-end people, and huge back-offices. At least up to the advent of e-banking.

The pace of dramatic change for retail banking varies from country to country, but common trends are emerging:

- The focus of banking is shifting from transactions management toward sales of financial products. As banks merge, they are increasingly centralizing and streamlining their processes.
- Barriers to entry for the retail banking segment are being lowered, allowing competitors from other industries to come in and try innovative approaches mainly with a massive use of technological delivery channels.
- The growing variety of delivery channels for banking enables new entrants to thrive.

The two main forces changing the competitive environment in retail banking are technological change and aggressive new competitors:

1. Technological change is creating huge problems for traditional banks with extended and costly branch networks. The major technological issues affecting the retail banking business are the rise of telephone banking and the impressive diffusion of the Web-based

banking. These innovations make branch networks less important and national boundaries irrelevant. Computer banking, either through the Internet or proprietary networks, is gaining a growing and growing importance.

2. New unrelated competitors are entering the retail banking market. In the United Kingdom, the country's two biggest retailers, Sainsbury's and Tesco, have gone into partnership with the Bank of Scotland and the Royal Bank of Scotland, respectively.[8] Sainsbury's Bank offers a savings account, two credit cards, and personal loans and mortgages, with more services to follow. Tesco Personal Finance offers only a savings account and a credit card, but aims to expand its range.

These trends do not indicate that traditional branch banking is going to die, but that the competitive scenario is changing. High-street banks have expensive branch networks and relatively outdated procedures, with far greater operating costs than their new, more flexible rivals.[9] Despite growing competition, retail banking can still generate remarkable profits—at least in the United Kingdom.[10] So high have been the returns that a number of U.K. banks experienced that they have sold their investment-banking arms to direct more attention toward this lucrative sector. This strategy (known as specialization) is proving effective for those banks that decide to specialize.

Nevertheless, the general trend is that the retail banking industry, rather than being the dominant business of commercial banks, will become a specialized niche as the core business of a few high-street banks. Global banks will offer retail banking service and products in the context of a wide spectrum of services and products from other banking businesses.

PRIVATE BANKING

One of the most interesting trends affecting the banking industry is the development of domestic private banking services. These services, once provided only to aristocrats, are gaining popularity and seem to be an attractive, fast-growing market. Retail banks are no longer targeting only the super rich, who hold a small proportion of the total wealth, but also people with, relatively speaking, high income.[11] Private banking is basically an asset management service and represents a natural area for banks in time of margin squeezing and increased competition.[12] Risks of adverse market movements are transferred, at least partially, to customers, while banks increase their fee-based income. Nevertheless, commercial banks must be aware of actual and potential competitors including traditional private banks, investment banks, converted building societies, and insurers. Private banking creates opportunities for commercial banks, but also adds new problems in the following areas:

- Bank organization.[13]
- Culture needed to manage private banking.[14]
- Risk management.

For our purposes, the most important aspect is the effect of private banking on risk assessment and management of commercial banks. As banks diversify while entering the private banking market, they must manage new types of risk. Since private banking is basically an asset management service, the importance of financial risk management becomes overwhelming. As international financial markets integrate, banks need effective financial risk measurement and management techniques on a global basis. They must define their asset allocation according to their own and their customers' risk/return ratios, set limits to control losses, and set aside reserves to cover potential losses. That is why financial risk management is becoming a key issue for modern bank management.

GLOBAL INVESTMENT BANKING

Investment banking is by far the most globalized segment of the financial service industries. Commercial banks today are starting to offer investment-banking and merchant banking services to larger corporations, thus entering in direct competition with prestigious investment houses.[15] These services include:

- Identifying possible merger targets.
- Financing acquisitions of other companies.
- Dealing in customers' securities (i.e., security underwritings).
- Providing strategic advice.
- Offering hedging services against market risk.

To provide customers with a broader spectrum of services, commercial banks in search of globalization are boosting takeovers of investment banks. All the major competitors have developed, or are in the process of developing, facilities in the world's leading markets. The aim is to provide multinational corporations with a broad range of financial service products, including conventional investment banking such as merger and acquisition (M&A) advice, market trading, financial lending and fund management, at both the institutional and retail levels. Relationship banking is replacing transaction-based banking: What is important is to increase the loyalty of the client to the bank, almost irrespectively of the service needed or required.

Diversification is not the whole story. To face the rising costs and squeezing margins created by competition, investment banks need partners with large amounts of available capital.[16] Investment banks have been taking bigger risks in search of higher returns. This policy has taken two distinct forms. One has been to increase the riskiness of their existing businesses. This can happen, for example, when an equity dealer underwrites the whole lot, thus taking the full risk of adverse market movements. The other form is *proprietary trading*. It means that investment bank desks operate like in-house hedge funds, and hedge funding is renounced as being one of the riskiest financial businesses.

Proprietary trading also increases the need for capital to cope with unavoidable trading losses, and favors consolidation between investment and commercial banks, which are much better capitalized.[17] Consolidation and the undertaking of riskier operations emphasize the need for effective risk management techniques to measure the risk incurred by aggressive desks in their operations. Commercial banks that have swallowed investment banks must learn how to manage the new risks they are taking on.

RECENT TRENDS IN THE GLOBAL BANKING INDUSTRY

The global banking industry has been undergoing deep transformation. The following trends can be outlined:

- The technological breakthrough caused by the eruption of e-banking and e-finance.
- Worldwide consolidation and consequent restructuring.
- Increasing competition in terms of both markets (geographic diversification) and products.
- "Contamination" among different industries, thanks to a progressive relaxation of regulations and huge interindustry acquisitions.
- A slowing population growth and increasing average life expectancy and per capita income. Since Western governments need to cut expenditures for old-age benefits to keep deficits under control, there will be an increase in the importance of private pensions, mutual funds, and private banking operations.

- The growing importance of a clear strategic intent in the banking industry. Banks, especially commercial banks, will be obliged to rethink their strategic positioning. While some banks are opting to offer a vast variety of products/services on a global scale, others are focusing on some specific market segment (retail banking, private banking, corporate banking) or specific geographic area.
- New competitors are entering the financial service business. In the retail banking industry, large department stores in the United Kingdom have entered the market for personal and mortgage loans, primarily to retain their customers.

These trends are having and will have a major impact on banks' and financial institutions' risk management process. Contamination also means that firms in the different subindustries will face risks that were once specific to another subindustry. The relaxation of the *Glass-Steagall Act* in the United States, and similar processes of deregulation in many other leading countries, are forcing even commercial banks to dedicate growing attention to market risk management and liquidity risk management, in addition to the more traditional credit risk and interest rate risk.

CONSOLIDATION

One of the most important trends affecting the financial service industry is consolidation. The U.S. market saw a merger boom in 1996; in Europe the same process culminated in 1997, with the merger between the Swiss banks UBS and SBC creating one of the largest banks in the world. The first months of 1998 saw the creation of the world's largest financial group—Citigroup—formed by the merger between Citibank and Travelers.

This trend is likely to continue, at least for the foreseeable future.[18] Consolidations take place for the following reasons:

- To take advantage of economies of scale. These are *horizontal mergers or acquisitions* (e.g., two or more institutions of the same type merge).
- To have access to distribution channels. This is referred to as *interindustry consolidation.* For example, large insurance companies often seek a fast way to access a widespread network of points of sales, such as bank branches, through which they can sell their products.
- To widen the range of products that the bank can offer both actual and potential clients. This process is known as *contamination* and can be achieved by entering into a new market. For example, the

acquisitions of investment banks by commercial banks are aimed at widening the services offered by the parent bank through its business units (they may also be, and often are, legal entities separate from the acquiring bank). Entering into a new market through an acquisition is often much easier than starting a new business from scratch.

- To enter a new geographic market. This type of consolidation is known as *international diversification.* For a foreign commercial bank, any national market has significant barriers to entry, because it is difficult to establish an efficient and effective network of branches in foreign countries in a limited period. Most often, acquiring a domestic bank is the only feasible way to access that market. In addition, foreign banks face regulatory limitations in many countries. When allowed, acquiring a domestic bank is a way to circumvent these regulations.

HORIZONTAL CONSOLIDATION

The horizontal consolidation boom started in 1996 in the United States, and "merger mania" boomed in 1997 in Europe, where banks were used to play on a domestic/international scale rather than on a global scale. The forces driving consolidation in European banking are overcapacity, deregulation, relaxation of domestic protectionism, and increased competition driven by the single currency started on January 1, 1999.

Commercial banks pursue horizontal consolidation to reach critical mass in terms of the financial resources, skill, and geographic diversification needed for competing on a global scale. The forces driving commercial banks are the search for more profitable businesses and the need for efficiency, obtained by lower costs per transaction and by the elimination of overlapping branches and activities. Traditional services (e.g., retail and corporate banking) are now only slightly profitable, while the ongoing disintermediation and the need for economy of scale to spread high overhead costs are forcing commercial banks to increase size.

No single model defines the ideal bank of the future, but it is generally agreed that size will be a source of competitive advantage. As a general rule, the bigger the bank, the lower the per unit transaction cost ratio. Not surprisingly, profits are higher where the banking industry is concentrated; overcapacity is a major problem for European banks.[19] Greater size permits banks to afford the huge costs of technological improvements and justifies acquiring banks with specific skills and products in countries where the acquiring bank is weak. At the moment it seems that a dominant position in the domestic market is still a prerequisite for being a major player, at least, on a European scale. Table 1.1 reports the results of a study by Morgan Stanley[20] showing the percentage of total assets in the banking system owned by the top five banks in selected European countries.

Both in Europe and North America, banks have pursued horizontal consolidation primarily on a domestic basis.[21] It is quite obvious that the European banking industry will continue its process of consolidation. But, with few exceptions, consolidation in the commercial banking sector will likely be national in character. The most important exception is the acquisition of Bankers' Trust by Deutsche Bank in 1999, that created the largest bank in the world in terms of total assets.

Cross-border mergers, with all the problems involved even on a regional scale, have not yet taken place. Nevertheless, the adoption of a single European currency is likely to promote a massive wave of cross-border M&As in the financial service industry in Europe. It is similar to the consolidation that took place in the United States at the beginning of the twentieth century. Furthermore, the rise of the single currency will likely favor cross-border transactions aimed at creating a true pan-European bank, but this seems pursued more through joint ventures or strategic alliances rather than through mergers or acquisitions. At the moment, massive transatlantic mergers still seem to come. Investment banking is probably the subindustry that has seen the most impressive process of consolidation in the past few years, with four American houses at the top.[22] The most global business in the financial-service industry, investment banking is also where consolidation is most likely to lead to economies of scale big enough to exclude smaller competitors from the market. A particular kind of consolidation is taking place between

TABLE 1.1   Concentration in the Banking Industry in Some European Countries (C5 Index)

Country	Percentage
Sweden	86
Holland	81
Finland	74
United Kingdom	57
France	47
Italy	29
Germany	17

Source: Peter Lee, "Eurogigantism," Euromoney, Feb. 1998.

insurance companies and commercial banks. This phenomenon, known as *bancassurance,* sees insurance companies buying small banks, or being bought by large commercial banks, to realize a synergy in their distribution channels. Banks widen the spectrum of their products and services, while insurance companies find this is an easy and attractive way to distribute their products.[23]

CONTAMINATION—THE RISE OF GLOBAL PLAYERS

Consolidation is also taking place also on an interindustry basis. By interindustry consolidation, we mean M&As taking place between firms of different subindustries in the financial service industry (e.g., insurance companies acquiring commercial banks or commercial banks acquiring investment banks). There can be cost-saving potential, particularly in computer systems. But complexity explodes. Top managers have to handle a far more complicated business; front-line service staff have to sell a richer mix of products.

Integrated banking—or one-stop shopping, as it is known—is not new, but it is the ambition of many banks. Many banks have taken actions to ensure capability in all forms of debt, equity, and advisory services. Examples are Bankers Trust's acquisition of Wolfensohn, considered an M&As boutique, and the 1998 takeover of Alex Brown. European commercial banks, on the other hand, have tried to enter the lucrative investment-banking business by acquiring U.S. or British investment banks to provide more services to their clients.[24] Investment banks also have to worry about diversification. Fund-management firms that used to be excellent customers are now powerful competitors. On the other hand, some investment banks have bought or built their own fund managers. Indeed, SBC's merger with UBS has created one such monster. To defend themselves against squeezing revenues, some investment banks have sought higher profits in even riskier operations, but many more have had to merge or find parent companies with large amounts of capital, as previously remarked. In Europe, huge commercial banks and insurers have been ready suppliers of fresh capital for the investment banking industry.

One of the largest and most impressive mergers, between Citibank and Travelers, has originated Citigroup, giving life to one of the largest financial supermarkets in the world. This approach is based on the assumption that the financial service industry is a unique industry. Retail banking, corporate banking, private banking, investment banking, leasing, and mutual and pension funds can be considered segments of the global financial service industry rather than different industries.

The strategic implications of such an approach to the financial service industry is straightforward: banking conglomerates must act as *global players,* offering the whole spectrum of financial services on a global (worldwide) basis.

To be a global player, a banking conglomerate must satisfy three characteristics:

1. *Size.* It must be big enough to play on a global basis.
2. *High degree of contamination.* It must cover the full spectrum of financial products and services.
3. *High degree of geographic diversification.* A significant portion of its assets must be outside its original domestic market.

In Europe, the "global player strategy" has been pursued with a strong commitment only by Deutsche Bank that has not been followed by Dresdner and Commerzbank. Ubs-Sbc and Credit Suisse-Wintherthur both have the structure—in terms of products and services offered and size— to be global players, but they still seem domestic-centered. Only Holland can deploy two global players—ING and ABN Amro—but they probably lack sufficient size.

The key issue is whether mergers can provide synergies, so that two plus two actually make five, and not just four—or even less. Contamination without the necessary skills and competence in the acquired business can lead to negative results.

For our purposes, the most important aspect of this phenomenon is risk management. Global players are subject to all the risks that financial firms can encounter: credit, market, interest rates, liquidity, business and operations, and complexity (i.e., the risk in managing different businesses on a geographically diversified basis).

STRATEGIC REFOCUSING

Although contamination is a major trend affecting the banking industry, many banks that do not have the size, competence, or will to become global players have decided to specialize in well-defined subindustries, relying on their specific skills and competence and efficiency rather than on a variety of products and services. Their intent is to be financial boutiques (not financial supermarkets) targeting specific segments of the financial service industry.

Some European banks, especially some British and Spanish banks, are focusing on previously neglected activities such as retail banking.[25] Although retail banking has a low profile, there will always be a place for "excellent" retail banks.[26] Lloyds TSB considers its focused strategy a key reason for its success.

Also, some institutions in the field of investment banking pursue the strategy of specialization. Although consolidation and diversification seem to be the winning strategies, the supporters of specialization argue that investment bank customers are highly sophisticated and will pick the best provider for each service they buy. The British investment bank BZW, the investment bank arm of Barclays, has been partially sold out in a process of specialization. Without its equities business, BZW has metamorphosed from a big investment bank into a medium-sized one.[27]

Strategic focusing (or refocusing) has affected French banks, too. Many of them have given up their global ambitions to concentrate on the business they are best able to perform. Bad loans, low margins, and increasing costs are forcing French bankers to rethink the way they do business. Banque Indosuez decided to close offices in 15 countries,[28] including commercial banking operations in the United States.[29] As opposed to Barclays, Indosuez's strategy can be regarded as a geographic downsizing rather than a downscoping. Paribas, once one of the top investment banks in Europe, chose to achieve global coverage in certain areas, while pursuing other business streams on a more ad hoc basis.[30] At the end, in 1999, Paribas merged with the retail bank BNP, creating a group in France.

From the risk manager's viewpoint, strategic focusing means that the firm is concentrated on the type of risk typical of the activity undertaken. Focused strategy poses fewer risk management problems than diversified strategy. What is required is excellence: focused firms must be able to manage specific risk better than their diversified competitors.

Managing risk for a globally integrated firm requires integrated risk management, which is much more complex than the mere sum of credit, market, and operational risk. Hence, risk management is a source of competitive advantage. It is becoming a strategic issue that must involve top managers instead of just being a matter for high skilled professionals and researchers.

RISK MANAGEMENT AND STRATEGY

Risk management is becoming a key issue in financial management. The trends outlined, especially in deregulation, globalization, and contamination are making risk management a primary strategic activity for financial firms, rather than a mere support activity. Good risk management creates a key competitive advantage, which also explains the impressive growth in importance of risk managers.

Risk management can have four meanings:

1. In a strict sense, it means only *risk measurement* (e.g., assembling data and identifying and quantifying classes of risk: credit risk, market risk, operational risk).
2. In a broader sense, risk management is intended to be *risk control,* aimed at monitoring the risks run by departments and individuals in the firm.
3. Additional risk control involves supervising the correctness of business units' behavior with respect to firmwide risk management guidelines, and the execution of actions aimed at restoring the denied risk profile.
4. The risk manager provides guidelines for capital allocation within the firm, integrating business performance and risk management with strategic planning.

Thus, risk management includes risk measurement and risk control, and the use of these tools to fine-tune the firm's risk/return ratio.

Risk measurement is the crucial first step. Market risk measurement has reached a high degree of sophistication. Thanks to Value at Risk class models, it is now possible to accurately quantify the maximum probable loss over a given time horizon for a portfolio of financial assets. Many argue that VaR models are able to capture only normal market movements, while risk managers should be able to measure extreme events, too. Regardless of the weaknesses implicit in VaR class models, they are far more sophisticated than credit risk models. The 8% ratio imposed by the Basle Committee proved ineffective in the recent Asian crisis. Nevertheless, capital adequacy requirements have been issued to minimize damages in case of crises, not to better the risk assessment process.

Even the best risk manager cannot prevent the occurrence of dramatic events. Sometimes, they are totally unpredictable. Nevertheless, he or she must implement actions that will limit the impact of such events, should they actually occur. This is basically what risk management units in banks and other financial institutions do, and it is the primary function of risk managers.

A risk manager's second function is to control risk by monitoring it and taking appropriate actions to achieve the desired level. This means that if traders have taken positions that imply more risk than he or she is authorized to take, the risk manager should be able to independently take appropriate actions to reduce that risk. For example, if equity traders are long and the VaR of this portfolio is higher than the maximum-accepted VaR, then risk managers could independently hedge the long equity position by going short in the futures market. Usually, risk managers do not have this power and refer to front-end people themselves to take the suggested actions. Usually, risk managers have more in common with portfolio managers. They rarely have firm-wide power to force traders and portfolio managers to reduce excessive risk.

The third function refers to the cultural role that risk managers should play within a financial service company. Risk managers can—and actually should—help CFOs and CEOs evaluate the performance of business units or individuals on a risk-adjusted basis. Better returns can always be achieved by taking greater risks. Risk managers can and should measure performance on a risk-adjusted basis and communicate these measures to top executives. These measures are largely different from and provide an alternative to traditional accounting performance measures top managers are well acquainted with. This also requires a corporate culture willing to accept and to inculcate the culture of risk management as opposed to the culture of mere performanc evaluation.

The fourth and most significant function of the risk manager is to provide guidelines for effective capital allocation to risk and business areas within the firm. Efficient allocation means the firm's resources will be put at risk in the most efficient way for the optimum quality (in terms of relative risk) of returns. Capital is usually allocated on an undifferentiated basis. That is why banks should develop a "shadow risk-pricing mechanism" to allocate capital with business units on a risk-adjusted basis. This allows for the allocation of capital where it produces the most efficient risk/return combination. Quantifying (i.e., measuring) risk is the prerequisite for allocating capital (deciding which projects to undertake and which not to undertake). The risk management then becomes a business driver.

Risk management is a key factor in the modern financial service industry. Globalization and contamination will strengthen this unavoidable process. That is why it is essential to study risk management in detail and make it an integral part of a bank's managerial concerns.

In this book, we concentrate on market risk management, even though credit risk management still plays an important role in banking management. In Chapter 2, we briefly review the classic approach to financial risk management, asset and liability management. In Chapter 3, we review how regulatory bodies have regulated financial risk to avoid banking crisis. In Chapter 4, we review the fundamentals of Value at Risk and its applications.

NOTES

1. A precise definition of financial risk is provided in Chapter 2. Financial risk includes not only market risk but also other types of risk, such as liquidity and interest-rate risk.

2. Peter Rose, *Commercial Bank Management,* New York: McGraw Hill, 3d ed., 1998, 24.

3. Suzanne Miller, "Commercial Banks: Giants with Nowhere to Hide," *Euromoney*, February 1988.

4. *Ibid.*

5. Peter Rose, *Commercial Bank Management,* New York: McGraw Hill, 3d ed., 1998, 24.

6. The discussion about retail banking is mainly drawn from Rebecca Ream, "The Battle for the High-Street," *Euromoney*, February 1998.

7. For example, in 1980 the big-four high-street banks in the United Kingdom generated almost 70% of the industry's profits. The main exception was the United States, where geography and past regulation meant that no banks operated in every state and that most banks stuck to their traditional strongholds. Rebecca Ream, "The Battle for the High-Street," *Euromoney*, February 1998.

8. These banks have few branches in England while the supermarkets have few outlets in Scotland, so the banks gain access to new markets without cannibalizing their own operations. Rebecca Ream, "The Battle for the High-Street," *Euromoney*, February 1998.

9. An important development has been the move to centralize transaction processing, which reduces paperwork for individual branches and substantially cuts staff numbers and costs. Canadian retail banks have pooled their check-clearing activities and maintenance of their ATMs. Another important response aimed at cutting overhead costs is the reduction in the number of branches. Since 1985, competitive pressure has reduced the number of French banks by half, while Swedish banks have decreased by over 80%. Many countries have liberalized financial regulations, triggering a merger and acquisition spree. British Banks have cut costs by drastically reducing their branches and overhead costs. For example, the number of NatWest branches has fallen to about 1,750 from a peak of around 3,600 in the late 1980s. Rebecca Ream, "The Battle for the High-Street," *Euromoney*, February 1998.

10. The United Kingdom's Lloyds TSB, for example, is the second bank in Europe by market capitalization, with a return on equity (ROE) of 33.5%, thanks largely to its focus on retail banking. "Dine or Be Dinner," *Euromoney*, November 1999, and "Lloyds TSB: A Lesser Quest for Perfection," *Euromoney*, October 1999.

11. Say, more than $200,000 a year.

12. It is estimated in the United Kingdom that 1 million people could be potential targets for private banking services; C. Brown-Humes "The domestic market," *Financial Times,* November 26, 1997.

13. Some commercial banks (such as Lloyds TSB) manage retail and private banking within the same legal entity. Other commercial banks, such as NatWest, prefer to manage private banking through a separate arm.

14. Private banking requires a customer-led culture rather than a product-led culture, typical of traditional retail banking. The focus is on the customer, on how added value can be provided, and on the products and services available in the market rather than just within the bank.

15. Although the Glass-Steagall Act prevented commercial banks from underwriting corporate securities, the Federal Reserve Board has permitted some well-capitalized U.S. banks to underwrite selected stocks and bonds issued by their customers. Banks have also entered into the guarantee market, backing the debt issued by their customers and allowing their customers to raise funds at lower costs. The Glass-Steagall Act has been recently relaxed.

16. For example, fund-management firms used to be excellent customers, relying on investment banks to buy and sell the shares and bonds they invest in and supply research on their investments. But today's fund managers are huge—firms such as AXA of France and

America's Fidelity manage more than $500 billion—and many have invested in their own analysts and traders. Not unreasonably, fund managers are demanding more and more from investment bankers for less and less money.

17. In Europe, huge commercial banks and insurers have been ready suppliers of fresh capital for the industry. Deutsche Bank and Dresdner Bank have both bought British investment banks. ING, a Dutch banking and insurance conglomerate, also has purchased a U.S. investment bank.

18. A simple proportion shows us why consolidation is far from over. In 1997, the United States has more than 9,000 commercial banks. Britain has 212; Canada 53. So if the American banking system were to become as concentrated as Britain's, it would have, at the most, 1,000 banks; if like Canada's, just 500.

19. In Germany there are more than 3,500 different banking institutions.

20. Peter Lee, "Eurogigantism," *Euromoney,* February 1998.

21. For example, UBS and SBC in Switzerland and the merger between Bayerische Vereisbank and Hypobank in Germany.

22. Merrill Lynch, Goldman Sachs, the recently merged Salomon Smith Barney, and Morgan Stanley-Dean Witter Discover (also newly merged).

23. A recent example is the merger between Credit Suisse and the insurance company Wintherthur.

24. Examples are the acquisition of Morgan Grenfell by Deutsche Bank and Kleinwort Benson by Dresdner Bank; and ING's takeover of Barings after the well-known Leeson's crash.

25. Barclays seems to have decided to focus on old-fashioned retail banking, having sold its equity investment banking to Credit First Suisse Boston, and is planning to put retail banking back at the forefront of its operations. Lloyds TSB has never deviated from the domestic retail banking path. The German Dresdner bank, one of the largest in Germany, and still among the largest in the world in terms of total assets, has refocused its strategy on its core banking business by selling stakes in industrial companies.

26. "Commercial Banks: Giants with Nowhere to Hide," *Euromoney,* February 1998.

27. Barclays Capital (this is the new name of the company) is an excellent example of strategic refocusing pursued by downsizing and downscoping.

28. Jonathan Ford, "Breaking the Foreign Taboo," *Euromoney,* March 1996.

29. As a matter of fact, Banque Indosuez implicitly admitted to not being able to compete with the global players like the Anglo-German investment banks in London or the U.S. investment banks. Indosuez chose a reduced focus: to become the leading integrated investment bank in France, the Middle East, and Asia. Indosuez has limited its markets to those regions of the world where it already has a strong presence, abandoning its ambition to be a global player in investment banking. Jonathan Ford, *ibid.*

30. Since the main business stream for Paribas has been fixed income, Paribas intends to be a global player in treasury bonds, with a presence as a primary dealer in all the major markets. The equity business will be focused almost exclusively toward Europe. Jonathan Ford, *ibid.*

2

Risk Management Approaches in Banking Activity

Financial institutions—not only banks—increasingly recognize that financial risk management is a natural, core business of financial institutions. In fact, effective risk management systems can lead capital to a more effective (on a risk-adjusted basis) capital allocation and eventually to above-average profits. The 1990s have seen an escalating debate over risk management practice, especially financial risk management. This increase is basically due to the rapid proliferation of derivative contracts, both in type and number. This has created a need for accurate risk measurement techniques to cope with the risk across different positions. The growing demand for more accurate risk measurement techniques has led to the partial displacement of older but simpler approaches in favor of more complex models.

In this chapter, we briefly review the techniques most often used by banks and financial institutions to measure and manage financial risk, particularly interest rate risk. When compared with Value at Risk (VaR) models, these approaches can seem simple. Nevertheless, they still work well if the asset portfolio is highly unsecured and/or the trading portfolio is small compared with total assets. Since this was the situation of most Western commercial banks until the late 1980s or early 1990s, they were well able to do the job they had been created for. Basically, they captured and measured the impact of changes in interest rates on the banks' bottom line, by measuring the sensitivity of assets and liabilities to interest rate changes.

The chapter is organized to first classify the risks that banks face in their activity with special attention to the two most important kinds of risk: credit risk and financial risk. Then, we analyze in detail the risk-management process and its desirable characteristics. Finally, we briefly describe the basic features of the approach used most for managing interest rate risk (commonly known as asset and liability management, or A&LM) outlining the reasons that are leading to more complex and integrated models aimed at measuring financial risk.

TYPES OF RISK IN BANKING ACTIVITY

Banks, like all financial intermediaries, are among the most important actors in capital allocation, transferring funds from units with excess savings (typically, households) to units that need capital for their investments (typically firms).

Banks (and other financial intermediaries) do not act solely as brokers, connecting lenders and borrowers, but take positions for their own account. Lenders and borrowers differ greatly and, as a consequence, have different needs. On the one hand, lenders (depositors) usually deposit limited amounts of money, whereas borrowers usually require huge sums of capital for their investments. On the other hand, deposits are usually short-term, whereas loans granted to firms are often long-term.

The quintessence of banking activities is to transform maturities to fit the needs of lenders and borrowers and to manage the risk associated with the intermediation of funds. If we try to classify the risk incurred by banks (and financial institutions) in their activity, we first face a problem of taxonomy. Even in specialized literature, there is confusion about what is meant by each category of risk. It is beyond our scope to find a comprehensive classification of risks incurred by banks. We simply try to use a consistent terminology: once we define a term, we maintain that meaning throughout the book.

Traditionally, banks have faced two kinds of risk:

1. Risk of default in repaying the loans (often referred to as credit risk).
2. Risk of not being able to return deposits when requested (often referred to as liquidity risk).[1]

Figure 2.1 summarizes the main types of risk affecting banks' activities.

In the past two decades, the types of risk that banks[2] face have dramatically increased. This growth stems from the deep changes that have occurred in the financial industry and in the operations of banks where financial risk management is becoming more and more important. Based on Figure 2.1, we can define the most important types of risk a bank faces:[3]

- *Credit risk.* Risk of the loss arising from the failure of the counterpart to make the promised payment (i.e., the failure to honor and meet its legal obligation). Credit risk can occur on unsecured loans, on bonds/notes, and on derivatives not traded in organized exchanges (typically swaps, forwards, and other over-the-counter (OTC) derivatives).
- *Market risk.* Risk of losses sustained as a result of changes in the value of traded or tradable assets. This risk is due to changes in the prices of market factors[4] and is sometimes referred to as *price risk.*
- *Interest rate risk.* Risk[5] that assets will yield a lower return or liabilities will be more expensive because of a change in interest rates. This risk applies only to interest-sensitive assets and interest-sensitive liabilities and directly affects the margin of interest and, hence, the annual reported earnings.
- *Liquidity risk.* Risk of loss arising either from the inability either to make payments or to refinance obligations. When referred to negotiable instruments, liquidity risk is the risk of loss incurred due to a lack of potential buyers when the instrument is sold.
- *Legal risk.* Risk of loss arising from nonenforceability of contracts and/or breach of regulatory requirements.
- *Operational risk.* Risk of loss from a broad range of risks including processing failure and system failure.

FIGURE 2.1 Classification of Risks in Banking Activity

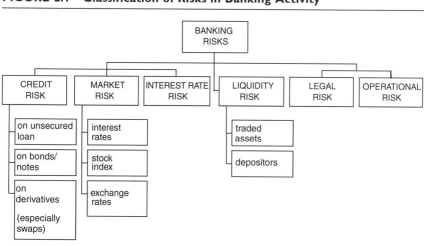

Financial risk usually refers to the whole spectrum of risks incurred with financial assets: market risk, interest rate risk, and liquidity risk.

Banks, like all other enterprises, are subject to *business risk*. Business risk is an industry-related risk; for banks it includes the risk of deep changes in the organization of markets, in the preferences of savers, in the regulatory framework, and in the whole banking-related business environment.

Market risk is increasing in importance in the context of banking management. Its growth stems from four basic factors:

1. The undergoing process of securitization that has caused the substitution of traditional forms of assets (typically, unsecured loans) with financial assets having a secondary market and, hence, a market price. Securitization has favored the adoption of marking-to-market techniques, making possible an immediate tracking of profits and losses on a portfolio of traded instruments.

2. The growing complexity of financial instruments (especially derivative instruments) commonly negotiated by banks. This change has underscored the need to replace traditional risk measurement techniques[6] with an integrated measure of risk. This measure is intended to be the cornerstone of an integrated and homogeneous financial risk management framework.

3. The increased volatility that interest rates, foreign exchanges, and stock prices experienced during the past 20 to 25 years, especially after the collapse of the gold-exchange standard in 1973. In addition, the globalization of financial markets has increased the volatility of market factors. This volatility is, at least partially, responsible for the crises that some financial institutions incurred during the late 1980s.

4. The increase in trading activities of banks and the resulting volatility of income.

Table 2.1 summarizes the main sources of risk (sometimes referred to as *volatility drivers*[7]) for the whole spectrum of banking activity.

Generally speaking, some elements of risk management will be highly quantitative because the risk can be represented with numbers generated by quantitative models that use probability theory and arbitrage/equilibrium-pricing theory. Some types of risk may not be easily quantified or may require qualitative or comparative types of measurement and control.[8] The growing importance of market risk has led regulators to include market risk among the main sources of risk for banks and financial intermediaries, and they have issued capital-adequacy requirements for market risks, not only credit risk. It is important to underline

TABLE 2.1 Risk Drivers in Banking Activities

Business	Type of Risk
Private banking/asset management	Credit risk (on loans to private clients) Market risk (change in the values of clients' portfolios)
Retail banking	Credit risk Interest rate risk
Foreign exchange trading	Market risk
Investment banking: securities/derivatives trading	Market risk (on positions held) Credit risk (mainly on derivatives)
Investment banking: corporate finance	Credit risk (loans to corporate clients) Market risk (on primary positions)

that risk taking for a bank is now more diverse than it was 20 years ago. It encompasses traditional forms of risk taking and increased trading in other asset classes. This change reflects the diversification of financial institutions that encompass activities in all asset classes (debt, currency, and equity) and in business ranging from balance-sheet activities to off-balance-sheet activities (underwriting and securities distributions) to pure fee-based activities (investment management, custody services, cash-management services, etc). This range of risks is forcing banks to adopt new techniques for managing risk in an integrated and transparent framework and to measure risk-adjusted returns that enable more accurate evaluation of performance and a more efficient allocation of capital between business units and types of activities.

THE RISK MANAGEMENT PROCESS

Risk management in this context is a complex and multidimensional process, with many actors at stake, each having a different perspective and objective. There is often a surprising confusion between the concept of risk management and the capital structure of a financial firm (especially a bank): it is often assumed that being well capitalized means undertaking sound risk management practices. This is anything but true: it is only when good risk management breaks down and the problem becomes unmanageable that reliance on insurance in the form of equity (or subordinated loans) capital comes into play. Therefore, capital by itself is not a substitute for adequate risk management. Capital, per se, means little if not coupled with effective risk management. Eventually, it acts like a backstop or last-ditch defense.

Risk management practices have at least two aspects:

1. The internal point of view.
2. The regulatory point of view.

The internal point of view refers to the consideration of risk management as a core business practice for banks and financial institutions. Under this approach, risk management is needed even in the absence of any regulatory burden in the same way manufacturing firms manage their production lines or their distribution systems. Regulators have a different standpoint: their objective is to prevent a single firm's (a bank) failure from becoming a crash of the whole banking system. If a bank fails, it is a problem for its depositors; if many banks fail, it is a problem for the whole economy.

A limited number of failures can, paradoxically, be a good event for the financial industry, indicating that competition is wiping out of the market firms that perform poorly or are inefficient. In general, the inspections and checks that regulators carry out on regulated firms are not only to check statutory compliance with rules and restrictions but also to investigate the adequacy of internal controls and, therein, the whole risk management process. Among more progressive regulators, indications that a firm is well controlled lead to less intensive and less frequent investigation by the regulator and thus a lighter regulatory burden.

The risk management process can be summarized in the following two steps:

1. Identifying the types of risk to face and their possible sources, and measuring (when possible) the exposure to each of these sources.
2. Foreseeing probable future evolution of risk sources and setting up rules aimed at limiting the impacts of such negative events.

Therefore, risk management is a two-stage process. The *first stage* is about identifying risk within the business process and, if possible, quantifying its magnitude and sources. The *second stage* is about setting limits and parameters into which the risk is constrained and controlled, to meet the goals of the business with a sensible and considered risk profile. So to be successful in risk management, it is important not only to identify and measure but also to limit and control. In looking at a firm's risk management, a regulator will, therefore, view how a firm and its management use its internal controls to achieve these twin aspects of risk management.

As with any control structure, quality-control mechanisms, such as feedback loops and spot checks, can ensure that the system is functioning properly and can enable the timely detection of errors.

FINANCIAL RISK MANAGEMENT: MAIN CHARACTERISTICS

Financial risk management can be considered as one of the more complete areas of the risk management framework, in terms of both qualitative and quantitative standards and techniques. The basic risk management necessity here is to identify the sources of risk that a bank is exposed to and to analyze how that risk profile may evolve over time in terms of profit and loss variations. This makes it possible to ascertain that potential profit and loss variations are within the framework of the organization's aspirations in terms of risk and return, overall financial stability, and longevity.

Financial risk management relies heavily on quantitative techniques (especially statistical and econometric techniques) to describe the behavior of financial markets. This aspect is usually referred to as financial modeling. As shown in Chapter 5, financial modeling plays a key role in assessing financial risks. Data are the cornerstone of this financial risk management operation, especially for marking-to-market the portfolios under examination. The whole process therefore relies on the quality and adequacy of the data that are fed into the quantitative aspects of the market risk management process. The reliance of data and the computational power of financial risk management software play an important role. The most satisfying approach to Value at Risk is based on numerical simulation (described in Chapter 3), which requires the generation of an incredibly high number of different scenarios to derive the profit-and-loss distribution of the portfolio under examination.

Generally speaking, market risk management involves a series of five distinct steps:[9]

1. Collecting all the transactions.
2. Aggregating transactions to form a portfolio of similar transactions.
3. Decomposing the portfolio into the underlying risk factors. This entails the breakdown of each instrument into its pure risk components.
4. Valuation of the decomposed portfolio using current prices and rates for relevant risk factors to estimate the earnings of the portfolio.

5. Risk measurement, by repricing the portfolio using a set of simulated market prices and rates. This is the essence of the class of models that includes VaR models.

Traditionally, banks have devoted much of their attention to the credit risk on unsecured loans, focusing on the creditworthiness of clients and on credit-collection techniques and procedures. For several decades, credit risk on loans meant risk *tout court.* The first attempts to measure and manage financial risks, and particularly, interest-rate risk, gave way to a broad class of model, known under the general name of *asset and liability management* (A&LM).

The main objectives of A&LM models were:

- To measure the exposure of a bank's portfolio to interest-rate changes.
- To measure the impact on profit (the bottom line) of a change in interest rates.
- To identify a strategy for hedging a portfolio of assets and liabilities against interest-rate changes.

In the next sections, we briefly review the main concepts of A&LM, and then we turn to Value at Risk and its innovative approach for measuring market risk.

THE TRADITIONAL APPROACH TO MANAGING FINANCIAL RISK: ASSET AND LIABILITY MANAGEMENT

Asset and liability management techniques go back to the mid 1970s when the increasing volatility of market rates favored the adoption of new and more adequate techniques for the strategic management and operations of financial intermediaries (particularly banks). Asset and liability management generally refers to a set of methodologies aimed at identifying, measuring, and controlling the risk associated with balance-sheet and off-balance-sheet positions, and at favoring an integrated management of these same positions. The final objective is to maximize risk-adjusted shareholders' value.

Traditionally, A&LM techniques have been divided into two broad categories:

1. Strategic A&LM.
2. Operational A&LM.

Strategic A&LM techniques include all asset and liability categories of both the banking and the trading book. People who speak of A&LM usually mean strategic A&LM. Operational A&LM (also called portfolio risk management) is a set of tools for identifying, measuring, and evaluating financial risk with the final objective of supporting, in real time, the decision process on short-term trading negotiations.

Although A&LM was intended to be a complex system of tools and techniques for managing different types of risk, it has tended to focus on interest rate risk management since it is usually easily measurable and manageable (given the high number of instruments suited for interest rate hedging). To better understand the differences between VaR and other more traditional approaches, it is useful to briefly look at the main approaches to A&LM and their most important characteristics.

The most used A&LM approaches (almost exclusively aimed at interest rate risk) are:

- The current earnings approach.
- The economic value approach.
- the dynamic simulation approach.

We also review the Basle Committee approach to financial risk and the sensitivity analysis approach.

The Current Earnings Approach

Under the *current earnings* approach, the target variable is given by current earnings. Changes of interest rates affect directly the interest margin (the difference between interest received and paid) and, therefore, earnings. In addition, changes in interest rates affect the market value of instruments subject to trading. When these instruments are negotiated, the net effect can be a profit or loss and consequently can add to or subtract from current earnings.

Some simplifying assumptions are needed to make this approach workable:

- Exposure to risk is calculated as it is at the time the analysis is performed (static analysis).
- The analysis is performed for a time horizon of about 12 months.
- A unique shock on interest rates, taking place at the time of the analysis, is taken into account.
- The reinvestment rate is the prevailing rate after the shock has occurred.

The objective of this approach is to estimate the risk pending on the portion of the margin of interest, given the asset and liability structure at the time the analysis is performed and to derive indexes of net exposure to interest rate risk. In the context of the current earnings approach, the most used technique is the *gap analysis.*

Under this approach, all the assets and liabilities that mature or reprice within the time horizon are explicitly taken into account in terms of the associated cash flows. We refer to these assets and liabilities as *RSA* (*rate-sensitive assets*) and *RSL* (*rate-sensitive liabilities*), respectively. We define *GAP* as the difference between *RSA* and *RSL:*

$$GAP = RSA - RSL \qquad (2.1)$$

The expected variation of the margin of interest for a given change Δi is given by

$$E(\Delta IM) = RSA * \Delta i - RSL * \Delta i \qquad (2.2)$$

For example, if a bank has *RSA* equal to $100m and *RSL* equal to $80m, the expected impact on the margin of interest of a change of interest rates equal to 1% is given by

$$E(\Delta IM) = \$100m * 0.01 - \$80m * 0.01 = \$200,000 \qquad (2.3)$$

From Equation 2.1, we can derive that having *RSA* = *RSL* immunizes a bank against interest rate risk. A good hedging strategy would then be to have a *GAP* equal to zero. On the other hand, a bank will benefit from a positive gap if interest rates are expected to rise and will be exposed to interest rate risk if interest rates are expected to fall. The reverse is true if *GAP* < 0.

The main drawback of this technique is that the gap is calculated by a crude difference between *RSA* and *RSL,* irrespective of the exact time when assets and liabilities mature or reprice. This drawback can be limited by clustering the cash flows generated by assets and liabilities into maturity "buckets": time intervals where assets and liabilities mature or reprice. The underlying hypothesis is that all assets and liabilities reprice at the midpoint of each bucket. For the k-th bucket, Equation 2.1 then becomes

$$E(\Delta IM_k) = \frac{(RSA_k - RSL_k) * \Delta i * T_k}{365} \qquad (2.4)$$

where T_k is the number of days from the midpoint of the k-th bucket to the end of the time horizon.

The total impact on the margin of interest is given by

$$E(\Delta IM) = \Sigma_k E(\Delta MI_k) \qquad (2.5)$$

The analysis can be refined down to where time buckets are taken to be equal to one day only.

The Market Value Approach

The *market value* approach is aimed at measuring the market value of the bank, by defining a new target variable given by the difference between financial assets and financial liabilities. It does not take into account tangible assets. The market value is defined as

$$W = FA - FL \qquad (2.6)$$

where W is the market value of the bank; FA represents the current price of financial assets and FL the current price of financial liabilities. If we consider only fixed-rate assets and liabilities, duration can be used to measure the exposure of W to interest rate risk.[10] For a change in interest rate equal to Δi, the price change for a fixed-rate asset is equal to

$$\Delta P = -D^* * P * \Delta i \qquad (2.7)$$

where D^* is the modified duration. Henceforth, the market value change for the bank can be expressed as in Equation 2.8:

$$\Delta W = \Sigma_k(-D_{k\,A}^* * VA_k * \Delta i) - \Sigma_j(-D_{j\,L}^* * VL_j * \Delta i) \qquad (2.8)$$

where VA_k is the current price of the k-th asset in the portfolio, and $D_{k\,A}^*$ is the modified duration for the k-th asset.

If we assume a parallel shift of the yield curve, Equation 2.8 becomes

$$\Delta W = \left[\Sigma_k(-D_{k\,A}^* * VA_k) - \Sigma_j(-D_{j\,L}^* * VL_j)\right] * \Delta i \qquad (2.9)$$

Given that the duration of a portfolio is just the weighted average of the durations of single assets and liabilities included in the portfolio, Equation 2.9 becomes

$$\Delta W \cong \left(D^*_A * VA - D_j^*{}_L * VL_j \right) * \Delta i \qquad\qquad (2.10)$$

or, in an even simpler way,

$$\Delta W \cong D^*_w * W * \Delta i \qquad\qquad (2.11)$$

where

$$D^*_w = \frac{\left(D^*_A * VA - D^*_L * VL \right)}{W}$$

D^*_w can be either positive or negative. If D^*_w is positive, the market value of net worth increases as interest rates fall; if D^*_w is negative, the market value of the bank decreases as interest rates fall.

The estimation error is due to *convexity;* this means that the higher the Δi, the higher the error associated with Equation 2.11. The error is somewhat lower than it would be in the case of a portfolio of assets or liabilities alone because the presence of both assets and liabilities creates a "compensation effect." The error on one side is at least partially offset by an error equivalent in magnitude but different in sign.

The condition for hedging against interest rate risk is that

$$D^*_w = \frac{\left(D^*_A * VA - D^*_L * VL \right)}{W} = 0 \qquad => \qquad (2.12)$$

$$D^*_A * VA = D^*_L * VL$$

Equation 2.12 can be transformed into

$$D^*_w = \frac{\left(D^*_A * (W + VL) - D^*_L * VL_j \right)}{W} = 0 \qquad =>$$

$$\frac{\left(D^*_A * W \right)}{W} + \frac{\left(D_A{}^* - D^*_L \right) * VL}{W} \qquad => \qquad (2.13)$$

$$D^*_A + \left(D_A{}^* - D_L{}^* \right) * Lev = 0$$

where *Lev* is the leverage ratio (Debt/Equity at market values). If $D_A{}^* > D_L{}^*$, D^*_w grows as the leverage ratio increases. If $D_A{}^* > D_L{}^*$, reducing *Lev* is an effective way for reducing D^*_w and, hence, the exposure to interest rate risk.

The Sensitivity Analysis Approach

The *sensitivity analysis* approach is similar to the *market value* approach. Sensitivity analysis measures interest rate risk on the basis of "earnings at risk": the amount of future potential losses caused by an interest rate movement. We define as *interest rate position sensitivity* (IRPS) the difference between the market value of all assets and liabilities (on and off balance), determined by discounting future cash flows by current market rates, and the present value of all assets and liabilities, assuming a change (no limitation on the type of change) in the yield curve. Therefore we define as *interest rate exposure* (IRE)

$$IRE = VAs - VA \qquad (2.14)$$

where *VAs* is the present value of assets and liabilities after the change in interest rates, and *VA* is the present value of assets and liabilities before the change in interest rates. An advantage of this approach is that it does not require the use of duration, while conveying the same basic results. An important plus is that it allows for a nonparallel shift in the yield curve.

The linkage between the sensitivity analysis approach and the market value approach is given by the concept of *present value of a basis point* (pvbp): the price change of an asset or liability due to a change of 1 basis point (0.01%). The relation between interest rate exposure, pvbp, and duration is given by the equation

$$\Delta VA = VAs - VA = 100 * \text{pvbp} = \frac{-D^* * VA}{100} \qquad (2.15)$$

in the case of a shift of 100 basis points in the yield curve.

The Basle Committee Approach for Interest Rate Risk

The measurement scheme for interest rate risk proposed by the Basle Committee in 1993 unifies the current earnings approach and the market value approach.

Its main characteristics are:

- The definition of standardized maturity buckets where *RSA* or *RSL* mature or reprice.
- The definition of a system of weights for each bucket. These weights are an estimate of duration for each bucket, adjusted to take into account the differences in volatility of rates along the yield curve.

Duration is calculated on the basis of a theoretical bond maturing at the mean point of each bucket, assuming a market rate of 8% and a coupon rate of 8%. This proposal is quite simplifying, although easy to apply. There is a general tendency to consider it more suited for regulatory purposes than for risk management purposes. At the time of this writing, there is no capital charge for interest rate risk. The Basle Committee has proposed a capital charge for interest rate risk in the banking book for banks whose interest rate risks are above the average.[11]

Simulation Analysis Models

Simulation analysis models represent the most sophisticated technique used for A&LM purposes. They rely on the forecast of future possible scenarios, defined by the interaction of all the possible variables that may evolve over time and that are assumed to affect, directly or indirectly, future values of assets and liabilities.

Simulation techniques are based on econometric models that permit the simulation of macroeconomic scenarios and possible strategies that could be pursued by the bank. Although difficult to implement, and computer intensive, simulation analysis is the only approach that can forecast the effects of decisions taken or events occurring at any moment within the time horizon chosen. In addition, simulation analysis models can be continuously upgraded, using past real data as feedback.

As shown in the following chapters, simulation techniques are extensively used for VaR models, and although difficult to implement, they provide the most accurate and comprehensive results.

FROM A&LM TO VALUE AT RISK—MEASURING FINANCIAL RISK IN AN INTEGRATED FRAMEWORK

Financial institutions, from commercial banks and investment banks to mutual funds, have always regarded financial risk in a nonintegrated framework. Different techniques are used to measure the exposure to different sources of financial risk (interest rates, currencies, and stock indexes). It is incorrect to assume that financial institutions—before the adoption of VaR models—had no risk models at all. The traditional A&LM is now less and less relevant and is being increasingly replaced by an overall risk management framework. The main differences between A&LM and VaR are:

- A&LM is balance-sheet oriented, whereas VaR is risk oriented.
- A&LM is not easily adapted to off-balance-sheet transactions, particularly derivatives; whereas risk management of derivatives is a key issue in VaR models.

- A&LM measures interest rate risk through the use of gaps and duration that are not easily translatable across other asset classes.
- A&LM is not intended to provide an overall risk measure and is not easily adapted to an adjusted risk/return framework.
- A&LM is mainly interest rate based; it is not intended to measure sources of market risk other than interest rate risk.

Analyzing the financial risk profile of a bond, a stock, and a stock option demonstrates that VaR represents a quantum leap in financial risk management when compared to traditional A&LM techniques. Financial risk is usually measured estimating sensitivity parameters of asset price in response to market factor changes, for example, duration or modified duration for bonds, "the Greeks" (delta, gamma, vega, theta, rho) for options, or the Capital Asset Pricing Model (CAPM) beta for stock. Different users will have different needs and ways of analyzing and measuring financial risk. Traders would most likely express the riskiness of a position in terms of its peculiar risk measurement technique. Accountants, on the other hand, having to measure the risk that a position faces, would more likely state that the whole notional is at risk—the notional is equal to the risk exposure.

In fact, at least from a theoretical point of view, the market rates could evolve in such a way as to lead the actual value of the position to zero. Finally, top managers just want a simple and understandable measure of risk. At the same time, this measure should be immediately understandable for those who are not used to financial theory and must consider all types of market (and possibly financial) risk. For example, one could well ask what the risk equivalent (in terms of option δ or stock β) is for a bond with a duration of 4.5 years. The use of different approaches for measuring risk among different instruments and users can easily lead to a Tower of Babel situation where everybody speaks his own language and nobody understands exactly what is going on.

One of the greatest features of the VaR approach is to provide a unique measure of risk that allows a direct comparison of relative riskiness among instruments subject to different financial risks. It provides an integrated framework through which all financial risk can be homogeneously measured and aggregated to provide useful information for top managers' needs.

The line of reasoning leading to use of VaR can be explained starting from the accountants' viewpoint. Suppose that a U.S. bank is long in a DEM-denominated asset (e.g., foreign currency) worth 1 m DEM. Accountants would say that exposure to currency risk is equal to the whole capital amount. Assuming a current exchange rate of 0.5 USD/DEM, the exposure to currency risk would be $500,000. From the risk manager's standpoint, it is highly unlikely that the DEM will depreciate (at least in the short term) so much, vis-à-vis the USD, as to completely lose its value in terms of USD. The accountants' approach overestimates actual risk.

The VaR approach simply tries to measure the exposure to risk for each position and for a whole portfolio by defining an a priori confidence level and a time horizon. The longer the horizon, and the higher the confidence level, the higher will be the exposure to risk for a given position or portfolio. Assume that the current USD/DEM spot rate is equal to 0.5 and that, over a 1-day time horizon, with a probability of 95% (from historical data or based on an assumed probability density function of future expected spot rates), the USD/DEM exchange rate does not exceed a negative variation greater than −0.05.

This means that, at a 95% confidence level, the 1-day-ahead exchange rate will be higher than 0.45 $/DEM.

The minimum 1-day-ahead value the position can attain at the 95% confidence level is $450,000 (corresponding to a USD/DEM exchange rate of 0.45). The maximum probable loss is $500,000 − $450,000 = $50,000. This maximum probable loss is known as Value at Risk.

The comparison of risk across different instruments, using the concept of VaR, offers two great advantages:

1. It favors the communication among traders operating on different desks. They can now compare, using a common yardstick, the risk of the position they trade with the risk of positions traded by other people.
2. It favors the communication to top managers and CEOs. Once aware of the logic and the intrinsic limitations of any VaR-based model, they can appreciate much more deeply the aggregate exposure to financial risk of a portfolio by means of a unique, meaningful number.

So far we have emphasized the importance of the VaR for measuring risk. There are at least three other important areas where VaR based models can be successfully applied:

1. Setting up market risk limits.
2. Evaluating performance on a return/risk basis.
3. Estimating capital requirements to support risk taking.

Item 3 is discussed in the next chapter.

NOTES

1. The terms credit risk and liquidity risk in the context of derivatives are used to define two categories of risk: the default of one of the counterparts to honor his or her obligation and the risk of incurring substantial losses when selling a not-commonly-traded financial instrument in a thin market.

2. This is particularly true for Western European banks, which have always operated in a government-protected environment.

3. See S. Das, *Risk Management and Financial Derivatives,* McGraw-Hill, NY: 1998, 548–550.

4. The terminology is used somewhat loosely. By market factors, we mean interest rates, stock indexes, and exchange rates. These prices will be referred to later also as risk factors since they are the main source of financial risk.

5. This type of risk is applicable to nontrading assets and liabilities apart from issued or bought floating-rate notes.

6. Usually created to measure exposures for each different type of financial instrument (*duration* and *convexity* for bonds; *delta, gamma, vega,* etc., for options; and *beta* for stock).

7. See C. Matten, *Managing Bank Capital,* New York: John Wiley & Sons, 1996, 65.

8. For example, market risk, given the availability of extensive data and sophisticated techniques, is relatively easy to quantify in numerical terms. On the other hand, quantification of operational risk is, per se, difficult, and, in many respects, has more to do with interaction of humans with IT application and with business processes and procedures.

9. Das, *Risk Management and Financial Derivatives,* McGraw-Hill, NY: 1998, 554–555.

10. The concept of duration for measuring financial risk will be reviewed in greater detail in Chapters 4 and 6 through 9.

11. Basle Committee on Banking Supervision, 1999. Consultative Paper: "A New Capital Adequacy Framework." Basle: Bank for International Settlements.

3

Financial Risk Management and Regulations

Not surprisingly, governments are scared by the possibility of bank failures. During the twentieth century, deposit-insurance schemes were established to protect savers. The growing instability of markets and the risk that a single bank crash could lead to a crash of the whole banking system has led to a much stricter set of rules to ensure that the failure of a single bank will not lead to a crisis of the whole banking system. Regulation on banking activity is based on three "pillars": capital requirement, supervisory review, and market discipline. The most important of these rules are the capital-adequacy standards, which require banks to set aside money against future possible losses.

Although capital requirements are a less than sophisticated approach and are severely criticized for this reason, their introduction was a quantum leap in the definition of common regulatory standards, at least among advanced nations. This approach stems from the fact that globalization of banking activity requires responses that cannot be implemented on a local scale since the regulatory bodies of single nations can do little or nothing to prevent global banking crises.

Market risks have surged to a new importance in recent years because banks are relying more on market instruments to finance operations, capital markets have globalized, and regulations that put limits on market-based assets that could be held by commercial banks have become less strict, as in the case of the reform of the Glass-Steagall Act in the United States.

Regulators have traditionally been more interested in credit risk rather than in market risks since credit risk was considered the typical risk incurred by banks. The 8% capital charge imposed on weighted assets was intended to protect also against other kinds of risks, typically market and operational risk. In the first half of the 1990s, regulators had to recognize the importance of market risk in commercial banking activity, too, and have issued regulations aimed at defining capital requirements for both credit risk and market risks. Later, in 1996, regulators finally recognized that models for market risks implemented by banks are by far more accurate than the approach proposed by the Basle Committee. Banks are now allowed to use internal models for assessing capital requirements for market risks. Banks also have developed sophisticated techniques for managing their credit exposures, developing and implementing internal models in an effort to overcome the weaknesses of the Basle approach.

The current approach was heralded as a great advance when it was adopted in 1988 because each bank's capital requirement supposedly is based on risk. Nevertheless, it has many serious drawbacks, the most important of which is that it favors lending to lower credit standing counterparties.

This chapter focuses on the regulatory approach for measuring and managing market risk, since the objective of VaR models is just to measure market risk. Regulatory approach to credit risk, starting from the Basle Agreement of 1988, is briefly reviewed in the Appendix to Chapter 3 since the tendency is to an even more integrated framework encompassing credit and market risk.

Finally, the *standardized approach* and the *internal model approach* are compared, and the *precommitment approach* is outlined.

THE STANDARDIZED APPROACH

The first set of proposals from the Basle Committee aimed at measuring and facing market risks was issued in 1993. These proposals define a highly structured and standardized approach, sometimes referred to as *standard model.* The final document, after the responses were received, was reissued in 1995.

In January 1996, the Basle Committee issued a new document, "Amendment to the Capital Accord to Incorporate Market Risks," commonly known as "The Amendment," that allowed, within a given methodological framework, to use internal models to calculate the capital charge for market risk. The Basle Committee defines market risk as "the risk of losses in on- and off-balance sheet positions arising from movements in market prices."

The standardized model uses a building-block approach to first determine the capital charge for each risk category (i.e., interest rate, equity, foreign exchange, and commodities). Then, the four measures are simply summed up to obtain the global capital charge related to market risk.

Interest Rate Risk

The model encompasses all fixed rate and floating rate debt securities, zero-coupon instruments, interest rate derivatives, nonconvertible preference shares, and hybrid products such as convertible bonds, although they are treated like debt securities only when they trade like debt securities (i.e., when their price is below par), and are treated like equities otherwise. Simple interest rate derivatives such as futures and forward contracts, including FRAs, and swaps are treated like a combination of short and long positions in debt contracts. Options are treated separately.

The interest risk capital charge is the sum of two components separately calculated: one is related to "specific risk," which applies to the net holdings for each instrument; the other is related to "general market risk," where long and short positions in different securities or derivatives can be partially offset.

Specific Risk

The capital charge for specific risk is designed to protect the bank against an adverse price movement in the price of an individual security due to factors related to the individual issuer. Offsetting is thus restricted to matched positions in the identical issue, including derivatives. The capital charge applies whether it is a net long or net short position. Even if the issuer is the same, but there are differences in maturity, coupon rates, call features, and so on, no offsetting is allowed since a change in the credit quality of the issuer may have a differential effect on the market value of each instrument (i.e., prices may diverge in the short run).

Weighting factors apply to the market value of the debt instruments, and not their notional amount. Table 3.1 shows the specific risk charge for various debt positions.

A specific risk charge also applies to derivative contracts in the trading book only when the underlying is subject to specific risk. For example, an

TABLE 3.1   Capital Charges for Specific Risks

Debt Category	Remaining Maturities	Capital Charge (%)
Government	N/A	0.00
Qualifying	6 months or less	0.25
	6 to 24 months	1.00
	over 2 years	1.60
Other	N/A	8.00

Details about each debt category are reported in the Amendment.

interest rate swap based on LIBOR (London Interbank Offered Rate) won't be subject to specific risk charge, while an option on a corporate bond will.

All over-the-counter derivative contracts are subject to counterpart credit risk charge according to guidelines of the 1988 Accord, even where a specific risk charge is required.

General Market Risk

Capital requirements for general market risk capture the risk of loss arising from changes in market interest rates. Banks can choose between two methods, the *maturity* method and the *duration* method. The duration method is just a variant of the maturity method.

The maturity method uses "maturity bands," within which net positions are identified across all on- and off-balance sheet items. The first step in the maturity ladder method consists of allocating the marked-to-market value of the positions to each maturity band. Fixed rate instruments are allocated according to the residual term to maturity, and floating rate instruments according to the residual term to the next repricing date. Derivatives, like forwards, futures, and swaps, should be converted into long and short positions in the underlying positions. For example, a long 2-month forward on a 3-month T-bill is equivalent to a long 5-month T-bill plus a short 2-month T-bill. Options are treated separately.

The second step is to weight the positions in each of 13 time bands by a factor designed to reflect the price sensitivity of those positions to annual changes in interest rates, ranging from 0.2% for positions under 3 months to 12.5% for positions over 20 years.

The third step is to offset the weighted longs and shorts in each time band, resulting in a single short or long position for each band. A 10% capital charge on the smaller of the offsetting positions will be levied to adjust basis risk and gap risk resulting from the differences in maturities and instruments in each time band. (It is called "vertical offsetting.")

In addition, banks are allowed to conduct two rounds of "horizontal offsetting," first between the net positions in each of three zones, and subsequently between the net positions in the three different zones.

The total capital charge is given by the sum of weighted long/short position for each band, vertical offsetting, and horizontal offsetting. Netting the positions within a band and aggregation across bands basically assumes perfect correlation among debt instruments.

Treatment of Options

There are three approaches:

1. The *simplified approach.*
2. The *delta-plus method.*
3. The *scenario approach.*

The first approach applies to banks that only buy options. The other two methods should be used by banks that also write options.

The Simplified Approach

Under the simplified approach, the capital charge is the market value of the underlying security multiplied by the sum of specific and general market risk charges for the underlying, less the amount the option is in the money (if any), bounded at zero.

If the position is only a long call or a long put, the capital charge is the minimum between the market value of the underlying security multiplied by the sum of specific and general market risk charges for the underlying and the market value of the option.

The risk numbers thus generated are then added to the capital charge for the relevant category (i.e., interest related instruments, equity, foreign exchange, and commodities).

Suppose the bank is long 100 shares currently valued at $10, and has a put on this quantity of shares with a strike price of $11. The capital charge would be

+ $1,000 * 16% (8% for specific risk plus 8% for general market risk) = $160

− the amount the option is in the money: ($11 − $10) * 100 = $100
Total $60

Delta-Plus Method

Under the delta-plus method, the option is first considered as its delta equivalent in the underlying instrument. Delta capital charge = Delta * ΔV, where ΔV denotes the change in the value of the underlying. For interest rate products, it is calculated according to the assumed changes in yield in the maturity band. For equities and foreign exchange and gold, the price change is taken as 8%, while for commodities it is taken as 15%.

Then, two additional capital charges are added.

The first one adjusts the capital charge for gamma risk or convexity risk:

Gamma capital charge = ½ Gamma * ΔV^2

It is simply the second-order term in the Taylor expansion of the option price formula. (See Chapters 10–12 for more details.)

The second one compensates for vega risk:

Vega capital charge = vega * 25% annualized volatility
of the underlying

In fact, it is the absolute value of the impact of a 25% increase or decrease in volatility. Consider a short position in a European one-year call option on a stock with a striking price of $490. The underlying spot price is $500, the risk-free rate is 8% per annum, and the annualized volatility is 20%. The option value is $65.48, with a delta and gamma of −0.721 and −0.0034, respectively, corresponding to a $1 change in the underlying price; its vega is 1.68 associated with a change in volatility of 1 percentage point.

The three components of the capital charge are:

delta equivalent: $500 * 0.721 * 8%   = $28.84
gamma adjustment: ½ * 0.0034 * ($500 *8%)^2 = $ 2.72
vega adjustment: 1.68 * (25% * 20)   = $ 8.40

Total $39.96

Scenario Matrix Approach

The scenario matrix approach adopts as capital charge the worst loss for all the scenarios generated by a grid that allows for a combination of possible values of the underlying price, the volatility, and the cost of carry, with the range of values to be considered being the same as for the delta-plus approach.

For the delta-plus method and the scenario approach, the specific risk capital charges are determined separately by multiplying the delta equivalent of each option by the specific risk weight.

Equity Risk

The instruments covered are stocks, convertible securities that behave like equity, and commitments to buy or sell equity securities. General market risk charge is 8%. Capital charge for specific risk is 8%, unless the portfolio is both liquid and well diversified, in which case the charge is 4%.

Equity derivatives are treated the same way as interest rate derivatives.

Foreign Exchange Risk

The instruments covered are foreign currencies, with the exclusion of "structural positions," and gold. There are two steps in the calculation of the capital charge. After the exposure in each currency has been measured, the net long and net short exposures in all currencies are translated into an overall capital charge according to a rule called the *shorthand method*.

The measurement of the exposures is straightforward. It consists of the net spot position, the net forward position, the delta equivalent for options, accrued interest and expenses, and other future income and expenses that are already fully hedged.

The capital charge is the absolute value of 8% of the greater of the net open long positions and the net open short positions in all currencies, plus 8% of the absolute value of the net open position in gold plus the gamma and vega adjustments for options.

Commodities Risk

Commodities are broadly defined as physical products that can be traded on an organized market, such as agricultural products, oil, gas, electricity, and precious metals (except gold, which is treated as a foreign currency). Commodities' risks are often more complex to measure than other financial instruments as markets are less liquid, prices are affected by seasonal patterns in supply and demand, and inventories play a critical role in the determination of the equilibrium price.

The standardized model for commodities is somewhat similar to the maturity ladder approach for interest rate products. The idea being to design a simple framework that captures directional, curve risk as well as time spread risk.

THE 1995 BIS MARKET RISK PROPOSAL: THE 1996 AMENDMENT

The most important innovation in the 1995 BIS Market Risk Proposal and in the Amendment was that, for the first time, regulators, recognizing the superiority of many financial risk management models implemented by commercial and investment banks, accepted that capital adequacy requirements could be determined on the basis of the so-called internal models rather than on the basis of the standardized approach. Internal models should satisfy some qualitative and quantitative prerequisites to qualify for capital adequacy purposes. The prototype of these internal models is undoubtedly J.P. Morgan's RiskMetrics™.

The Accord treated all instruments equivalently, whether in the trading or nontrading book, introducing the requirements to face market risk in addition to credit risk. The initial Accord still applies to the nontrading items both on-balance sheet and off-balance sheet. Market risk must now be measured for both on- and off-balance sheet traded instruments. However, on-balance sheet assets are subject to market risk capital charge only, while off-balance sheet derivatives, like swaps and options, are subject to both market risk and credit risk capital charges.

The bank's overall capital requirement will be the sum of:

- *Credit risk capital charge,* as proposed in the initial 1988 Accord, which applies to all positions in the trading[1] and banking books, *excluding debt and equity traded securities in the trading book, and all positions in commodities and foreign exchange.*
- *Market risk capital charge* for the instruments of the trading book on- and off-balance sheet.

This proposal was adopted by the U.S. regulatory agencies in July 1995, and became mandatory to all financial institutions with a significant trading activity, as of January 1, 1998. The new capital requirement related to market risks should largely be offset by the fact that the capital charge calculated under the 1988 Accord to cover credit risk will no longer need to be held for on-balance sheet securities in the trading portfolio. The capital charge for general market risks and specific risks should be, on aggregate, much smaller than the credit risk capital charge for large trading books. Furthermore, banks adopting the internal models approach should realize substantial capital savings depending on the size of their trading operations and the instruments they trade. While the regulators are not specific about the modeling requirements and the choice of the relevant risk factors, banks will have to satisfy some minimum qualitative and quantitative requirements before they can adopt the internal model approach.

Since we are more interested in internal financial risk management models, such as VaR class models, we will analyze in greater detail the BIS qualitative and quantitative requirements that banks must meet to use internal models for capital adequacy requirements.

INTERNAL MODELS APPROACH: GENERALITIES

The regulators accept that institutions will use different assumptions and modeling techniques, simply because trading financial products relies on proprietary expertise both in trading and modeling markets. Model risk is thus an issue, and will stay an issue since it is inherent to the trading of financial instruments. Indeed, the ability of a trading institution to stay profitable relies, at least in part, on the skill of its financial engineers and traders to build the appropriate pricing and hedging models. State of the art modeling provides institutions with a unique competitive edge. These models are kept relatively secret, although most of them are based on published papers in academic journals. For example, J.P. Morgan has revealed on the Internet its full technical documentation about the well-known Risk-Metrics VaR software. However, the implementation and calibration of these models require an understanding of the products and the markets and a strong capacity to model financial markets with statistical tools.

Using internal models for regulatory purposes is a controversial issue, since errors in the modeling of the model or in its calibration can lead to large overestimation or underestimation of the market risk. From a regulatory standpoint, the risk relies on the possibility of underestimation and the consequent scarcity of capital set to cover actual risk. Recognizing this relevant—but to a certain extent unavoidable—weakness of any internal model, regulators requires institutions to scale up their VaR number derived from their internal model by a factor of three, referred to in the following as the *multiplier*. The multiplier, sometimes known as the hysteria factor, is equal to 3, unless the model does not meet backtesting requirements. In this case, the multiplier is equal to 4. Not surprisingly, the use of multipliers has been deeply criticized. Its existence seems to be inconsistent with the acceptance by regulators of internal models. These criticisms are acceptable from a managerial viewpoint, but not if we share the regulatory viewpoint. We should consider the existence of multipliers for at least two reasons:

1. Multipliers should be viewed as an insurance against model risk, imperfect assessment of specific risks, and other operational risks.
2. Multipliers can be considered a safety factor against extreme market moves.[2]

INTERNAL MODELS: QUALITATIVE REQUIREMENTS

Before an institution can expect to be eligible to use its own internal model to assess regulatory capital related to market risk, it should have sound risk management practices already in place. The institution should have a strong risk management group that is independent from the business units it monitors and that reports directly to the senior executive management of the institution. In a paper issued in 1998, the Basle Committee has focused its attention on the existence of an effective internal control system in banking organizations as the unifying framework of which risk measurement techniques are only one of the five cornerstones (the other cornerstones are: control environment, control activities, information and communication, and monitoring).[3]

The internal models should not be used only for calculating regulatory capital, but should be fully integrated in the daily risk management of the institution. In addition, the regulators require that systematic back-testing and stress testing be conducted on a regular basis, to test the robustness of the internal model against various market conditions and crises. Improvements should be implemented if the model fails to pass the tests (e.g., when backtesting exhibits too many days where the trading losses are greater than VaR).

Implementing a VaR model is a massive and intensive system endeavor. The aim is to build a truly integrated, global, real-time system that records all positions centrally in a data warehouse, and map them to the risk factors tracked by the VaR model. Part of the challenge of implementing such a system is a need to have in place controls to ensure that the model inputs, and therefore the risk measures, are reliable and accurate. A formal vetting system is needed to approve the models, their modifications, assumptions, and calibration:

- Model parameters should be estimated independently of the trading desks to avoid the temptation by the traders to "choose" volatility numbers and other key parameters to make their position smaller.
- The financial rates and prices that feed the risk management system should come from sources independent of the front office and be located in a financial database independently controlled by risk management.

INTERNAL MODEL: QUANTITATIVE AND MODELING REQUIREMENTS

The internal model approach should capture the magnitude of all market risks of the trading positions. Although each institution has some discretion in the choice of risk factors, these risk factors should be selected with great care to guarantee the robustness of the VaR model. Oversimplification and failure to select the right risk factors inherent in the trading positions may have serious consequences, as the VaR model may miss components of basis risk, curve risk, or spread risk. These shortcomings should be revealed when backtesting the model, and may lead to penalties in the form of a multiplier greater than three.

Recalling the Basle Committee's classification, market risks can be broken down into four categories: interest rate risk, equity risk, exchange rate risk, and commodity price risk:

1. *Interest rate risk* applies only to the trading book. The base yield curve in each currency (government curve or swap curve) should be modeled with a minimum of six risk points. The model should also incorporate separate risk factors to capture spread risk.

2. *Equity price risk* should incorporate risk factors corresponding to each of the equity markets in which the trading book holds significant positions. At a minimum, a risk factor should be designed to capture market wide movements in equity prices (e.g., the broad market index in each national equity market to assess both market risk and idiosyncratic risk) according to the Capital Asset Pricing Model (CAPM). The most extensive approach would have risk factors corresponding to each asset.
3. *Exchange rate risk* should include risk factors corresponding to the individual currencies in which the trading and banking books have positions.
4. *Commodity price risk* should incorporate risk factors corresponding to each of the commodity markets in which the trading and banking books have significant positions.

The 1996 amendment requires VaR to be computed on uniform quantitative inputs:

- A 99 percent (one-tailed) confidence level.
- A 10-day horizon.

In the initial phase of implementation of the internal model, however, the BIS allows the 10-day VaR to be proxied by multiplying the 1-day VaR by the square root of 10 (i.e., about 3.16). The effective VaR number used for regulatory capital purpose, corresponds to the maximum of yesterday's VaR, and three times the average VaR over the past 60 days. Institutions are allowed to take into account correlations among risk categories. Volatilities and correlations should be estimated based on past historical data with a minimum history of 250 days (i.e., approximately one year). Market parameters should be updated at least once every three months, or more frequently if market conditions warrant. If empirical correlations between risk categories are unavailable, then the aggregate VaR is calculated as the simple arithmetic sum of the VaR for each block (i.e., equity, interest rate, FX, and commodities). In that case, the aggregate VaR doesn't benefit from the risk reduction resulting from diversification across risk classes.

The internal model should capture not only linear risks, known as delta risks, but also nonlinear risks, like convexity risk (gamma) and volatility risk (vega) inherent in options positions. The choice of the method is left to the institution, whether it chooses to implement full Monte Carlo simulation or other pseudoanalytic methods based on the Greeks. Anyway, a penalty component will be added to the multiplicative factor if backtesting reveals that the bank's internal models incorrectly forecast risk. The purpose of this penalty is to give incentives to banks to improve the accuracy of their models, avoiding optimistic projections.

Banks that cannot meet all the requirements for the internal models are allowed to use a combination of standard models and internal models, although they are expected to move toward a fully internal models framework. Each risk category, however, must be measured according to only one approach. If a combination of approaches is used, then the total capital charge is determined by a simple arithmetic sum, without accounting for a possible correlation effect between risk categories.

The new 1998 regulatory framework views specific risk and consequently credit risk, as an outgrowth of market risk. As such, it should be modeled with assumptions which are consistent with the market risk model. This is a significant improvement with respect to the 1988 Accord, where credit risk capital charge was calculated according to somewhat arbitrary ratios that didn't correctly account for the specificity of the instrument.

NEW CAPITAL REQUIREMENTS: COMBINING CREDIT RISK AND MARKET RISK

Under the 1996 amendment, banks are now allowed to add a new category of capital, Tier 3 capital, which mainly consists in short-term subordinated debt subject to certain conditions, but only to meet on a daily basis market risk capital requirement. The total capital adequacy requirements are obtained by summing the credit risk charge to the market risk charge applied to trading operations.

In particular, the market-risk charge for day t is given by

$$MRC_t = \max(k * \frac{1}{60} \Sigma_j \text{VaR}_{t-i}, \text{VaR}_{t-1})$$
(3.1)

where k is the hysteria multiplicative factor (usually equal to 3; see Table 3.2). Banks should first allocate Tier 1 and Tier 2 capital to meet credit risk capital requirements according to the 1988 Accord, so that together they represent 8% of the risk-weighted assets, adjusted for the positions that are no longer subject to the 1988 credit risk rules (i.e., the traded instruments on-balance sheet like bonds and equities, which are already subject to specific risk).

Then, the bank should satisfy a second ratio of eligible capital to the risk-weighted asset equivalent. The risk-weighted asset equivalent is simply the sum of the risk-weighted on-balance sheet assets, the risk-weighted off-balance sheet items, and 12.5 times the market risk capital charge, where 12.5 is the reciprocal of the minimum capital ratio of 8%.

TABLE 3.2   Penalty Factors Due to Inaccuracy

Number of Exceptions	Multiplier
4 or fewer	3.00
5	3.40
6	3.50
7	3.65
8	3.75
9	3.85
10 or more	4.00

BACKTESTING OF INTERNAL MODELS

The backtests must compare daily VaR measures calibrated to a one-day movement in rates and prices and a 99 percent (one-tailed) confidence level, against two measures of the profit and loss (P&L):

1. The actual net trading P&L for the next day.
2. The theoretical P&L that would have occurred if the position at the close of the previous day had been carried forward the next day.

VaR is computed at the end of the day. The portfolio is traded all the time, and its actual composition keeps changing during the next trading day. Risk management is also active, and decisions to alter the risk exposure of the bank's position. Assuming that the risk factors are correctly modeled and that markets behave accordingly, then we expect the absolute value of actual P&L over the past 250 days to be greater than VaR only five days, on average.

Backtesting should be performed daily. In addition, institutions must identify the number of times when its net trading losses, if any, for a particular day exceed the corresponding daily VaR. This BIS multiplicative factor can become higher than three if the number of exceptions during the previous 250 days is greater than five and can rise up to four if the number of exceptions reaches ten or more during the period, as shown in Table 3.2.

However, there is some doubt on how seriously this rule will be enforced since exceptions to the rule are already envisaged when abnormal situations occur, such as a market crash, a major political event, or a natural disaster. In addition, the regulators should acknowledge that all the financial institutions, including the regulators, are learning by doing. It may thus not be appropriate to penalize an institution by applying a higher multiplier if the institution reacts quickly and subsequently implements improvements to its VaR model after it has recognized its weaknesses.

STRESS TESTING OF INTERNAL MODELS

In developing the VaR model, many assumptions are necessary to make it practical. In particular, most market parameters are set to match normal market conditions. This is somewhat contradictory with the concept of maximum loss at the 99% confidence level. How robust is the VaR model? How sensitive are the VaR numbers to key assumptions? Stress testing aims to address these questions. The objective of stress testing is to assess the VaR models' robustness to extreme market conditions (i.e., the situations this class of model is *not* suited for).

The best approach to backtesting is "historical simulation" where each day, the position would reevaluated based on the past 250 days' closing market data. Then, the "historical distribution" of the changes in the position value would be compared with the "theoretical distribution" derived from the internal VaR model. This approach permits revisiting over time some key assumptions made in the VaR model that, according to the historical simulation, are revealed to be inconsistent with market data, and may produce a biased picture of the bank's exposure.

Stress testing consists in generating market "extreme scenarios," although plausible, that may violate key assumptions in the VaR model. Stress testing should assess the impact on VaR of the breakdown of some otherwise stable relationships, like relative prices, correlations, and volatility. It should also investigate some causal relationships between market factors, between market and credit risk, and other exceptional relationships that may be triggered by low probability events.

One of the most important field of investigation of stress testing in extreme conditions is the relation between:

- Market factors and portfolio value.
- Market risk and credit risk.

For example, the debt crisis of the 1980s reminds us that although the distinction between general market risk, specific risk, and credit risk is important to bear in mind, we still cannot ignore that—especially in extreme situations—different risk categories are strongly interrelated. On the other hand, although the recent East Asian crisis started as a financial crisis, it is having strong drawback on the credit risk of Western banks' loans to East Asian government and private institutions.

Other scenarios that require simulations are the oil shocks of the 1970s, recent crises like the October 1987 market crash, the European Monetary System crises of 1992 and 1993, credit spreads widening, and the fall in the bond markets in May 1994 consecutive to the Fed tightening. For Europe, it could include the possibility that the one or more countries leave the EMU because of a political or macro-economic crisis. These stress scenarios should simulate large price movements, combined with a sharp reduction in market liquidity for several consecutive days, and a dramatic change in instantaneous volatilities and correlations. When the market crashes, it is the correlation structure that breaks down with correlations tending to the extremes, either +1 or −1.

The impact of these stress tests will vary greatly depending on the bank's positions in the markets affected by the simulated crises. Accordingly, additional stress scenarios may be run to reflect specific concentration risk in one geographic region or in one market. Stress testing may allow the bank to derive some kind of confidence interval on its VaR numbers.

THE PROS AND CONS OF THE STANDARDIZED APPROACH AND THE INTERNAL MODELS

The standardized approach has undergone many critics. The standard model is considered the least adequate method for determining capital charges for the following reasons:

- The standard approach ignores diversification across sources of risk. As long as financial instruments are not perfectly correlated with each other, diversification reduces overall risk.
- The capital charges are somewhat arbitrary and only loosely related to the volatility of each asset category. This fact can introduce a distortion in the portfolio allocation of a bank, since banks can move away from assets where capital charge is abnormally high.

Internal models overcome these weaknesses but, at least from the standpoint of regulators, suffer from the limitation of being implemented by the controlled banks themselves. There is, or there could be, a *moral hazard* to artificially lower VaR exposure and, hence, capital requirement. In addition, at least in the short run, it is sometimes difficult to distinguish when actual losses exceed VaR figure over a specified confidence level only by chance or as a consequence of the inaccuracy of the model. Verification, therefore, is not an easy task, since even the most accurate model can be exceeded by actual figures with unexpected frequencies.

Regulators have defended themselves by imposing safety factors like the multiplier of three to translate VaR into capital charge. These conservative measures, paradoxically, can be dangerous indeed since they may discourage the most sophisticated banks to improve their internal model, at least for regulatory capital purpose and may also induce a distorted allocation of capital.

In recognition of the weaknesses inherent in both the standard approach and the internal model approach, P. Kupiec and J. O'Brien, two senior economists at the Board of Governors of the Federal Reserve Board, have proposed an alternative approach, the so-called Precommitment Approach (PCA). The PCA would require a bank to precommit to a maximum trading loss over a fixed subsequent period. This maximum loss precommitment would be the bank's market risk capital charge. Upon verification by regulatory bodies, if the bank were to incur trading losses exceeding its capital commitment, it would be subject to penalties. Violation of the limit would also bring public scrutiny to the bank, which also would provide a further feedback mechanism for sound management.

The main advantage of this approach is that it is incentive-compatible; it forces the bank to develop more and more sophisticated risk measurement systems. Under the PCA, the bank's maximum loss precommitment can reflect the bank's internal assessment of risks, including formal model estimates as well as management's subjective judgments. The PCA approach is an interesting initiative since it aims at replacing regulatory capital requirements, based on ex-ante estimates of the bank's risks, with a capital charge that is set endogenously through the optimal resolution of an incentive contract between the bank and its regulators. We can regard the PCA as a put option written on the bank's assets and issued to the regulators. The value of this liability for the bank increases with the penalty rate, set by the regulator, and the riskiness of the bank's assets, while it decreases with the striking price of the put (i.e., the precommitment level). When the bank increases the risk of its assets, it increases the value of its precommitment liability. The optimal design of the incentive contract becomes bank specific and should be such that the bank finds itself the right trade-off between the riskiness of its trading book and the level of pre-committed capital with the objective to maximize the shareholder value.

The issue at hand is whether capital charges should be based on internal models more than on standardized models. Models, by the way, are only one of the important elements of risk measurement. Experience, judgment, and controls are often more important than formulas in translating the models' results into actual capital. Precommitment attempts to take these multiple factors into account.

APPENDIX: REGULATIONS AND CREDIT RISK MANAGEMENT

The Basle Accord (1988)

The landmark Basle Accord of 1988 provided the first step toward tighter risk management. Basically, the Basle Accord set minimum capital requirements that must be met by commercial banks to face credit risk.

This approach reflected the traditional view that regarded credit risk as the most typical and important source of risk in banking activity. Only later, central bankers started recognizing the importance of market risks, issuing capital requirements for market risk, too.

Actually, the Basle Accord of 1988 set out principles—laid out in the "International Convergence of Capital Measurement and Capital Standards" document, published in July 1988—that led subsequently to agreements in the field of risk management.

This Accord was initially developed by the Basle Committee on Banking Supervision, and later endorsed by the central bank governors of the Group of Ten.[4] The most important result of the 1988 Accord was the definition of a common measure of solvency (known as the Cooke ratio), which only covers *credit risk* and deals only with the identity of banks' debtors.

Although we focus on market risk, a brief discussion of the 1988 Basle Accord on credit risk provides a useful insight into the regulatory viewpoint about risk management in banking activity. The 1988 Basle Accord defined two minimum standards for meeting acceptable capital adequacy requirements:

1. An assets-to-capital multiple.
2. Risk-based capital ratio.

The first standard is an overall measure of the bank's capital adequacy. The second measure focuses on the credit risk associated with specific on- and off-balance sheet asset categories. This measure is a solvency ratio—the well-known Cooke ratio—and is defined as the ratio of capital to risk-weighted on-balance sheet assets plus off-balance sheet exposures, where the weights are assigned on the basis of counterparts' credit risk.

The Asset-to-Capital Multiple

A simple test for determining the overall adequacy of a financial institution's capital is the assets-to-capital multiple. This test calculates the multiple by dividing the bank's total assets, including specified off-balance sheet items, by its total capital. The off-balance sheet items included in this test are direct credit substitutes (including letters of credit and guarantees), transaction-related contingencies, trade-related contingencies, and sale and repurchase agreements. All of these items are included at their notional principal amount.

At present, the maximum multiple allowed is 20. In general, this test does not set the capital requirements. However, a bank with large off-balance sheet activities may trigger this multiple as the minimum requirement.

The Solvency Ratio (Cooke Ratio)

The Basle Accord requires capital to be equal to at least 8% of the total risk-weighted asset of the bank. Capital, however, is intended in a broader way than the usual definition of equity since its goal is to protect deposits.

Capital consists of three basic components: Tier 1, or core capital, Tier 2, or supplementary capital, and Tier 3, or subsupplementary capital.

Tier 1 includes common stockholder's equity, noncumulative perpetual preferred stock, and minority equity interests in consolidated subsidiaries, less goodwill and other deductions.

Tier 2, or supplementary capital, includes hybrid capital instruments, like cumulative perpetual preferred shares and qualifying 99-year debentures, which are essentially permanent in nature and have certain characteristics of both equity and debt; limited life instruments, like subordinated debt with an original average maturity of at least five years. In the 1995 BIS amendment to the original Accord, a third tier of capital has been added only to meet market risk requirements.

Tier 3, or subsupplementary capital, consists of short-term subordinated debt with an original maturity of at least two years. It must be unsecured and fully paid up. It is also subject to lock-in clauses that prevent the issuer from repaying the debt before maturity, or even at maturity should the issuer's capital ratio become less than 8% after repayment.

According to the original Accord, Tier 1 and Tier 2 capital should represent at least 8% of the risk-weighted assets, as a protection against credit risk. At least 50% must be covered by Tier 1 capital. Capital represents the numerator of the Cooke ratio. Risk-weighted assets represent the denominator. In determining the Cooke ratio, it is necessary to consider both the on-balance sheet and specific off-balance sheet items.

On-balance sheet items have risk weightings from zero% for cash and OECD (Organization for Economic Cooperation and Development) government securities to 100% for corporate bonds and others. Off-balance sheet items are first expressed as a credit equivalent and then are appropriately risk-weighted by counterpart. The risk-weighted amount is then the sum of the two components: the risk-weighted assets for on-balance sheet instruments and the risk-weighted credit equivalent for off-balance sheet items. Table 3A.1 summarizes the risk capital weights by asset categories.

The computation of credit equivalence for off-balance sheet items is complicated and well beyond the scope of this book. The 1988 Basle Accord has been highly criticized on several fronts:

- It does not account for the portfolio risk of the bank. From financial theory, it is known that correlations between components of the portfolio may significantly alter the total portfolio risk. It

TABLE 3A.1 Risk Weights by Asset Category

Risk Weights (%)	Asset Category
0	Cash and gold bullion, claims on OECD governments like Treasury bonds, insured residential mortgages.
20	Claims on OECD banks and OECD public sector entities like securities issued by U.S. government agencies, claims on municipalities.
50	Uninsured residential mortgages.
100	All other claims like corporate bonds and less developed country debt, claims on non-OECD banks, equity, real estate, premises, plant, and equipment.

means that credit risk can be offset by diversification across issuers, industries, and geographical locations.

- It does not account for netting. If a bank matches lenders and borrowers, its' net exposure may be small.
- It does not take into account market risk and other types of risk. In fact, assets are recorded at book value, which may substantially differ from current market values. This omission is particularly significant for trading portfolios of banks with many positions in derivatives.

Recognizing these weaknesses, the Basle Committee has moved to issue regulations more suited for measuring and facing market risk. Regulatory aspects of financial risk management have been described in detail in Chapter 3.

SHORTCOMINGS OF THE BASLE APPROACH

The main critics to the Basle Approach center on the weights assigned to single assets' categories used to determine the capital required to face credit risk. The "risk-based" standard requires less capital for loans to governments and financial institutions than for corporate loans because loans to OECD countries are considered to be less risky than loans to corporates or non-OECD countries. In addition, these weights are also used to determine how much capital to set against any credit-like exposure in derivatives.

Asian crisis shows that this approach can be very misleading, since it makes no distinction between loans to banks in America and loans to banks in South Korea (or Japan), nor between loans to blue-chip companies and to firms on the edge of bankruptcy. This, perversely, gives banks a moral hazard to lend to riskier borrowers, because such loans permit higher interest rates than high-quality loans while requiring the same capital coverage.

Three recent developments have brought the inadequacies of this regime into the light:

1. Since the early 1990s, when bad loans nearly bankrupted banks such as Citicorp and Barclays, banks have become far more sophisticated in managing their loan portfolios. Some have developed complex computer models to do the job (we brief some of these models later in this Appendix). Banks are now confident that they can safely reduce the amount of capital they need to well below the amount required by regulators using these models.

2. There has been an explosion in the use of credit derivatives. These allow banks to trade their credit-risk exposures cheaply, and so make it much easier to reduce the riskiness of their loan portfolios. This has further emphasized the insufficiency of current regulations. The use of credit derivatives can lead to counterintuitive results. In fact, it would actually increase the amount of capital that has to be set aside, as the bank would receive no credit for risk hedging but would need additional capital to cover possible losses on the derivative.

3. This development occurred in January 1997, as new rules differentiated between assets in a bank's trading portfolio and those in its loan portfolio. Banks can now use sophisticated risk models to calculate how much capital they need to cover possible trading losses. Predictably, this has led some banks to label their low-risk loans as assets held for trading, in effect circumventing the capital standards governing loan portfolios.

All this has put pressure on regulators to rethink the rules on credit risk. Bankers would like to be able to determine their own capital requirements for loans, based on their credit-risk models. This could benefit borrowers as well because loans would become cheaper if bank capital were used more efficiently. And, since banks that understand their risks better are safer banks, well-tuned models could give taxpayers, who must bear the cost of bailing out bust institutions, something to be pleased about. Regulators are, obviously, less enthusiastic, although such a step has been taken for assessing capital requirement for market risks.

There are many reasons to regard unfavorably the idea of internal-based models of credit risk for regulatory purposes, at least as many as there are for accepting the bankers' approach. By the way, the problem is centered on the Latin question: *Quis custodet custodes?* ("Who guards the guardians?").

In addition, as seen in Chapter 2, banks need capital not just as a protection against bad loans, but also for risks that cannot be quantified, including such operational hazards as employee fraud and computer failure. Experience with the new rules for banks' trading portfolios shows that models need not be perfect since regulators can impose a substantial comfort margin by requiring banks to hold three times as much capital as the models recommend.[5] They also reserved the right to raise this amount, should a bank's portfolio behave differently from the predictions of its model.[6] Even so, a number of banks say the change has released significant amounts of capital, which can be returned to shareholders or used more profitably.

RECENT DEVELOPMENT OF REGULATORY BODIES ON CREDIT RISK

Years 1999 and 2000 have seen the issues of several documents from the Basle Committee about credit risk management. Of particular interest is that the Basle Committee has recently decided to introduce a new capital adequacy framework to replace the 1988 Accord. As in the case of market risk, a consultative paper with the proposal of the Committee has been sent to banks and associations within the G-10 countries to stimulate discussions and to receive suggestions.

This new capital framework consists of three pillars: minimum capital requirements, a supervisory review process, and effective use of market discipline. With regard to minimum capital requirements, the Committee recognizes that a modified version of the existing Accord should remain the "standardized" approach, but that for some sophisticated banks, use of internal credit ratings and, at a later stage, portfolio models could contribute to a more accurate assessment of a bank's capital requirement in relation to its particular risk profile. It is also proposed that the Accord's scope of application be extended, so that it fully captures the risks in a banking group.

This point deserves more attention. The Basle Committee recognizes that the current approach to credit risk is outdated, but it also underlines that it is still not possible to allow the use of internal credit models, as in the case of market risk. While working on a revised version of the standardized model, the Committee regards internal rating models as an intermediate step to internal credit models based on a portfolio approach. The use of ratings (be they external or internal) certainly represents a step toward a better correlation between risk and capital charge; nevertheless, the most important point is the methodological framework to be used so that these ratings can be validated by regulators for capital charge purposes. The use of internal ratings, possibly in addition to external ratings, is obliged. Apart from the United States, most European corporations are not rated. In addition, small- and medium-size firms, that constitute the backbone of the German and Italian economies, cannot afford—or have no interest to pay—the huge fees requested by rating houses to produce their ratings. Although the Accord should focus on internationally active banks, its underlying principles should be suitable for application to banks of varying levels of complexity and sophistication. The final objective of the "new" Accord is to reduce risk weights for high quality corporate credits, and to introduce a higher-than-100% risk weight for certain low quality exposures. A new risk weighting scheme to address asset securitization, and the application of a 20% credit conversion factor for certain types of short-term commitments are also proposed.

At the time of this writing, the use of internal models seems far in the future. "Looking further ahead, the Committee will closely monitor developments in portfolio credit risk modeling for its possible use in regulatory capital calculations."[7]

The Committee is also examining the capital treatment of a number of important credit risk mitigation techniques and the possibility of introducing capital charges for interest rate risk in the banking book and operational risk. Notably, together with credit risk in the banking book, interest rate risk in the banking book and operational risk are of far greater importance for the vast majority of banks than market risk (as in the case of U.S. Savings & Loans, of German Landes- and Hypo-banks, and of a large number of Italian banks).

Players in the industry have started to introduce internal credit models for managerial purposes, while models for quantifying operational risk are still to come. It is hoped that, especially for credit risk, advances in the industry will induce regulators to continue their process of innovation, allowing a more efficient use of capital without threatening the stability of the whole system.

RECENT DEVELOPMENT IN CREDIT RISK MANAGEMENT: INTERNAL CREDIT RISK MODELS

The purpose of banks' credit risk models is simple: how much of a bank's lending might plausibly turn bad? Armed with the answer, banks can set aside enough capital to make sure they face even the worst probable scenario. No model, of course, can take account of every possibility. Credit risk models try to put a value on how much a bank should realistically expect to lose in the 95% or 99% of all the possible future scenarios.

This requires estimating three different things:

1. The likelihood that any given borrower will default.
2. The amount that might be recoverable if that happened.
3. The likelihood that the borrower will default at the same time others are doing so.

This last factor is crucial. In effect, it will decide whether some unforeseen event is likely to wreck the bank. This is the equivalent concept of correlation for market risk. If credit risk among borrowers is highly correlated, the possibility that a single event causes the failure of the bank is by far greater than it would be if low, or no, correlation among borrowers exists. Broadly speaking, the less likely it is that many loans will go bad at the same time, the lower the risk will be of a big loss from bad loans.

While models work quite well in theory, they are much more difficult to implement. Many of the banking industry's brightest rocket scientists have been given over to the task. Some of the most recent and renouned models have been proposed by banks and consulting firms. Credit Suisse Financial Products has launched "CreditRisk+" which attempts to provide an actuarial model of the likelihood that a loan will turn bad, much as an insurance firm would produce a forecast of likely claims.

McKinsey issued a model linking default probabilities to macroeconomic variables, such as interest rates and growth in gross domestic product (GDP). J.P. Morgan's "Credit-Metrics™" applies a theoretical model of when borrowers default, using credit ratings for bonds and drawing on another model developed by KMV, a Californian firm, which calculates the risk that a firm will default by looking at ranges in the price of its shares.

These models go from calculating the probability that any one borrower will default, to estimating the chances that two or more borrowers will default at the same time. This leads to a series of loss probabilities for the bank's entire portfolio of loans that allows for the construction of a simulated distribution of losses for the bank. Using an approach taken from VaR models,[8] this will indicate the maximum loss that the bank needs to prepare for by setting aside capital. "Value-at-Risk" models, developed to estimate how much of a bank's trading portfolio it could lose over a given time horizon and probability level because of adverse movements in financial prices, have been prodromic to credit-risk models. This may seem strange given that credit risk is the most traditional kind of risk that banks have been used to cope with. Credit-risk models are much more difficult to implement and test than VaR models, which generally deal with publicly traded assets that can provide a vast amount of data for implementation and testing. In fact, it is far harder to treat data on the market value of loans or on how much of the value of bad loans banks eventually recover.

A substantial amount of work is needed to estimate how much of a loan can be recovered if it turns bad and how long the recovery procedures take. That leaves it uncertain whether the output of credit risk models is statistically valid and can reasonably be used for determining how much capital is needed to face credit risk. Unfortunately, this will not be clear until after the next recession.

NOTES

1. The trading book means the bank's proprietary positions in financial instruments, whether on- or off-balance sheet, which are intentionally held for short-term trading, and/or which are taken on by the bank with the intention of making profit from short-term changes in prices, rates, and volatilities. All trading book positions must be marked-to-market or marked-to-model every day. For market risk capital purposes, an institution may include in its measure of general market risk certain nontrading book instruments that it deliberately uses to hedge trading positions.

2. We return to this point in greater detail in Chapters 5 to 9 and 13 to 16. One of the strongest criticisms to VaR models based on the assumption of normality of portfolio assets'/liabilities' or market factors' returns is that this assumption does not account properly for large market movements that can be justified only under a non-normal statistical approach.

3. Basle Committee on Banking Supervision, 1998 Framework for Internal Control Systems in Banking Organizations, September.

4. Members of the G-10 are Belgium, Canada, France, Germany, Italy, Japan, the Netherlands, Sweden, United Kingdom, and the United States, plus Luxembourg and Switzerland.

5. As required for assessing capital adequacy for market risk.

6. This is known as the "Precommitment approach."

7. Basle Committee on Banking Supervision, "A New Capital Adequacy Framework," June 1999, Executive Summary.

8. See Chapter 4 for further details.

4

A Simple Introduction to Value at Risk

C ommercial banks, investment banks, insurance companies, nonfinancial firms, and pension funds hold assets that may include stocks, bonds, currencies, and derivatives. Each institution needs to quantify the amount of risk its portfolio may incur in a day, week, month, or year. For example, a bank must assess its potential losses to set aside enough reserves to cover them. The growing importance of the Treasury, run as a profit center, and the ongoing process of securitization have emphasized the importance of market risk for banking management.

Credit rating and regulatory agencies also must assess likely losses on portfolios since they need to set capital requirements and issue credit ratings. How can these institutions judge the likelihood and magnitude of potential losses on a given portfolio? The Value at Risk (VaR) approach and methodologies can be used to estimate these losses.

While the concept of VaR is simple, the implementation of VaR-based models is all but an easy task. Given some weaknesses implied in the theoretical rationale of the approach and in the statistical estimates used to build VaR models, results must always be interpreted with caution and must be fostered with a strong cultural background about financial risk management (this is especially true for CEOs and senior managers).

This chapter provides an overview of the Value at Risk approach and methodologies; it gives the reader a general understanding of what VaR is and how it can be used to measure market risk. An in-depth analysis of VaR (both from a theoretical and methodological point of view) goes beyond the scope of this chapter and will be pursued in the following chapters.

WHAT IS VALUE AT RISK?

Value at Risk is a statistical concept and is itself just a number: it is the maximum loss that an institution (in our case a bank) can be confident it would lose on a portfolio of assets due to "normal" market movements. This definition implies that losses greater than the VaR are suffered only with a specified small probability.

P. Jorion, in a milestone book on VaR, defines the VaR this way: "VaR summarizes the expected maximum loss (or worst loss) over a target horizon within a given confidence level."[1]

From Jorion's definition, we can figure out the most important characteristics of VaR:

- *VaR is a summary measure.* While summary measures assessing the exposure to specific sources of risk have existed for a long time, VaR provides a unique measure of risk that takes into account all possible sources of market risk in an integrated framework. This characteristic makes VaR particularly appealing and easy to communicate to senior management.
- *VaR requires that it is possible to express future profits and losses on a portfolio* (hereafter P&L) *in stochastic terms* so that each future expected P&L (or intervals of P&Ls) can be associated with its probability to occur. This can be done by observing historical data and projecting them into the future or assuming an appropriate probability/density function for expected P&Ls.
- *VaR depends on the time horizon chosen.* Heuristically, for a given portfolio, we expect the VaR for a one-day time horizon to be smaller than the VaR for a one-month time horizon. This is nothing more than common sense: expected P&Ls on a given stock for a one-month holding period are commonly expected to be larger (in absolute values) than the expected P&Ls on the same stock for a one-day holding period.
- *VaR depends on the probability level chosen.* In fact, we expect actual future losses to exceed the VaR with a given probability (for example 5%) over the specified time horizon. The higher the level of probability, the smaller (but also the less useful) the VaR.

In other words, *VaR is a simple way to describe the magnitude of the likely losses on a given portfolio.* The VaR approach is flexible because it can be adapted to the needs of different financial institutions simply by choosing the appropriate time horizon and probability level. One of its main weaknesses is that the concept of VaR does not require any specific theoretical assumption on the behavior of financial markets. Consequently, a good amount of judgment and subjectivity is required to implement VaR-based risk measurement systems. The choice of different models describing the market behavior leads to results that can be, and often actually are, dramatically different from each other.

The Choice of the Time Horizon

The choice of the time horizon is mainly subjective and related to the business of the bank/financial institution and to the kind of portfolio under analysis. For a bank trading portfolio invested in high liquid currencies, the choice of a 1-day time horizon is probably the best one. For an investment manager with quarterly portfolio rebalancing and reporting focus, a 90-day is more appropriate. Ideally, the time horizon corresponds to the longest period needed for an orderly portfolio liquidation.[2] If the time horizon is shorter than the time needed for an orderly portfolio liquidation, the liquidity risk must be explicitly incorporated into the model.

Banks and financial institutions typically use a 1-day time horizon to mark-to-market effectively their assets portfolio, given the large amount of daily trading and the importance of financial assets in their balance sheet. For nonfinancial firms, larger periods (even 1 month) may be appropriate as well. Time horizon is fundamental especially when comparing VaRs of two different portfolios; it makes no sense to compare the VaR on a 10-day time horizon with the VaR on a 1-day time horizon. The former is, *ceteris paribus,* larger than the latter.

We do not have to calculate different VaRs for different time horizons. In fact, under a set of restrictive but commonly accepted assumptions, the VaR for a t-day time horizon is approximately $\sqrt{t}$ times the VaR computed using a 1-day time horizon.[3] For example, if the computed VaR for a given portfolio over a 1-day time horizon at 95% confidence level is $1,000,000, the VaR for the same portfolio over a 10-day time horizon (at the same confidence level) is $1,000,000 * \sqrt{10} \cong \$1,000,000 * 3.16 \cong \$3,160,000$, where the symbol "$\cong$" means "approximately equal to." Apart from the statistical assumptions needed to scale the risk by this simple linear transformation, one should always remember that a computed VaR applies to a given portfolio and that the (sometimes implicit) assumption underlying the risk scaling is that the original portfolio remains unchanged throughout the new (and longer) time horizon. This may not be reasonable, especially for longtime horizons.

The Choice of the Probability Level

Finance theory provides no guidance about the magnitude of the probability level Ω;[4] this probability mainly depends on how the risk management system wants to interpret the VaR numbers. Should a loss occurring with probability equal to 5% or 1% be considered as "extreme"? From the risk manager's side, it is a matter of choice. Commercial banks using VaR systems have chosen different levels of probability. The same can be said for nonfinancial firms that have reported using VaR systems to measure and manage their financial risk.

Table 4.1 summarizes the confidence level (equal to $1 - p$) used by some banks and nonfinancial firms.[5]

The Choice of the Probability (Density) Function of Expected Returns

The computation of VaR requires that the probability density function of expected returns (or expected price changes of the portfolio) is known[6] or can be approximated with a known distribution. The most (almost exclusively) used distribution is the normal distribution. This assumption significantly simplifies the computational burden required for calculating the VaR and provides the risk manager with an enormous statistical toolkit. Reliance on normality is enhanced because almost all the known inferential statistical methods start with the assumption of normality, which is theoretically justified on the basis of the Central Limit Theorem. A great portion of empirical studies on assets' returns do not support the assumption of normality, indicating that empirical distributions of assets' returns have higher peaks around the mean and heavier tails than the normal distribution. In the following chapters, this assumption is relaxed and the consequences for the calculation of VaR are shown. We assume that the asset returns are normally distributed.

TABLE 4.1   A Summary of Confidence Levels

Company Name	Confidence Level (%)
Bankers Trust	99
Citibank	95.4
J.P. Morgan	95
Bank of America	95
Mobil Oil	99.7

A FORMAL DEFINITION OF VaR

It is now possible to give a formal definition of VaR:

> *Given a probability of ω percent and a holding period of t days, an entity's VaR is the loss that is expected to be exceeded with a probability of only x percent on the t-day holding period.*

VaR is the value for which

$$Prob[abs(loss) > VaR] < \Omega \qquad (4.1)$$

For example, a portfolio with VaR equal to $10 for a 1-day period and 95% of probability means that this portfolio will have a loss exceeding $10 for a 1-day period in 5% of the times only. This is equivalent to saying that, given an infinite number of 1-day periods, the loss will be larger than $10 in only 5% of the periods.

If the P&Ls probability density function over the chosen time horizon is known in advance, the computation of VaR is straightforward. If the probability density function is normal, the calculations required are easy since every normal distribution can be standardized to the well-known Z-distribution tabulated in every book of statistics.

The next paragraphs provide simple examples of VaR computations.

A NONPARAMETRIC APPROACH

The method for calculating VaR shown in this section is nonparametric (i.e., it does not require any assumption about the probability distribution of returns). Suppose, as a market index fund's manager, our objective is to calculate the daily VaR for our fund at 95% confidence level. Also suppose that the current value of our fund is $10m.

To calculate VaR without assuming any probability function of market returns, we must rely on historical data. Through a computer simulation, we have constructed an hypothetical time series of the market index values made up of 1,001 observations. (Details about the computer simulation are given in the Appendix of this chapter.)

As the market index fund's manager we can rely on 1,001 historical daily index values to calculate the daily VaR at 95% confidence. The following five steps are needed:

1. Convert the time series of 1,001 market index values into a series of 1,000 market index returns.

2. Using the historical 1,000 daily returns, compute 1,000 possible values of the fund over a 1-day time horizon and hence 1,000 simulated 1-day variations of the value of the fund. The underlying assumption is that over 1,001 days we can explore the full range of possible market index daily returns.
3. The simulated variations of the fund are ordered, and an observed frequency distribution is figured out.
4. The amount of variation that has, at its "left," 5% of all the simulated outcomes is figured out.
5. The absolute value of the amount found at Step 4 is the daily Value at Risk.

The complete procedure is described in the Appendix to Chapter 4. The time series plot of the market index values and the simulated frequency distribution of fund's variations are shown in Figures 4.1 and 4.2 respectively.

Table 4.2 shows the computed VaR for different combinations of confidence levels and time horizons. The VaR for different time horizons has been computed by scaling the 1-day VaR multiplying 1-day VaR by $\sqrt{t}$. As expected, VaR has a negative correlation Ω (the lower the probability to be exceeded, the higher the computed VaR) and a positive correlation with the time horizon (the longer the time horizon, the higher the expected losses).

FIGURE 4.1   Market Index Plot

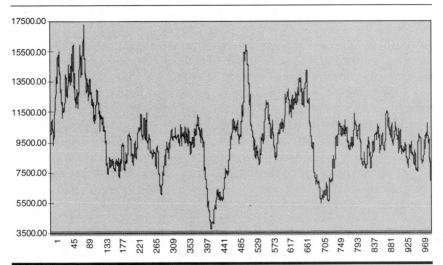

FIGURE 4.2 Simulated Frequency Distribution

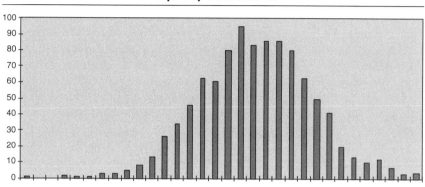

VaR can be used to get a first measure of the reserves to set aside because of the expected loss on the portfolio. For example, the amount of reserves to set aside quarterly for the portfolio of assets at hand can be approximated by

$$1 - \text{quarter VaR} = 1 - \text{day VaR} * \sqrt{60}^7 \qquad (4.2)$$

At 95% confidence level, this is approximately equal to \$6,118.

A PARAMETRIC APPROACH

In this section, we use a parametric approach to calculate VaR for a portfolio made up of an asset denominated in a foreign currency. A parametric approach requires knowing or assuming the probability distributions

TABLE 4.2 Summary of VaR Computations

Confidence Level (%)	Time Horizon			
	1 Day	2 Days	5 Days	10 Days
90	616	871	1,377	1,948
95	790	1,117	1,766	2,498
97.5	923	1,305	2,064	2,919
99	1,182	1,672	2,643	3,738

of assets' return in advance. Throughout this example, we assume the probability density function of assets' returns to be normal.

Suppose, as the risk manager of a U.S. bank, our objective is to measure the daily VaR at 95% confidence level on our DEM2,000,000 asset. Let us suppose that spot exchange rate is 0.50 $/DEM. It means that the DEM-denominated asset is worth $1,000,000 at the current exchange rate. We know, from past experience or just by judgment, that daily changes of $/DEM exchange rate follow a normal distribution with zero mean and standard deviation equal to 0.05. This distribution is shown in Figure 4.3 (variations are expressed in basis points).

Given the well-known properties of the normal distribution, we know that about 66% of the distribution is between −1 standard deviations and +1 standard deviations and about 95% is between −2 and +2 standard deviations. For our problem, we must find the value that leaves at the left 5% of the distribution. From basic statistic courses, we know that this value corresponds to −1.645 standard deviations. Formally:

$$\int_{-\infty}^{-1.645\sigma} N(x) = 0.05 \qquad (4.3)$$

Since we are using the American notation, a decrease in the $/DEM means that the dollar is appreciating versus the DEM. If the US$ appreciates,

FIGURE 4.3   Distribution of Expected $/DEM FX Variations

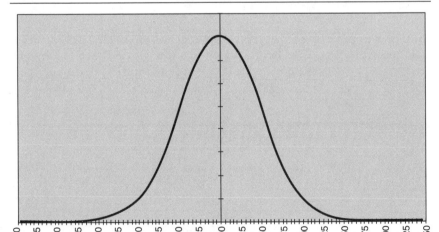

the value (in terms of our domestic currency, i.e., the US$) of our DEM-denominated asset decreases. In other words, fewer dollars are needed to buy one deutsche mark. Our objective is to measure the effects of this risk on the DEM-denominated asset.

We can now calculate corresponding expected variation of $/DEM exchange rate at −1.645 standard deviations:

$$\text{Maximum probable variation} = 1.645 * \sigma = 1.645 * 0.05$$
$$\cong 8.23\% \tag{4.4}$$

It means that with a current exchange rate of 0.50 $/DEM, out of 100 repeated 1-day outcomes, 95% of the times the 1-day $/DEM exchange rate will be greater than $0.5 * 0.0823 = 0.4589$.

The VaR can be computed from Equations 4.4 and 4.5 by multiplying the maximum probable variation by the exposure in the DEM-denominated asset:

$$\text{VaR} = \text{exposure} * abs(\text{maximum probable variation})$$
$$= DM2,000,000 * (0.5 - 0.4589) = \$82,300 \tag{4.5}$$

Heuristically, given that daily expected $/DEM exchange variations are normally distributed with zero mean and standard deviation equal to 0.05, the maximum probable loss expected over a 1-day time horizon on a $1,000,000 DEM-denominated asset is equal to $82,300. Equivalently, it is possible to affirm that the bank's risk manager can be 95% confident that the dollar value of the DEM-denominated asset on a 1-day time horizon is greater than $835,500.

Assuming normality, VaR for a single asset can be easily calculated by a simple closed-form formula:

$$\text{VaR} = \alpha \sigma P \sqrt{t} \tag{4.6}$$

where α is the Z-score corresponding to the probability level ω chosen. For example, if $\omega = 5\%$, then α is equal to 1.645; if $\omega = 2.5\%$, then α is equal to 1.96; and if $\omega = 1\%$, then $\alpha = 2.33$.

σ is the standard deviation of returns of the asset on a given time horizon.

P is the current market value of the asset.

$\sqrt{t}$ is the adjustment factor needed to scale the variance of the asset's return. For example, if we want to calculate VaR for a monthly time horizon and we have computed σ on a daily basis, the adjustment factor is equal to $\sqrt{30}$.

MARKING-TO-MARKET AND VaR WITH DELTA FACTORS

The application of VaR requires valuing all the assets at their market values (this is often called "marking-to-market"). This is a simple task if assets are traded in a liquid market since prices can be directly derived from the market itself. If assets are traded in an illiquid market, it is necessary to perform specific evaluation models that allow the calculation of prices based on prices of similar assets that are commonly traded.[8]

After assigning market values to all the assets in the portfolio, it is necessary to estimate the probability density functions of the price changes for all those assets and, hence, for the portfolio as a whole.[9] The number of assets in the portfolio of a financial institution like a bank is extremely high. It has been already discussed how it is possible to apply two approaches, both based, at least partially, on historical data. For each asset in the portfolio, it is necessary to complete either of the following processes:

- Compute the frequency distribution (sometimes called the "observed" probability distribution) of price changes and compute VaR based on the sample percentile.
- Use historical data and/or judgment to estimate the mean and the variance of price changes assuming they are normally distributed over the chosen time horizon.

In the first case, the required percentile is simply observed. In the latter, it is calculated from a known distribution. Even with a limited number of assets, this process becomes soon computationally cumbersome unless the portfolio under examination can be directly observed and has been tracked in the past so that a unique probability/frequency distribution is needed. Most often, a portfolio of "new" instruments cannot be tracked because observations are not available at all or there is an insufficient number of observations to provide a sound basis for statistical inference.

A simplified approach consists of identifying the basic market rates and market prices that affect the value of a portfolio of assets. These basic market rates are known as *market factors* or *risk factors*. It is necessary to identify a limited number of basic risk factors simply because otherwise trying to come up with a portfolio level quantitative measure of market risk explodes in complexity. Thus, expressing the assets' values in terms of a limited number of basic risk factors is an essential step in making the problem manageable.

Typically, risk factors are identified by decomposing the instruments in the portfolio into simpler instruments more directly related to basic risk factors and interpreting the actual instruments as portfolios of the simpler instruments.[10] "Decomposing" the risk of an asset into its basic components is known as *risk mapping*. Chapters 10 to 12 will be devoted to the description of risk-mapping procedures for many types of assets.

The reliance on risk factors for describing assets' price changes is a parsimonious approach since it only requires the estimation of the frequency distribution/probability density functions of price changes for a limited number of factors. If we assume that market factors' changes follow a multivariate normal distribution, we only need to calculate the vector of expected changes and the variance-covariance matrix of market factors' changes.

Nevertheless, a further step is necessary. In fact, price changes of market factors must be translated into price changes of single specific assets to calculate VaR. The easiest way is to define, through financial theory, and to estimate, using statistical end econometric tools, a set of coefficients linking a specific asset's price changes to market factors' price changes. As a first approximation, we will assume this relationship to be linear. Given n market factors named $F_1, F_2, \ldots, F_n$ price changes for asset j can be expressed as

$$\Delta A_j = \sum_{i=1}^{n} \delta_{ij} * \Delta F_i \qquad (4.7)$$

The price changes of asset j can be expressed as the sum of price changes of market factors multiplied by a parameter representing the linear relationship between market factors' changes and single asset price changes. This parameters are specific to each asset or class of assets and are usually referred to as *delta parameters*. Delta parameters play a special role in the context of VaR.[11] In the context of option pricing, delta coefficient represents a linear approximation of the option's price changes due to price changes of the underlying asset. Formally:

$$\delta = \frac{\partial C}{\partial S} \qquad (4.8)$$

where S is the spot price of the underlying asset. If $\delta = 0.5$, it means that a change, for example, of \$1 in the price of the underlying asset will cause a change of \$0.5 in the price of the call option. Similarly, VaR δs can be expressed as

$$\delta_{ij} = \frac{\partial A_i}{\partial F_j} \qquad (4.9)$$

where A_i is a given asset and F_j is the j-th market factor.

For a single risk factor, the closed-form formula for calculating a single asset's VaR becomes:

$$\text{VaR} = \alpha \sigma_{RF} \delta P \sqrt{t} \qquad (4.10)$$

In the next section, we illustrate risk decomposition and the use of delta parameters to calculate VaR for an interest rate swap (IRS).

MARKING-TO-MARKET AN IRS

Swaps are agreements between two parties to exchange cash flows in the future according to a prearranged formula. The first swap was negotiated in 1981, and since then the market has been growing very rapidly. In the context of VaR, swaps and forwards/futures belong to the class of linear derivatives. Linear derivatives[12] are so called since their risk can be adequately described by linear VaR models.

Definition

An interest rate swap (IRS) is a contract in which "one party, B, agrees to pay the other party, A, cash flows equal to interest at a predetermined fixed rate on a notional principal for a number of years. At the same time, party A agrees to pay party B cash flows equal to interest at a floating rate on the same principal for the same period."[13] The currencies of the two cash flows are the same and the swap can range from 2 to 15 years.

Pricing

With no risk of default, an IRS can be valued through decomposition. An IRS, in fact, can be valued as a long position in one bond combined with a short position in another bond.[14] Suppose that a swap has been agreed between a company and a bank. The bank pays the floating rate cash flows while the company pays the fixed rate cash flows. We can figure out the swap as composed by two contemporaneous transactions:

1. The company has lent the bank the notional at the floating rate.
2. The bank has lent the company the notional at the fixed rate.

From the bank's perspective, an IRS is a portfolio composed of two bonds: the floating rate note issued and the fixed rate bond underwritten.

The value of the swap can be defined as:

$$V = B_{fix} - B_{float}$$ (4.11)

where V is zero at the origination of the contract. In fact, at the beginning of the contract both the floating rate note and the fixed rate bond are worth par. During its life, the contract can have either a positive or a negative value. Since the swap is a zero-sum game, if the value of the swap increases for one party, it decreases of the same amount for the other party.

Defining Risk Factors and δ Parameters

Investors enter into swaps to change their exposure to interest rate uncertainty by exchanging interest flows. Since a swap can be considered a portfolio of bonds, the value of the swap depends on the market interest rate r:[15]

$$V = f(r)$$ (4.12)

For the sake of simplicity, we assume the yield curve to be flat and that only parallel shifts of the yield curve take place. So a unique market interest rate can be considered the risk factor used to measure the risk of an IRS.

The next step is to define a linear relationship between the market interest rate changes and swap rate changes so that it is possible to apply an equation like

$$\Delta V = \delta \, \Delta r$$ (4.13)

The relationship between bond price changes and interest rate changes can be expressed linearly through modified duration. Modified duration measures the changes of the price of a bond in response to variation of the interest rate. Modified duration is then the delta parameter of Equation 4.12.

Modified duration for a coupon bond D^* is defined by Equation 4.14.

$$D^* = \left(\frac{-1}{P}\right)\left(\frac{dP}{dr}\right) = \frac{D}{(1+r)}$$ (4.14)

where P is the price of the bond.

    dr is the change in market interest rate.

    D is the "standard" duration.

Duration, as originally proposed by Macauley, is the weighted maturity of each bond payment where the weights are proportional to the present value of each cash flow. The relationship between modified duration and duration are expressed in Equations 4.15 and 4.16.

$$D^* = \left(\frac{-1}{P}\right)\left(\frac{dP}{dr}\right) = \frac{D}{(1+r)} \tag{4.15}$$

where

$$D = \frac{\left[\dfrac{\sum t^* C_t}{(1+r)^t}\right]}{\left[\dfrac{\sum t}{(1+r)^t}\right]} \tag{4.16}$$

Since duration is a linear measure of risk, the duration of a portfolio of securities is just the weighted average of individual durations, as expressed in Equation 4.17:

$$Dp = \sum x_i * D_i \text{ where } \sum x_i = 1 \tag{4.17}$$

Since an IRS can be decomposed into a portfolio of bonds, the duration of the swap is just the sum of the durations of the two legs.

Up to this point, two additional steps have been performed to calculate VaR for an IRS:

1. A market factor (r) has been identified.
2. A linear delta coefficient, the modified duration, has been identified for measuring risk in term of a risk factor's variations.

Measuring Risk for an IRS

From Equation 4.15, which defines modified duration, we can derive the formula to approximate the change of price of a bond caused by a change in the interest rate:

$$dP = -D^* P \, dr \tag{4.18}$$

The fixed rate of a swap is described and valued as if it were a fixed rate bond while the floating leg as if it were a floating rate note. The fixed leg subjects the investors to interest rate risk up to the maturity of the swap. For the floating leg, the risk depends on the timing of reset on the floating rate leg. With continuous resetting, this leg has no risk. Since the coupon is reset at discrete time intervals, only one (the next) is set on the floating rate at any given time.

This means that the investors are exposed to interest rate risk up to the maturity of this payment. Just before the reset, in fact, the floating rate leg behaves exactly like a cash investment with fair value equal to the principal. Just after the reset, the floating rate note becomes a short-term fixed-rate note.[16] If we consider a situation where the floating-rate note is about to be reset, this leg has no risk, so we can consider the risk on the fixed rate leg only and we can rewrite Equation 4.13 as:

$$dV = -D^* P \, dr \tag{4.19}$$

assuming small variations of r (hence Δr and ΔV are substituted by dV and dr respectively). Turning back to the example let us assume that the schedule of payments for the fixed rate leg of an IRS is given in Table 4.3. The yield curve is supposed to be flat at 4% and all the payments are yearly at 4%. We assume the bank is long on the fixed rate leg (i.e., it has "bought" the fixed rate bond). It means that is if the interest increases, the value of the fixed rate leg decreases and vice versa.

For the reasons already underlined, we concentrate only on the fixed rate leg of the swap. To measure the value changes of the fixed rate leg, we have to calculate the appropriate delta-coefficient (i.e., the modified duration). Calculations are shown in Table 4.4.

At time zero, with a yield curve flat at a rate of 4%, the value of the fixed rate leg is 1,000 (i.e., the notional of the swap). The modified duration is 3.42 years. We can approximate the value changes of the fixed rate leg of the swap just by applying Equation 4.18.

We used modified duration to simulate price changes of an equivalent fixed rate bond at time zero. Calculations are shown in Table 4.5. The actual price is computed by discounting all the cash flows with the new

TABLE 4.3 Fixed Rate Leg for an IRS

Year	CF	PV of CF	CF × Time (yr)
1	40	38.46	38.46
2	40	36.98	73.96
3	40	35.56	106.68
4	1,040	889.00	3,555.99

TABLE 4.4   Price and Duration for Table 4.3

Price	1,000.00
Duration	3.56
Modified duration	3.42

rate, while the expected price is calculated applying Equation 4.18 and then computing back the new price.

The linear model approximates in a fairly good way the price variations caused by parallel movements of the yield curve. We must also consider that Equation 4.17 works well for small movements, while we have simulated fairly large movements (±2%). As described in Chapters 10 to 12, the prediction capability of duration-based models can be improved by introducing a quadratic term able to describe in a more adequate fashion the behavior of duration when interest rate changes.[17]

Since we have supposed the floating rate note to have zero risk, we can approximate the VaR of the whole swap by simply taking the VaR on the fixed rate leg.

Calculating VaR

The final step consists of figuring out the amount of the risk factor's changes at the desired percentile cutoff level. This amount can be derived from a frequency distribution taken from past experience or by assuming that changes of interest rates are distributed in accordance with a known pdf. Suppose that interest rate changes are normally distributed with zero mean and a standard deviation of 50 basis point on a 1-year time horizon. Applying the parametric approach, we have calculated the VaR for different probability levels and a 1-year time horizon. Calculations are reported in Table 4.6.

TABLE 4.5   Simulated versus Actual Price Changes for a Fixed Income Security

Δ Rate (%)	Expected	Actual
+1	965.80	964.54
+2	931.60	930.70
−1	1,034.20	1,037.17
−2	1,068.40	1,076.15

TABLE 4.6   VaR for an IRS on a 1-Year Time Horizon

Confidence Level (%)	Δ Rate	VaR
90	0.8	28.123
95	1.0	33.508
99	1.2	39.834

FROM SINGLE-ASSET RISK TO PORTFOLIO RISK

So far we have calculated VaR for single assets only; we still have not considered VaR for a portfolio of assets. The risk of a portfolio of assets, as modern portfolio theory states, is not just the sum of the risks of every single asset in portfolio, but also the covariances between price changes of the assets themselves. In the context of VaR, it means that we must consider the covariances between risk factors to correctly calculate VaR for a portfolio. As long as market factors are not perfectly correlated, diversification will reduce risk and, hence, VaR. The process of portfolio risk aggregation will be given in-depth coverage in the context of delta-normal models in Chapters 13 to 16. A simple example will illustrate the basic effects of diversification on VaR measures.

Suppose that an Italian bank holds a long position in a 10-year 10 million DEM-denominated German T-bond (hereafter called "bund"). The risk manager wants to calculate the VaR of the bund at 95% confidence level on a 1-year time horizon. The position is exposed both to foreign exchange risk and to interest rate risk. We will calculate separately the VaR for each of the risks and then aggregate the risks providing a unique VaR that incorporates both foreign exchange risk and interest rate risk. The computation of VaR will be performed through a parametric approach, assuming normality of risk factors' changes.

We first calculate the foreign exchange risk and the related VaR (for simplicity, VaR_1). The risk factor is the ITL/DEM exchange rate with a $\sigma_{dem/itl} = 0.7\%$ on a 1-year basis. The delta parameter is equal to 1 since changes in the exchange rates completely affect the value of the position. Applying Equation 4.10, we have:

$$VaR1 = 1.65*0.7\%*1*10m*1100 = 127.050.000 \text{ ITL} \qquad (4.20)$$

supposing a current exchange rate of 1100 ITL/DEM.

We will now calculate the VaR related to interest rate risk (VaR_2). The German bund is supposed to be quoted at par, to have a modified duration (i.e., the delta parameter of this example) of 7.3 years. In addition, the 1-year estimated volatility of returns is assumed to be 0.8%. The calculation of VaR_2 is shown in Equation 4.21.

$$VaR = 10 \text{ million DEM} * 0.008 * 1.65 * 7.3 * 1 * 1100 = 1,059,960,000 \quad (4.21)$$

Since for a long position in a German bund, the holding bank is exposed both to interest rate risk and currency risk, in case of a perfect correlation between movements between return of the bund and the exchange rate, the VaR of the position is simply equal to 70,143,292. If the correlation coefficient between changes in interest rates (the bund's risk factors) and in ITL/DEM exchange rate is equal to 0.4, the VaR of the position is given by:

$$VaR = \sqrt{\left[VaR_1^{\,2} + VaR_2^{\,2} + \left(2 * 0.4 * VaR_1 * VaR_2 \right) \right]} = 1,116,866,706 \quad (4.22)$$

The effect of diversification is given by the difference between the undiversified VaR (the mere sum of VaR_1 and VaR_2) and the diversified VaR (1,187,010,000 − 1,116,866,706 = 70,143,294). It may seem contradictory that for showing the effect of diversification we chose an example of a single instrument subject to two sources of risk instead of choosing two or more different instruments. The contradiction is only apparent: the heart of VaR is the process of risk decomposition of any asset in the portfolio into simpler basic instruments (whenever possible). So a bund subject both to interest rate risk and foreign exchange risk can be decomposed into two simpler instruments, one subject to interest rate risk only and the other subject to foreign exchange risk only. The German bund can be regarded as a portfolio composed by a long position in an ITL denominated fixed income bond and a long position in DEM-denominated asset subject only to foreign exchange risk.

The process of aggregating risk from single assets to provide the portfolio risk can be generalized for more than two assets. The computational burden becomes more and more cumbersome, and we have to rely on matrix algebra to make the problem workable.[18] An example will show how diversification works for a portfolio composed of more than two assets. Table 4.7 gives a snapshot of an Italian bank's assets in the trading book. For each asset, the current exposure, the currency of denomination, and the delta parameter are provided and the relevant risk factor identified.[19]

Note that the long-term U.S. T-bond has been decomposed into two assets subject to two sources of risk (the other having been neutralized).

TABLE 4.7 Calculation of VaR for a Portfolio of Financial Assets

Assets	Risk Factors	Currency of Denomination	Exposure	Delta	Standard Deviation of Market Factors (%)	VaR	Exchange Rate	VaR in ITL
BOT	1 IT short-term ir	ITL	10,000,000,000	0.5	1.1	90,750,000	1	90,750,000
BTP	2 IT long-term ir	ITL	20,000,000,000	4.2	0.9	1,247,400,000	1	1,247,400,000
U.S. T-Bond	3 US long-term ir	USD	10,000,000	7.3	0.8	963,600	1,600	1,541,760,000
U.S. T-Bond	4 ITL/USD exc. rate	USD	10,000,000	1	6.0	990,000	1,600	1,584,000,000
Stock	5 Market index	ITL	5,000,000,000	1.3	10.0	1,072,500,000	1	1,072,500,000

Undiversified VaR	5,536,410,000
Diversified VaR	3,078,529,186
Gain from diversification	2,457,880,814

We will use a parametric approach based on normality of risk factors' changes. Therefore the 1-year standard deviation of each risk factor has been provided.

Assuming a current ITL/USD exchange rate of 1600 ITL/USD, the VaR for each single asset is shown in ITL. The VaR for every single asset has been computed applying Equation 4.9 and is shown in the last column of Table 4.7.

To calculate the risk for the whole portfolio, we must consider the correlation between each pair of risk factors. This process can be easily and elegantly handled with a matrix notation. Denoting with X the vector of individual VaRs and with Θ the correlation matrix between risk factors, the VaR for the whole portfolio can be computed by Equation 4.23:

$$\mathrm{VaR}_p = \sqrt{X'\Theta X} \tag{4.23}$$

where

$$X' = [90,750,000; 1,247,400,000; \ldots; 1,072,500,000] \tag{4.24}$$

and Θ is shown in Table 4.8.

The VaR for the whole portfolio (95% confidence level, 1-year time horizon) is ITL 3,078,529,186, significantly lower than the undiversified VaR equal to ITL 5,536,410,000. The gain from diversification is equal to ITL 2,457,880,814 given by the difference between the undiversified VaR and portfolio VaR. Obviously, if the correlation between each pair of risk factors were 1, the undiversified VaR and the portfolio VaR would have been the same, as predicted by Markowitz's portfolio theory.

Some aspects must be remarked. The first, and perhaps most important, aspect to underline is that diversification[20] plays a key role in the

TABLE 4.8   Correlation Matrix for Risk Factors

	1	2	3	4	5
1	1	0.6	0.1	0.7	−0.1
2	0.6	1	0.2	0.8	−0.3
3	0.1	0.2	1	−0.5	0.2
4	0.7	0.8	−0.5	1	0.4
5	−0.1	−0.3	0.2	0.4	1

calculation of VaR for a portfolio of asset, so that it is possible to construct a zero-VaR portfolio—a portfolio that, based on the cross-correlation between risk factors, is completely immunized against financial risk.

This is a well-known result of MPT: a risk-free portfolio can be constructed when assets are perfectly and negatively correlated ($\rho = -1$) and assets are given the same weight in the portfolio. The second aspect is that the VaR for a given asset cannot be analyzed on a stand-alone basis, but instead it must be valued in the context of the portfolio this asset is going to be added to. Although VaR on a stand-alone basis is always non-negative, the contribution to VaR provided by the introduction of an asset in a portfolio can be positive or negative depending on the correlation of the added asset's returns to the returns of assets previously held in the portfolio.

The third aspect is that this relatively simple approach is valid under the assumptions of linearity of risk and normality of returns. If one of these assumptions is violated, a different set of calculations is needed and results obtained this way can be misleading. Equation 4.23 is particularly important because it provides a closed-form formula for computing VaR for a portfolio of assets under the linearity and normality assumptions. Equation 4.23 represents the "heart" of the delta-normal class models that will be deeply analyzed in Chapters 13 to 16. Nevertheless, since diversification plays an important role in all the most commonly used VaR models, it can be considered a general feature of the VaR approach instead of being considered a characteristic of a single class of models. Since VaR computations under the assumptions of linearity and normality closely resemble modern portfolio theory, it was much easier to introduce this effect in the context of delta-normal models instead of relying on a more general approach.

VaR IN PRACTICE: THE CASE OF CHASE MANHATTAN BANK

To conclude Chapter 4, we will review an example of real implementation of VaR approach in a financial institution, including the approach chosen, and compare it with the concepts examined throughout this chapter.[21]

Chase Manhattan Bank (hereafter Chase) uses VaR to evaluate 1-day market risk for all trading positions. It means, with the terminology adopted in this chapter, that Chase has a 1-day time horizon. The main objective of VaR is to monitor price risk as it intermediates a broad range of financial instruments over several different financial markets. VaR is also used to:

- To set position limits.
- To allocate capital.
- To analyze performances on a risk adjusted basis.[22]

The approach used to calculate VaR is a parametric approach, but the distributions of daily changes are obtained using historical data. The assumptions underlying this choice are:

- Distributions of returns are considered relatively stable over time, so historical distributions can be used to assess future variability of the returns.
- Distributions are closed to zero-normal distributions, so distributions can be described by using only one parameter (i.e., the standard deviation).

The VaR measures one standard deviation; since VaR is computed only in reference with the left tail, it means that daily losses are not expected to exceed this VaR measure in more than about 15% of the cases. This is a much higher percentage than the one chosen by J.P. Morgan in its notorious RiskMetrics model (5% on a daily basis), even if RiskMetrics is not intended to be used for measuring trading risk.[23]

The risk measurement for individual securities includes the following three factors:

1. Size and sign (long or short) of the position.
2. Sensitivity (or elasticity) of its market value to changes in risk factors: these elasticities or sensitivity parameters correspond to the δ parameters discussed earlier.
3. Volatility of the markets (or corresponding *risk factors*).

When the market risk from single assets is aggregated, "value at risk is calculated as the standard deviation of a time series of daily changes in the market value of the portfolio. The market risk of the portfolio is determined by both the exposures of its components and the correlations between movements in the underlying financial prices. As a result, the risk for a portfolio of long positions is generally smaller than the sum of the risks for the individual positions. Similarly, the risk added to an existing portfolio by adding a new transaction is generally less than the risk for the new transaction on a 'stand-alone' basis."[24]

The Chase model also poses a penalty factor, increasing the VaR measures, in the case of illiquid securities, since closing the position can lead to an extra loss due to lack of liquidity.[25]

TABLE 4.9 Risk Factors Used by the Chase VaR Model

Type	Risk Factors	Delta Parameter
Fixed rate bond	Yield to maturity	Duration
Options	Price of underlying security Volatility Short-term interest rates	Delta
Forward FX contracts	Interest rates (domestic and foreign) Spot exchange rate	

Finally, in Table 4.9 we report the risk factors identified by Chase for some types of financial instruments.

CONCLUSION

The objective of this chapter was to provide a comprehensive overview on the VaR. We first defined the concept of VaR and how it can be formally defined for a statistical point of view. Then we examined two possible approaches for calculating VaR: the parametric approach, which assumes that assets' returns follow a known distribution, and the historical simulation approach. Under this second approach, VaR is computed from the sample quartile at the desired probability level. A third approach, the Structured Monte Carlo simulation (SMC) is analyzed in Chapter 17. Since the estimation of returns' probability density function becomes computationally expensive as the number of assets grows, we examined a more parsimonious approach based on the identification of a relatively small number of risk factors. The risk of all the assets in a portfolio is decomposed (some would say "mapped") isolating the effect of each risk factor on assets' price. The parameters that linearly relate risk factors' changes to assets' price changes are known as δ parameters. This way, price changes of every class of instruments can be obtained as a linear combination of risk factors' changes. The process of risk decomposition and the use of δ parameters were shown through an example of VaR calculation for an interest rate swap.

After examining how to calculate VaR for a single asset, the effect of diversification on VaR was shown. Under the assumptions of normality, diversification reduces risk and, consequently, VaR for a portfolio of assets when compared to the mere summation of VaRs for each single asset. Diversification, in other words, was explained in the context of delta-normal models. Finally, the Chase Manhattan approach to VaR implementation was briefly reviewed. In many pieces of literature, VaR is confused with delta-normal implementation, which is only one of the possible ways of calculating VaR. Again, the VaR approach does not require any assumption on the statistical features of risk and returns. Assumptions are introduced to transform a general concept into a manageable model yielding a VaR number with a reasonable computational effort.

That is why statistical assumptions are so important when computing VaR for a given portfolio. Chapters 5 to 9 analyzes in detail the statistical aspects of financial modeling, and through real data examples and numerical simulation, the effect on VaR measures of the different possible hypotheses are described.

APPENDIX: SIMULATING A STOCK INDEX TIME SERIES

In the following Appendix, the process of calculating VaR for the example provided in the section on Parametric Approach is described in detail. We used a computer simulation to generate a time-series of stock index values and returns. We started with an initial value (t_1) of 10,000; then using a computer package (Microsoft™ Minitab) we drew out 1,001 values from a standardized normal variable used as innovations.

The model used to generate the simulated series was a bilinear model in order to obtain a "jagged" series that could more closely resemble actual market index patterns. The coefficients have been selected in order to guarantee a realistic behavior. The model chosen was:

$$I_t = \mu + 0.99 * I_{t-1} + 0.05 * I_{t-1} * e_{t-1} + e_t$$

where μ = drift equal to 100, {e} is the vector of innovations, and e_t are NIID~(0,1).

Market index returns have been calculated as

$$R_t = \frac{\left(I_t - I_{t-1}\right)}{I_{t-1}}$$

The 1,000 daily market index returns have been ordered in order to obtain the "observed" probability function depicted in Figure 4.2 and the sample 5% percentile has been calculated to figure out the required VaR.

NOTES

1. P. Jorion, *Value at Risk*, New York: McGraw-Hill, 1997, 19.
2. *Ibid.*, 20.

3. This aspect is often referred to as the "scaling of variance." It is examined in detail in Chapters 5 to 9. For now, we simply assume this relation to hold. The required assumptions are that portfolio returns are normally and independently distributed along time.

4. In literature, this value is often associated with the Greek letter α. Since α is commonly used for indicating other variables, we prefer to use the Greek letter omega (Ω).

5. P. Jorion, *Value at Risk: The New Benchmark for Controlling Derivatives Risk,* New York: McGraw-Hill, 1997, 20; and T. Linsmeier and N. Pearson, *Risk Measurement: An Introduction to Value at Risk,* Working Paper, 4.

6. For example, from historical data.

7. We consider trading days only.

8. The liquidity of a market poses a great challenge to VaR models since it becomes difficult to assess—for example, from historical data—the volatility of a given asset since the actual loss on that asset can be much higher than predicted simply because of the market's lack of liquidity.

9. The process of calculating the VaR for the whole portfolio given the VaRs of single assets is briefly discussed later in this chapter and in great detail in Chapters 13 to 16.

10. T. Linsmeier and N. Pearson, *Risk Measurement: An Introduction to Value at Risk,* Working Paper, 5.

11. The name is a reminder of the well-known delta risk in the context of option pricing theory and there are many similarities between these two concepts. It is possible to say that options' delta is indeed a special case of VaR's delta.

12. P. Jorion, *Value at Risk: The New Benchmark for Controlling Derivatives Risk,* New York: McGraw-Hill, 1997, 127.

13. J. Hull, *Options, Futures, and Other Derivatives,* Englewood Cliffs, NJ: Prentice Hall, 1997, 111.

14. It can be equivalently decomposed into a portfolio of FRA.

15. Technically speaking, the value of the swap depends on the term structure of the interest rate. We examine in detail the pricing and risk decomposition of fixed income securities in Chapters 10 to 12.

16. P. Jorion, *Value at Risk: The New Benchmark for Controlling Derivatives Risk,* New York: McGraw-Hill, 1997, 134.

17. The effect that describes the way in which duration changes as interest rate changes is known as *convexity.*

18. This is intended to be only an example. A detailed analysis of calculating VaR for a portfolio of correlated assets is given in Chapter 13 to 16, especially Chapters 3 and 4.

19. See G. Lugianano, Lagestione Dei Risemi Finanziari Nella Banca, 1996, Il Mulino, pp. 194–195.

20. As pointed out in Chapters 5 to 9, this is particularly true under the normality assumption or as long as the Central Limit Theory applies. If returns follow a Pareto-stable distribution with finite mean and infinite variance, diversification effect progressively weakens as the rate of decline of the tails to the X-axis decreases. If returns follow a Pareto-stable distribution with infinite mean (and infinite variance) diversification does not reduce risk but instead increases risk. See C. Smithson and C. Smith Jr., *Managing Financial Risk: A Guide to Derivative Products, Financial Engineering, and Value Maximization,* Irwin, 1990.

21. Details about Chase Manhattan approach are taken from C. Smithson and C. Smith Jr., *ibid.,* 483.

22. This aspect of VaR is analyzed in Chapter 17.

23. J.P. Morgan, *RiskMetrics Technical Documentation.*

24. C. Smithson and C. Smith Jr., *Managing Financial Risk: A Guide to Derivative Products, Financial Engineering, and Value Maximization,* Irwin, 1990, 484.

25. By definition, a liquid position can be closed in a short time without incurring large losses.

5

Measuring Prices and Returns

This chapter provides a comprehensive overview of the main issues involved in measuring prices and returns of financial instruments. We show how returns can be used to measure the performance of single assets as well as a portfolio of assets. Two alternative methods for measuring returns are shown and compared; and the preference for log returns, given their desirable statistical properties, is assessed. Finally, the two methods are compared using theoretical point of view and using a real-data sample. Our conclusion supports the idea that log returns should be used when implementing a VaR-based risk-management system.

PERFORMANCE MEASUREMENT

Risk is often measured in terms of price changes. VaR is, by definition, the maximum expected change in the price (market value) of a portfolio, over a predefined time horizon, at a given probability level. Although we are often interested in the price of financial assets, the performance of securities is measured in terms of returns or price changes. This is because prices, being absolute numbers, provide no information on the performance of the underlying security. Loosely speaking, on the basis of a single price, we cannot say that stock A, quoted at $2.00 per share, performs better than stock B, quoted at $5.90 per share. Furthermore, from a statistical point of view, prices have some characteristics, such as not being stationary, that make modeling complex. On the other hand, both price differences and returns are better indicators of a security's performance and, at the same time, are much easier to model with statistical tools. As mentioned, statistical modeling plays a crucial role in the implementation of a VaR system and in the calculation of VaR measures, since the concept of VaR does not require any specific assumptions regarding the

TABLE 5.1   Prices, Price Changes, and Returns

Stock	Original Price	Final Price	Price Change	Return
A	$2.00	$2.5	$0.5	0.5/2 = 0.25
B	$4.00	$4.8	$0.8	0.8/4 = 0.20

path followed by price/ returns, their probability-density function or the structure of risk (e.g., conditional or unconditional). Statistical tractability, therefore, becomes an essential requisite of the time series of interest.

Contrary to prices, price changes do allow some kind of performance comparison between different assets. For example, it is possible to affirm that stock A performed better than stock B because, on a given time horizon, the price change of stock A was $0.5 while the price change of stock B was $-0.5.

Returns, on the other hand, provide an even better representation of security performance, since price changes are standardized by the original price, yielding a relative measure that makes comparison possible, even between securities with very different prices. Table 5.1 shows a very simple example.

Although the price change for stock B was greater then the price change for stock A, we cannot conclude that stock B performed better than stock B, since stock A grew by 0.25 (or, equivalently, 25%) while stock B grew by 0.20 (only 20%).

Financial theory assumes that returns (not price changes or prices) are the compensation for risk. Or, equivalently, it is assumed that the higher the expected return, the higher the risk. The importance of returns has been emphasized by the modern portfolio theory, which is based on a mean-variance approach, where the mean represents assets' expected return and variance their risk.

In the following sections, the properties of price changes and returns are examined in detail.

SINGLE-PERIOD RETURNS

The simplest form of price change is the one taken on a single-period (uniperiodal) time horizon. If we denote with P_t the price of a security at time t, and with P_{t-1} the price at time t minus one period, we define the price change at time t as

$$\Delta P_t = P_t - P_{t-1} \tag{5.1}$$

The time horizon is not restricted to a specific time period: it can be one-day, one-month, or whatever time period is chosen to be the period of interest. We also define as a single-period return, the relative price change:

$$R_t = \frac{\left(P_t - P_{t-1}\right)}{P_{t-1}} = \frac{\Delta P_t}{P_{t-1}} = \left(\frac{P_t}{P_{t-1}}\right) - 1 \tag{5.2}$$

In case of interest or dividends paid, Equation 5.2 can be adjusted, yielding Equation 5.3:

$$R_t = \frac{\left(P_t - P_{t-1} + D_t\right)}{P_{t-1}} = \frac{\left(\Delta P_t + D_t\right)}{P_{t-1}} \tag{5.3}$$

where D_t denotes the interest/dividend paid during the chosen period.

It is easy to translate returns into price changes. From Equation 5.3, we can rearrange the terms, obtaining Equation 5.4:

$$\left(R_t * P_{t-1}\right) - D_t = \Delta P_t \tag{5.4}$$

For example, if stock A

Has recorded a one-year return of 20% at the end of 1997,
Has paid a dividend of $0.5 per share during 1997, and
Had a price at the beginning of 1997 of $5,

the price change is given by Equation 5.5:

$$\Delta P_t = (0.2 * 5) - 0.5 = 0.5 \tag{5.5}$$

By Equation 5.1, P_t is then equal to $P_{t-1} + \Delta P_t = 5 + 0.5 = 5.5$.
P_t can also be obtained directly from Equation 5.6.

$$P_t = P_{t-1} * \left(1 + R_t\right) - D_t \tag{5.6}$$

Equations 5.2 through 5.6 are important because it is always possible to derive price risk from returns. This aspect is fundamental in the context of VaR, since it shows that it is possible to work with returns (given their desirable statistical properties) and then come back to calculate price risk. Over a short time horizon (e.g., on a daily basis) where the influence of dividends/interest most often is null, returns and price changes have the same sign, even if the magnitude is different.

Although returns are scale-free (independent of the price level of the security under examination), they are not unitless, since they are always defined with respect to some time interval. Therefore, a return of 20% is not a complete description of the performance of a security without the specification of the time horizon, in the same way that a VaR of $200 million means nothing until the time horizon and the confidence level are specified. This fact raises the issue of the relation between returns calculated on different time horizons, or multiperiodal returns.

MULTIPERIODAL RETURNS

If we denote by P_0 the price of a security (e.g., a stock) at the beginning of day 1; by P_1 the price at the end of day 1; and by P_k, the price at the end of day k, applying Equation 5.6 (considering interest or dividends being equal to zero), we have

$$P_1 = P_0 * \left(1 + R_1\right) \tag{5.7}$$

but also

$$P_2 = P_1 * \left(1 + R_2\right) \tag{5.8}$$

$$P_k = P_{k-1} * \left(1 + R_k\right) \tag{5.9}$$

where R_1 is the daily return over the first day, R_2 the daily return over the second day, and R_k the daily return over the k-th day.

By recursive substitution we have

$$P_k = P_0 * \left(1 + R_1\right) * \left(1 + R_2\right) * \ \ldots \ * \left(1 + R_k\right) \tag{5.10}$$

or, equivalently

$$\frac{P_k}{P_0} = \left(1 + R_1\right) * \left(1 + R_2\right) * \ \ldots \ * \left(1 + R_k\right) \tag{5.11}$$

From Equation 5.2 we can write

$$R(k) = \left(\frac{P_k}{P_0}\right) - 1 \tag{5.12}$$

where $R(k)$ is the return over a k-day time horizon. Therefore, rearranging Equations 5.11 and 5.12 we have

$$1 + R(k) = \left(1 + R_1\right) * \left(1 + R_2\right) * \ \ldots \ * \left(1 + R_k\right) = \prod_{j=1}^{k} \left(1 + R_j\right) \qquad (5.13)$$

Equation 5.13 is not only a mathematical equivalence but also defines a no-arbitrage condition. With no transaction costs, a buy-and-hold strategy must be equivalent to a strategy of sell and buy. The equality of the two strategies, represented by the right hand side (RHS) and left hand side (LHS) of Equation 5.13, is given by the fact that we start and finish with the same piece of stock so, by definition, the two strategies must be equivalent.

Although returns can be defined over any time horizon, a 1-year time horizon is often assumed as implicit unless stated otherwise.

On the basis of Equation 5.13, it is possible to annualize returns with different time horizons, making them immediately comparable:

$$\text{annualized } R(k) = [1 + R(k)]^{1/k} - 1 \qquad (5.14)$$

where k is the fraction of the year over which $R(k)$ has been computed.

For example, applying Equation 5.14, a quarterly return of 5% is equivalent to an annualized return of:

$$\text{annualized } R(k) = (1 + 0.05)^3 - 1 = 0.157625 = 15.7625\% \qquad (5.15)$$

Because returns are compounded, the annualized quarterly return of 5% is greater than the sum of the returns of three single quarter time horizons; that is, 5% * 3 = 15%. Nevertheless, when single-period returns are small (e.g., daily returns), the following approximation, based on a first-order Taylor expansion, can be applied:

$$\text{annualized } R(k) \cong \left(\frac{1}{k}\right) * \sum_{j=1}^{k} R_j \qquad (5.16)$$

Whether such an approximation is adequate depends on the particular application at hand; anyway, the importance of Equation 5.16 has decreased since the advent of cheap and convenient computing power. In some cases, the difference between the results provided by Equation 5.14 and Equation 5.16 can be very high. For example, the annualized 0.1% 1-day return is 44% when using Equation 5.14 but only 36.5% when using the approximation of Equation 5.16.

In Equation 5.14 we showed how multiple-day returns can be constructed from 1-day returns by aggregating the latter across time. This process is known as temporal aggregation. However, there is another type of aggregation known as "cross-section" aggregation: aggregation is across individual returns (each corresponding to a specific instrument) at a particular point in time. Cross-sectional aggregation is particularly important in the context of VaR, since it allows the calculation of returns for a portfolio of assets.

The return of a portfolio composed of n assets is given by:

$$R_p = \sum_{j=1}^{n} R_j w_j \qquad (5.17)$$

where w_j is the weight given to the i-th asset in the portfolio, with the obvious constraint that

$$\sum_{j=1}^{n} w_j = 1 \qquad (5.18)$$

PERCENTAGE RETURNS AND LIMITED LIABILITY

Although intuitive and easy to compute, percentage returns suffer some major drawbacks. First, the sometimes implicit assumption that actual returns are (approximately) normally distributed cannot be applied to percentage returns. If returns are defined as in Equation 5.2, the probability-density function of returns can be neither symmetric nor bell-shaped because of the limited liability principle. Under limited liability, a characteristic exhibited by most financial assets, the largest loss that an investor can realize is his total investment, and no more. In other words, for the holder of a financial asset, the worst possible scenario is that the asset itself has price zero. This means that expected one-period ahead returns can actually range from −1 (or −100%) to +∞, very different from what is predicted by a normal distribution.

It may be argued, of course, that by choosing the mean and the variance appropriately, the probability of returns smaller than −100% can be made arbitrarily small; however, it will never be zero, as limited liability requires. For example, if the expected return over a 1-year horizon is 15% and the standard deviation is 3%, the probability of an actual return smaller than −100%, as predicted by the normal distribution, is not distinguishable from zero.

On the other hand, if the expected return is −30% and the standard deviation is −30%, the probability that the actual return will be smaller than −100% is about 1% while, in reality, this occurrence is by definition impossible.

Second, if single-period returns are assumed to be normal, multiperi-odal returns cannot be normal. In fact, whereas the sum of n normally distributed variables is a normally distributed variable, the product of n normally distributed variables is not a normally distributed variable. Since the product of single-period returns has a precise economic mean-ing (multiperiod compounded returns), this fact leads to a strange para-dox. The paradox is that a 1-week percentage return can be assumed to be normally distributed when calculated as the standardized difference between the final and the initial price but, at the same time, it cannot be assumed normally distributed when calculated as the product of five 1-day returns if 1-day returns are assumed to be normally distributed!

Although percentage returns can be accepted, especially for very short time horizons, as a reasonable approximation of asset-price be-havior, their theoretical properties are unsatisfactory, especially when returns are scaled over time through the multiperiodal compounding pro-cess. This is a major drawback.

What is needed is a definition for returns that has the desired proper-ties and that, consequently, can be used effectively for financial model-ing. We derive this definition starting from Equation 5.13, which defines the effective rate-of-return over a k-day time horizon. Very often, practi-tioners express rates over any time horizon in terms of annual nominal re-turn. For example, an effective rate of 5% over a 6-month time horizon is often referred to as a 10% 1-year nominal rate. Obviously, the effective 1-year rate given by Equation 5.13 is greater than the nominal rate. In fact, the effective rate is 10.25%, versus a 10% nominal rate.

Generalizing Equation 5.13, given a nominal rate Rn, the effective 1-year rate (Re) is given by Equation 5.19, where m is the frequency of compounding within a year:

$$\text{Re} = \left(\frac{1 + Rn}{m}\right)^m - 1 \tag{5.19}$$

If $m \to \infty$ the term $(1 + Rn/m)^m$ converges to a finite number e^{Rn} (where e is the Neper number, approximately equal to 2.7178). When $m \to \infty$, we have so-called continuous compounding. Since

$$\text{Re} = \lim_{m \to \infty} \left(\frac{1 + R_n}{m}\right)^m - 1 = e^{Rn} - 1 \tag{5.20}$$

a nominal rate of 10% is equivalent to $e^{0.1} - 1 =$ a 10.52% 1-year effective rate with continuous compounding.

We can also derive the formula linking the 1-year effective rate with continuous compounding to the nominal rate. Supposing a $1 initial capital, by definition we have

$$e^{Rc} = \left(\frac{1 + Rn}{m} \right)^m \tag{5.21}$$

hence

$$Rc = m * \ln\left(\frac{1 + Rn}{m} \right) \tag{5.22}$$

For example, the effective 1-year rate, with continuous compounding equivalent to a 10% nominal rate with semiannual compounding is given by

$$Rc = 2 * \ln\left(\frac{1 + 0.1}{2} \right) = 2 * \ln(5.05) = 9.75\% \tag{5.23}$$

and the effective 1-year rate with continuous compounding (Rc), equivalent to a 1-year 10% effective rate, is

$$Rc = \ln(1 + 0.1) = \ln(5.1) = 9.53\% \tag{5.24}$$

Equation 5.22 can be used to define the equivalence between the 1-day effective return and the 1-day effective return with continuous compounding. Substituting the daily percentage return in Equation 5.22, we obtain

$$Rc = \ln(1 + R) = \ln\left(\frac{1 + P_t}{P_{t-1}} - 1 \right) = \ln\left(\frac{P_t}{P_{t-1}} \right) \tag{5.25}$$

If we denote by r_t the daily return with continuous compounding, we have

$$r_t = \ln\left(\frac{P_t}{P_{t-1}} \right) = \ln(P_t) - \ln(P_{t-1}) \tag{5.26}$$

Equation 5.26 is particularly important, since it is an alternative way to define an asset's return. Effective daily returns with continuous compounding, also called log returns, play a special role in financial theory and modeling. Although, especially for very short time horizons, percentual returns and log returns look similar, log returns have all the required theoretical properties that percentage returns miss. From a theoretical point of view, log returns are one of the fundamental bases for the option-pricing theory.

To underline the importance of log returns for calculating VaR, we quote a short passage from RiskMetrics Technical Documentation:

> *RiskMetrics measures change in value of a portfolio . . . in terms of log price changes, also known as continuously compounded returns . . . As previously stated, log price changes (continuously compounded returns) are used in RiskMetrics as the basis for all computations. (RiskMetrics™ technical documentation, fourth edition, 1996, J.P. Morgan/Reuters)*

We examine the properties of log returns in the next section.

PROPERTIES OF LOG RETURNS

Log returns overcome the drawback of percentage returns.

First, the principle of limited liability is never violated since log returns extend over the entire real line. In fact, by taking P_{t-1} as given, P_t can theoretically range from 0 to $+\infty$ over a given time horizon (let's say, 1-day). It means that the ratio P_t/P_{t-1} itself ranges from 0 to $+\infty$. Therefore, since

$$\lim_{P_t \to +\infty} \left(\frac{P_t}{P_{t-1}} \right) = +\infty \tag{5.27}$$

$$\lim_{P_t \to 0} \left(\frac{P_t}{P_{t-1}} \right) = -\infty \tag{5.28}$$

log returns seem better suited for modeling financial assets' behavior.

Second, from Equation 5.13 we have the definition of multiperiodal compounded returns.

Taking natural logarithms on both sides of Equation 5.13, we have

$$\ln [1 + R(k)] = \ln [(1 + R_1) * (1 + R_2) * \ldots * (1 + R_k)]$$
$$= r_1 + r_2 + \ldots + r_k = r(k) \tag{5.29}$$

TABLE 5.2   Cross-Rates on January 2, 1997

01-02-1997	ITL	USD	DEM
ITL	1.0000	0.0007	0.0010
USD	1520.50	1.0000	5.5497
DEM	985.13	0.6453	1.0000

Hence, the continuously compounded multiperiodal return is simply the sum of continuously compounded single-period returns. Taking logs transforms a multiplicative operation into an additive one, making calculations much easier. Furthermore, if r_1, r_2, ... rk are normally distributed, then $r(k)$ is normally distributed, too.

Third, deriving the properties of additive time series is much easier than deriving the properties of multiplicative time series. Furthermore, when options and other complex derivatives are priced, continuous compounding is used to such an extent that it has become a standard in financial modeling. This is easily understandable since calculus provides excellent techniques to deal with continuous series, whereas it is much more complex to work with discrete time series.

Finally, there are two other reasons for using log returns: the first is known as "Siegel's paradox," and is explained later; the other refers to cross-FX rates and can be illustrated through a simple example.

Table 5.2 reports the cross-rates between the Italian lira (ITL), the German mark (DEM) and the US dollar (USD) on January 2, 1997. Table 5.3 reports the same cross rates on December 31, 1997.

While the cross-rates on the main diagonal are obviously equal to one, the cross-rates outside the main diagonal are not symmetrical but the reciprocal of each other. Looking at Table 5.2, the cross-rate ITL/USD, expressed as the number of ITLs needed to buy 1 USD, is found at row 2, column 1, of the table itself (hereafter, "El(i,j)" will indicate the element of

TABLE 5.3   Cross-Rates on December 31, 1997

12/31/1997	ITL	USD	DEM
ITL	1.00	0.0006	0.0010
USD	1759.19	1.0000	1.7920
DEM	981.69	0.5580	1.0000

TABLE 5.4   Percentage Returns

Percentage Returns	ITL	USD	DEM
ITL	0	13.57%	0.06%
USD	−15.70%	0	−15.63%
DEM	−0.06%	13.52%	0

a table located at row i and column j). El(1,2) represents the cross-rate ITL/USD expressed as the number of USDs needed to buy 1 ITL with the obvious no-arbitrage relationship that El(i,j)=1/El(j,1). This form of representing currency rates allows us to analyze the effect of changes in the cross-rates from the standpoint of the investors of all three countries.

Tables 5.4 and 5.5 analyze the percentage and log returns of each of the three assets vis-à-vis the other two.

Table 5.4 analyzes percentage returns. El(2,1) represents the returns on a 1-year time horizon of the ITL vis-à-vis the USD. El(1,2) represents the return of the USD vis-à-vis the ITL.

Apart from the sign, the magnitudes of the two rates are different. Table 5.5, on the other hand, shows a much more symmetrical behavior, since |El(1,2)| = |El(2,1)|, where |a| stands for "absolute value of a." The return of the ITL vis-à-vis the USD is exactly equal, but different in sign, to the return of the USD vis-à-vis the ITL. Differently from what is indicated by percentage returns, log returns show that in response to a unique event, the ITL/USD exchange rate, the return for the two counterparts is exactly the same but opposite in sign.

Log returns, in addition, are necessary if the assumption of normality of cross rates is to be maintained. For example, if percentage returns of exchange rates ITL/DEM are assumed to be normally distributed, DEM/ITL returns cannot be, and usually are not, normally distributed.

TABLE 5.5   Log Returns

Log Returns	ITL	USD	DEM
ITL	0	14.58%	0.06%
USD	−14.58%	0	−14.52%
DEM	−0.06%	14.52%	0

Assuming e_t to be the exchange rate (units of domestic currency/1 unit of foreign currency) at the current time and e_{t-1} the exchange rate at time t-1, we define the single-period percentage return as

$$R_t = \frac{-\left(e_t - e_{t-1}\right)}{e_{t-1}} \tag{5.30}$$

The negative sign stems from the fact that a positive return is gained when the domestic currency appreciates vis-à-vis the foreign currency. In this case, the value of e decreases because fewer units of domestic currencies are needed to buy one unit of a foreign currency.

On the other hand, the cross-rate percentage return is given by:

$$R^*_t = \frac{-\left(e^*_t - e^*_{t-1}\right)}{e^*_{t-1}} \tag{5.31}$$

where $e^*_t = \dfrac{1}{e_t}$

Equation 5.27 can be transformed into

$$R^*_t = \frac{-\left(\dfrac{1}{e_t} - \dfrac{1}{e_{t-1}}\right)}{\left(\dfrac{1}{e_{t-1}}\right)} = \frac{-\left(e_{t-1} - e_t\right) e_{t-1}}{\left(e_t e_{t-1}\right)}$$

$$= \frac{-\left(e_{t-1} - e_t\right)}{e_t} = -\left[\frac{\left(e_{t-1} - e_t\right)}{e_{t-1}}\right]\left(\frac{e_t}{e_{t-1}}\right) = r_t \zeta \tag{5.32}$$

If we assume R_t to be normally distributed, the random variable $R_t * \zeta$ is, generally, not normally distributed (even if we assume ζ to be normally distributed as well), since the product of a normally distributed variable is not a normally distributed variable.

Empirical evidence confirms this theoretical result. We have examined daily exchange rates between the USD and five other currencies (GBP, CAD, DEM, JPY, and CHF). The sample data span from June 1, 1973, to May 31, 1987, for a total number of 3,510 observations for each series.

For each series we computed:

- The daily percentage return of the USD/foreign-currency exchange rate.

- The daily percentage return of the cross-rates (foreign currency/ USD).
- The daily log returns.

The significance of skewness and excess kurtosis (sample kurtosis − 3) has been tested using a standard t-test. In fact, asymptotically, the variance of the estimators of skewness and kurtosis are equal to $6/n$ and $24/n$, respectively.

The results are shown in Tables 5.6 and 5.7 and can be summarized in these terms:

- All the series show a significant level of kurtosis (this is not surprising for daily financial data).
- If a series is not skewed, the series of respective cross-rate returns is skewed, and vice versa.

For example, if the series of USD/CAD returns is skewed, the series of CAD/USD returns is not skewed. If we assume, for example, that the CAD/USD return series is normally distributed, we cannot, at the same time, assume that the USD/CAD is normally distributed. Percentage returns do not preserve normality of reciprocal rates, since a bias in one of the series is introduced. To confirm this behavior, we performed a numerical simulation, using Microsoft Minitab.

We assumed the initial exchange rate ITL/DEM to be 1,000 (or, alternatively, DEM/ITL equal to 0.001). Then, we simulated the behavior of ITL/DEM returns by drawing 10,000 numbers from a normal distribution with zero mean and a standard deviation equal to 1%. Using these 10,000 simulated returns, we derived the ITL/DEM exchange-rate path, using the following equations:

$$ITL/DEM(1) = 1000 * \left(1 + R_1\right) \tag{5.33}$$

$$ITL/DEM(2) = ITL/DEM(1) * \left(1 + R_2\right) \tag{5.34}$$

$$ITL/DEM(t) = ITL/DEM(t-1) * \left(1 + R_t\right) \tag{5.35}$$

and so on, recursively up to ITL/DEM(10,000).

The exchange rate DEM/ITL, for any t, is given by $1/(ITL/DEM(t))$.

TABLE 5.6 Analysis of Percentage Returns

					Percentage Returns					
	USD/GBP	GBP/USD	USD/CAD	CAD/USD	USD/DEM	DEM/USD	USD/JPY	JPY/USD	USD/CHF	CHF/USD
Skewness	-0.1472	-0.0013	0.0462	-0.1129	-0.0625	-0.1125	-0.2708	0.0760	-0.0346	-0.1489
Std. skewness	-3.5594	-0.0320	1.1177	-2.7308	-1.5108	-2.7213	-6.5500	1.8394	-0.8378	-3.6019
Kurtosis	5.6483	5.5147	7.3366	7.3171	5.9160	6.5163	8.2209	8.7191	5.2102	5.7823
Std. kurtosis	68.3065	66.6913	88.7244	88.4886	71.5439	78.8040	99.4185	105.4437	63.0089	69.9275

TABLE 5.7   Additional Analysis of Percentage Returns

	Log Returns				
	USD/GBP	USD/CAD	USD/DEM	USD/JPY	USD/CHF
Skewness	−0.0727	0.0796	0.0237	−0.1745	0.0557
Std. skewness	−1.7582	1.9248	0.5735	−4.2213	1.3480
Kurtosis	5.5651	7.3232	6.1769	8.4247	5.4625
Std. kurtosis	67.3005	88.5627	74.6997	101.8835	66.0595

From the DEM/ITL(t) series, we calculated the DEM/ITL returns. Descriptive statistics for the two series of percentage returns are shown in Table 5.8.

The standard error of the mean has been calculated as standard deviation/$\sqrt{n}$ where n is the sample size. Not surprisingly, the original series (ITL/DEM) has a mean, a skewness, and an excess kurtosis not statistically different from zero. This is not true for DEM/ITL returns. In fact, DEM/ITL returns are (negatively) skewed. On the other hand, if log returns R_t for a given exchange rate series are assumed to be normally distributed, this assumption can be held also for the series given by $R^*_t = 1/R_t$, since the two series would be equal in magnitude but opposite in sign. Kurtosis is not significant in either of the cases, evidencing that notation does not affect the tails of the distribution.

TABLE 5.8   Comparison of Cross-Rate Percentage Returns

	ITL/DEM Percentage Returns	DEM/ITL Percentage Returns
Average	−0.0012	−0.0087
Standard deviation	0.0099665	0.009971751
Standard error	9.966E-05	9.97175E-05
Skewness	0.0158367	−0.075528995
Excess Kurtosis	−0.0048802	0.00456231
t-stat average	−0.1245573	−0.872045947
t-stat skewness	0.646531	−3.083458329
t-stat kurtosis	−0.0996174	0.093127761

Finally, log returns for exchange rates have another appealing property: returns on a given foreign currency can be expressed as the sum of cross-rate returns, as in Equation 5.36:

$$r_{itl/usd} = r_{itl/dem} + r_{dem/usd} \qquad (5.36)$$

Looking back at Table 5.5, we have

$$r_{itl/usd} = -0.06\% - 14.52\% = -14.58\% \qquad (5.37)$$

This is obviously not true for percentage returns.

MEASURING RETURNS FOR A PORTFOLIO OF ASSETS

Since the VaR approach is intended to measure the price risk of a portfolio of assets over different time horizons, an important issue is the aggregation of single-asset returns both on a temporal and a cross-sectional basis. Table 5.9 summarizes the methods for temporal and cross-sectional return aggregations for both percentage and log returns.

We have already shown that temporal aggregation is performed through a multiplicative process for percentage returns and through an additive process for log returns. This is undoubtedly an appealing property of log returns, when compared to percentage returns. Nevertheless, percentage returns are easily aggregated on a cross-sectional basis. In fact, the return for a portfolio is simply the weighted average of the assets' returns, as reported in Table 5.9. The same does not apply to log returns. Given that the log of a sum is not the sum of logs, it follows that

$$r_p \diamond \sum_j w_j * r_j \qquad (5.38)$$

TABLE 5.9   Algorithms for Temporal and Cross-Sectional Aggregation

	Temporal	Cross-Section
Percentage returns	$R(k) = \prod_{j=1}^{k}\left(1+R_j\right)-1$	$R_p = \sum_{j=1}^{n} R_j * w_j$
Log returns	$r(k) = \sum_{j=1}^{k} r_j$	$r_p = \ln\left(\sum_{j=1}^{n} w_j * e^{r_j}\right)$

In empirical applications, the problem is usually minor. When returns are measured over short intervals of time, the continuously compounded return on a portfolio is close to the weighted average of continuously compounded returns of individual assets:

$$r_p \cong \Sigma_j \, w_j * r_j \tag{5.39}$$

For example, RiskMetrics assumes that a portfolio return is a weighted average of continuously compounded returns of individual assets. A common approach is to use simple returns when a cross-section of assets is studied and log returns when temporal aggregation of returns is the focus of interest.

An exact formula for cross-sectional aggregation can be derived from the following equation. Let P_0 be the initial value of a portfolio, P_1 the value at time 1 of the portfolio, and r_j the log return for the j-th asset in the portfolio. For the sake of simplicity, assume that the portfolio is composed of three assets, so P_1 can be expressed as

$$P_1 = w_1 * P_0 * e^{r1} + w_2 * P_0 * e^{r2} + w_3 * P_0 * e^{r3} \tag{5.40}$$

Equation 5.40 can be transformed into

$$\frac{P_1}{P_0} = w_1 * e^{r1} + w_2 * e^{r2} + w_3 * e^{r3} \tag{5.41}$$

Taking logarithms on both the sides of the equation we have

$$\ln\left(\frac{P_1}{P_0}\right) = \ln\left(w_1 * e^{r1} + w_2 * e^{r2} + w_3 * e^{r3}\right)$$
$$r_p = \ln\left(\Sigma_j \, w_j * e^{rj}\right) \tag{5.42}$$

6

Statistics for Prices
and Returns

A risk measurement model attempts to characterize the expected future changes of the value of a portfolio. The basic prerequisite is that we can figure out the temporal dynamic of expected returns and the distribution of returns at any point in time. Compared with prices, returns are much more appealing from an investment and a statistical point of view. Returns are much easier to model than prices and, not surprisingly, VaR-based risk management systems concentrates on return modeling.

The chapter is organized as follows:

- The concept of stochastic process and its importance for financial modeling are reviewed.
- The most important kinds of stochastic processes and their peculiar characteristics are reviewed.
- The random walk and its continuous counterpart (the Geometrical Brownian Motion) are analyzed in more detail given their importance in financial theory and VaR modeling.

Empirical evidence from selected time series is also provided.

STOCHASTIC PROCESSES AND RETURN MODELING

Actual future returns cannot be predicted with certainty. It does not mean that it is impossible to make any forecast, but that future returns can take any value—within a given range—and the probability of any possible outcome is defined by a probability density function (hereafter pdf). Returns can be treated as random variables, characterized by a given pdf. We denote one-period log returns by r.

Financial analysts are not interested only in one-period returns but in the complete path of future returns. To cope with such a need, we must be able to model returns evolving along time. In this context, returns can be considered as random variables evolving along time. We denote this variable as $r(t)$ where t is a time index. At any point in time (i.e., for $t = 1,2, \ldots n$), $r(t)$ is nothing but a random variable. The whole family of random variables $\{r(t)\}$ defines a stochastic process (or random function). The concept of stochastic process is crucially important in time series analysis and financial modeling, because once we have identified the stochastic process generating a series of observations, we can draw inferences from the series and forecast future outcomes.

Since $r(t)$ is a random variable, $r(t)$ can (at any point in time) assume different values. If we could repeat the experiment k times, we would observe k different values of $r(t)$. Thus an observed record of a random process (e.g., an observed series of returns) is merely one record out of a whole collection of possible series of returns that we might have observed. The collection of all the possible records is called the *ensemble* and each particular record is called *realization.* Statisticians used to say that an observed time series is "generated" by a stochastic process. Theoretically, a stochastic process could generate a large, even infinite, number of series. To make a parallel with classic inferential statistics, a stochastic process represents the population while the observed time series represents the sample.

The difference is that, whereas in classical experiments samples are taken randomly from the population and it is usually possible to take as many samples as needed, it is not possible for time series. The observed time series is the only sample we can ever have and, unfortunately, it is all but random.

A stochastic process is fully characterized by the joint probability distribution of the random variables compounding the process $[r(1), r(2), r(3), \ldots r(k)]$ as specified by their joint pdf $F[r(1), r(2), \ldots r(k)]$. The individual pdf $f[r(1)], f[r(2)], f[r(3)]$ represent the marginal distributions of $r(1), r(2), \ldots r(k)$. In general, we cannot construct the joint pdf $F[r(1), r(2), \ldots r(k)]$ from $f[r(1)], f[r(2)], f[r(3)]$ only since these functions tell us nothing about the joint variation of the k random variables apart from the special case where the k random variables are independently distributed. The joint pdf then becomes

$$F[r(1), r(2), \ldots r(k)] = f[r(1)] * f[r(2)] * f[r(3)] \qquad (6.1)$$

Notably, even if k tends to infinity (i.e., we have an infinite number of observations), under general conditions it is possible to estimate the probabilistic structure of the random process (the probability of any event associated with the complete overall behavior) from a large—but finite—number of observations.

STATIONARY PROCESSES

The class of random processes is far too large to enable designing methods of analysis that are suitable for all types of processes. Unless some restrictions about the probabilistic structure of the process are posed, stochastic processes are almost impossible to model with statistical tools. Our objective, on the other hand, is to define statistical methods that enable us to model assets' returns and to assess the probability of future outcomes on the basis of past information.

The most straightforward restriction is to assume that the statistical properties of a process do not change over time. These processes are said to be *stationary*. If $[r(t)]$ is such a process, then it follows not only that

$$f[r(1)] = f[r(2)] = f[r(3)] = \ldots = f[r(k)] \qquad (6.2)$$

but also that

$$F[r(1), r(2), \ldots r(k) \,|\, t] = F[r(1), r(2), \ldots r(k) \,|\, t+1] = \ldots$$
$$= F[r(1), r(2), \ldots r(k) \,|\, t+k] \qquad (6.3)$$

for any k.

Equation 6.3 defines the so-called *strict (or strong) stationarity*. Since a distribution is defined by its moments, an appealing approach from a practical point of view is to define stationarity of a process in terms of stationarity of the moments of its joint pdf. While theoretically not completely satisfactory (there are distributions that have infinite moments up to a given order but that can generate a strict stationary process), this is the most commonly used approach to define and test stationarity. Under this weaker condition, we do not insist, for example, that the marginal pdf of $r(1)$, $r(2)$, $\ldots$, $r(k)$ are identical, but only that the main features of these distributions should be the same (i.e., that their moments, up to a certain order, should be the same). Similarly, we do not insist that the $F[r(1), r(2), \ldots r(k)]$ must be identical over time but merely that, up to a certain order, its moments remain equal. Introducing the notion of "stationarity up to order m" as a weaker form of "complete stationarity," we replace the requirement that two probability distributions are equal with the lesser requirement that they agree up to a certain order m. We know that, under general conditions, the full infinite sequence of moments uniquely determines a distribution; the more moments we specify, the more accurately we determine the distribution.

Hence we might expect that there would be some "break point," m_0, such that processes which were stationary up to order m_0 or higher would, for all purposes, be considered identical to completely stationary processes. In the context of financial analysis, we consider as completely stationary a process stationary up to order 2. It is tempting to assume that a completely stationary process must be stationary up to any order, but this is not necessarily true since a process may be completely stationary even though not any of its moments exist. For example, a process consisting of a sequence of independent and identically distributed Cauchy variables is certainly stationary even if no joint moments exist. In general, provided that joint moments exist, a complete stationary process is stationary up to all orders.

GAUSSIAN PROCESSES

A stochastic process $[r(t)]$ is a Gaussian process if the joint pdf is multivariate normal pdf. A multivariate normal distribution is an extension of the univariate normal distribution as defined by Equation 6.4:

$$F[r(1), r(2), \ldots r(k)] = (2\pi)^{-k/2} \, |\Sigma|^{-1/2} \, \exp\left[\left(-\frac{1}{2}\right)(X - \mu)' \Sigma^{-1}(X - \mu)\right] \quad (6.4)$$

Equation 6.4 closely resembles the univariate normal distribution where the vectors of the means μ replaces the univariate means and the variance covariance matrix Σ replaces the univariate variance. We denote that a random variable X follows a multivariate normal distribution by $X \sim N(\mu, \Sigma)$.

In the context of time series analysis, the interpretation of μ for the stochastic process $[r(t)]$ is straightforward, since it is just the vector of the means of the random variables $r(1), r(2), \ldots, r(k)$:

$$\mu' = [\mu(1), \mu(2), \ldots, \mu(k)] \quad\quad\quad\quad (6.5)$$

where $\mu(j)$ is the mean of $r(j)$.

More interesting is the interpretation of the variance-covariance matrix Σ. The matrix Σ is a symmetrical matrix (positive semidefinite) where the elements on the main diagonal represent the variances of each random variable $r(j)$ and the elements off the main diagonal represent the covariances between each pair of random variables:

$$\Sigma = \begin{bmatrix} \sigma(1,1) & \sigma(1,2) & \sigma(1,3) & \ldots & \sigma(1,k) \\ \sigma(2,1) & \sigma(2,2) & \sigma(2,3) & \ldots & \sigma(2,k) \\ \sigma(3,1) & \sigma(3,2) & \sigma(3,3) & \ldots & \sigma(3,k) \\ \sigma(4,1) & \sigma(4,2) & \sigma(4,3) & \ldots & \sigma(4,k) \\ \ldots & \ldots & \ldots & \ldots & \ldots \\ \sigma(k,1) & \sigma(k,2) & \sigma(k,3) & \ldots & \sigma(k,k) \end{bmatrix}$$

The element $\sigma(j,j)$ represents the variance of $r(j)$ while $\sigma(i,j)$ represents the covariance between $r(i)$ and $r(j)$.

As the natural extension of the univariate normal pdf, the multivariate normal pdf (hereafter mN pdf) has the following four properties:

1. The *mN* pdf is completely and uniquely defined by its mean and variance. For k dimensions, it means that a *mN* pdf is characterized by $k(k + 1)/n$ parameters (k means + k variances + $k(k - 1)/n$ covariances).
2. If a stochastic process is Gaussian, the absence of correlation at any lag implies stochastic independence. In other words, if the elements of Σ off the main diagonal are all equal to zero, the random variables $r(1), r(2), \ldots r(k)$ are stochastically independent.
3. Linear transformations of a *mN* pdf give a *mN* pdf.
4. Isoprobability curves are ellipsoides that can be interpreted as the multivariate counterpart of confidence intervals.

For a process to be stationary, the joint pdf at time t must be equal to the joint pdf at time $t + k$ for any t and k. If we assume the process to be Gaussian, the vector of means and the variance-covariance matrix must remain unchanged. This implies that the correlation between $r(i)$ and $r(j)$ depends only on $j - i$. Although we derived this result from a *mN* pdf, this is a general result. For a stationary process up to order 2, the following three conditions must be met:

1. The means remain unchanged.
2. The variance of $r(t + k)$ remains unchanged for any point in t and k.

3. The correlation between $r(j)$ and $r(i)$ depends only on $j - i$ and not on time.

DISCRETE STOCHASTIC PROCESSES FOR MEASURING RETURNS

In this and the following paragraphs, we briefly review the most common stochastic process used for modeling asset returns. We treat discrete stochastic processes first. Later, we extend our analysis to continuous stochastic processes.[1] An important aspect for the analysis of stochastic processes is autocorrelation. The autocorrelation coefficient is a natural time-series extension of the well-known correlation coefficient between two random variables x and y:

$$r_{xy} = \frac{\text{Cov}(x, y)}{\sigma_x * \sigma_y} \tag{6.6}$$

Let $[X(t)]$ be a stochastic process. The kth-order autocorrelation coefficient is given by

$$\rho(1) = \frac{\text{Cov}\left(X_t, X_{t-1}\right)}{\sigma_t \sigma_{t-1}} \tag{6.7}$$

If $[X(t)]$ is a stationary process $\sigma_t = \sigma_{t-1}$, hence

$$\rho(1) = \frac{\text{Cov}\left(X_t, X_{t-1}\right)}{\sigma^2_t} = \frac{\gamma(1)}{\gamma(0)} \tag{6.8}$$

where

$$\gamma(k) = \text{Cov}\left(X_t, X_{t-k}\right) \tag{6.9}$$

and

$$\gamma(0) = \text{Cov}\left(X_t, X_t\right) = \sigma^2 \tag{6.10}$$

$\gamma(k)$ is known as autocovariance function and $\rho(k)$ as autocorrelation function (ACF). ACF plays a great importance in time series analysis and financial modeling.

Stationary up to order 2 requires that

$$\gamma(k) = \sigma^2 \text{ if } k = 0 \text{ and}$$
$$\gamma(k) \text{ is a function } k \text{ only if } k \neq 0 \tag{6.11}$$

The autocorrelation of a stochastic process is a crucial aspect for financial modeling. If a process describing financial returns is autocorrelated, it means that current returns depend, at least partially, on past returns making forecasts more accurate and hence future returns more predictable. It is easy to understand the importance of predictability in the context of VaR.

Another important property of stochastic processes is ergodicity. If a process is ergodic, it means that the sample mean, variance, and covariances converge to the population mean, variance, and covariances as the sample size increases. Ergodicity plays in time series analysis the same role that consistency plays in econometric modeling and forecasting. A condition, not proven here, for a process to be ergodic for the mean is that

$$\sum_t |\gamma(t)| < \infty \tag{6.12}$$

If a process is Gaussian, Equation 6.12 is a sufficient condition for the process to be stationary for the second moment. Estimates for the mean, the variance, and the ACF for (at least) a covariance stationary process can be obtained by replacing ensemble moments with their time series (sample) counterparts:

$$m = \left(\frac{1}{T}\right) \sum_t X_t \tag{6.13}$$

$$s = \left(\frac{1}{T}\right) \sum_t \left(X_t - m\right)^2 = g(0) \tag{6.14}$$

$$r(k) = \frac{g(k)}{g(0)} \tag{6.15}$$

Given their importance in financial modeling and theory, much attention will be devoted to autocorrelation coefficients and their sample estimates. The autocorrelation coefficients' sample estimates are, for small samples, negatively biased. A correction has been proposed by Fuller:

$$r(k) = g(k) + \left[\frac{T-k}{(T-1)^2}\right]\left[1 - g(k)^2\right] \tag{6.16}$$

THE WHITE NOISE PROCESS

Among the stochastic processes, the so-called *white noise* process plays a special role in financial theory, so it deserves a closer look. If returns follow a white noise process, they can be described by Equation 6.17:

$$r_t = \varepsilon_t \tag{6.17}$$

where the random variable ε_t is characterized by the following:

$$
\begin{aligned}
E(\varepsilon) &= 0 \\
E\left(\varepsilon_t \varepsilon_{t-j}\right) &= \sigma^2_e \text{ for } j = 0 \\
&= 0 \quad \text{for } j > 0
\end{aligned} \tag{6.18}
$$

A white noise process is a stationary process since both the mean and the variance are stable over time and the covariance is zero for any lag. Two observations are at hand:

1. A white noise process implies that returns are uncorrelated at any lag. If ε is also normally distributed, returns are stochastically independent (i.e., random) over time, and the joint probability function is nothing but the multiplication of marginal pdfs at any point in time.
2. The white noise process is well suited for representing the "innovation" term in financial modeling (i.e., variations that are unexplained by the model).

Last, but not least, Equation 6.17 can be restated as

$$\log\left(p_t\right) = \log\left(p_{t-1}\right) + \varepsilon_t \tag{6.19}$$

Hence, if the innovation term is normally distributed and if log returns follow a random process, *log prices* follow a discrete random walk process. The random walk defines a temporal behavior for log prices where the value taken at any time t depends only on the value at $t - 1$ plus a random innovation term. Random walks play a key role for modeling financial prices and returns.

AUTOREGRESSIVE PROCESSES

The most straightforward alternative to the white noise process is a process where value at time t depends on the past values. In the simplest autoregressive process, r_t depends (or is correlated) with r_{t-1}. Such a process is called a first-order autoregressive process and denoted by AR(1). A random walk process is a typical first-order autoregressive process for log prices.[2] An AR(1) for returns can be represented by

$$r_t = a_1 r_{t-1} + \varepsilon_t \tag{6.20}$$

where ε_t is described by Equation 6.20.

When compared with the white noise process, an AR(1) with $0 > a > 1$ process looks smoother since variations have a degree of persistence given by coefficient a. This increases the accuracy of forecasts. When $a \geq 1$ the process is nonstationary and shows a trend. The random walk process is a special case of nonstationary first-order autoregressive process. If $-1 < a < 0$, the series will look more jagged than the white noise series since there will be a bias toward reversal consecutive movements. If $a \leq -1$, the series will show an explosive oscillatory behavior.

If the process is autoregressive, it has a memory of its past values. If $a < |1|$, the memory of past values declines as time passes according to an exponential law and eventually vanishes. If $a \geq |1|$, past values definitively affect present and future values and the process shows a trend or explodes. A natural generalization of the AR(1) process is given by a broader class of autoregressive process, denoted by AR(p) where p is greater than 1, even infinite:

$$r_t = a_0 + a_1 r_{t-1} + a_2 r_{t-2} + a_3 r_{t-3} + \ldots + a_p r_{t-p} + \varepsilon_t \tag{6.21}$$

A formal treatment of these processes is beyond our scope. The condition for stationarity of an AR(p) process is that the roots z of the equation:

$$1 - a_1 z - a_2 z^2 - a_3 z^3 - \ldots - a_p z^p = 0 \tag{6.22}$$

are greater than 1 (lie outside the unit circle) in absolute value (i.e., all $z < |1|$).

For an AR(1) process, the condition for stationarity simply states that

$$z = \frac{1}{a} \tag{6.23}$$

hence, for z being $>|1|$ it follows that $a < |1|$. The mean of a stationary AR(p) process is given by $a_0 / \left(1 - a_1 - a_2 - \ldots - a_p\right)$.

An important distinction must be outlined between unconditional and conditional mean of the process. The unconditional mean is the mean taken independently from time. The sample mean is an unconditional mean. As the number of observations grow, it will converge to the ensemble mean, provided the process is ergodic. The conditional mean depends on the information set available at the time it is estimated. While the unconditional mean is a constant, the conditional mean needs a model to be specified. The model incorporates how past values are used to determine expected values. For example, provided that Equation 6.20 represents the model specifying conditional returns, the unconditional expected return is simply the mean of the process (i.e., zero since there is no drift term). Indeed, the conditional expected return at time t is a r_{t-1}.

MOVING AVERAGE PROCESSES

Another broad class of model is given by moving average (MA) models. An MA(q) model is given by Equation 6.24:

$$r_t = \varepsilon_{t-1} + b_1 \varepsilon_{t-1} + b_2 \varepsilon_{t-2} + \ldots + b_p \varepsilon_{t-p} \tag{6.24}$$

A white noise process is simply an MA(0) process. MA processes are appealing because they have a direct economic interpretation. They represent the shock that a market in equilibrium can receive and that leads this market temporarily out of equilibrium. If we suppose all b_j to be $<|1|$, all external shocks are completely absorbed after some time. If all b_j are $= 1$, shocks persists forever and the value of the observed variable is nothing less than the sum p (infinite indeed) past shocks. An MA(q) process, with q $< \infty$, is always stationary.

Interestingly, an AR(1) is equivalent to an MA(∞). In fact, an AR(1) can be written as:

$$r_t = a\, r_{t-1} + \varepsilon_t = a\left(a\ r_{t-2} + \varepsilon_{t-1}\right) + \varepsilon_t = a^2 r_{t-2} + a\ \varepsilon_{t-1} + \varepsilon_t$$
$$= a^3 r_{t-3} + a^2\ \varepsilon_{t-2} + a\ \varepsilon_{t-1} + \varepsilon_t \tag{6.25}$$

As long as the AR(1) process is stationary, the first term declines as the power of an increase. Hence:

$$r_t = \Sigma_j\ a^j \varepsilon_{t-j} \text{ for } j = 0, \ldots \infty \tag{6.26}$$

Notably, a random walk can be expressed as the infinite unweighted sum of all past random shocks. The actual price is then nothing else but the result of infinite past random shocks. Alternatively, we can interpret MA processes as providing forecasts of the dependent variable based on the linear combination of past errors, rather than on the linear combination of the variable itself.

GENERAL ARMA PROCESSES

A parsimonious way to represent a stochastic process is to use a mixed autoregressive-moving average process. These processes, known as ARMA, are able to capture many features of the process with considerably fewer parameters than required by an autoregressive or a moving average process. An ARMA(1,1) can be defined by Equation 6.27:

$$r_t = a_1 r_{t-1} + b_1 \varepsilon_{t-1} + \varepsilon_t \tag{6.27}$$

Stationarity of ARMA processes depend on autoregressive coefficients only.

Since, provided some conditions hold, an infinite moving average process is equivalent to a first-order autoregressive process, we can realize that a model such as ARMA(1,1) is really an infinite memory process. ARMA models are often used for modeling financial returns. The identification of the right autoregressive and/or moving average order is usually performed by examining both the autocorrelation and partial autocorrelation function. Once the order has been chosen, parameters are estimated through ML algorithms available in almost all econometric packages, although a recursive LS procedure is possible for AR processes.[3]

A possible approach to discriminate when two or more alternative models are available is the Akaike Information Criterion or AIC. This criterion penalizes overparameterization. If a more expensive model does not provide a sufficient advantage (in terms of the log of the MSE) over a more parsimonious model, the criterion "chooses" the more parsimonious one and penalizes the more "expensive" one.

THE RANDOM WALK

The Random Walk Defined

Random walk is the most commonly used model for describing the behavior of stock prices. A random walk (hereafter RW) is a first-order nonstationary autoregressive process. Prices are assumed to follow a random walk if

$$P_t = P_{t-1} + \varepsilon_t \tag{6.28}$$

where ε_t is normally distributed with zero mean and standard deviation equal to σ_ε. It is often assumed that prices grow at a constant rate over time, so a drift is usually added. RW can be rewritten as

$$P_t = \mu + P_{t-1} + \varepsilon_t \tag{6.29}$$

Notably, for Equation 6.28, $E(P_t) = E(P_{t-1})$ while for Equation 6.28, $E(P_t) = \mu + E(P_{t-1})$. The drift is assumed to be positive and constant. The RW expressed by Equations 6.28 and 6.29 does not ensure positive prices. To overcome this drawback, it is a common practice to use the natural logarithm of prices. Equation 6.29 can be rewritten as

$$\ln\left(P_t\right) = \mu + \ln\left(P_{t-1}\right) + \sigma \varepsilon_t \tag{6.30}$$

where ε_t is normally distributed with zero mean and unit variance. Since $\ln(P_t) - \ln(P_{t-1}) = r_t$, log returns also are assumed to be normally distributed with a mean equal to μ. To assume that log prices follow a RW is equivalent to assuming that log returns are generated by a Gaussian white noise process. If the log version of the RW is used

$$P_t = P_{t-1} e^{\mu + \sigma \varepsilon} \tag{6.31}$$

Since $e^{\mu + \sigma\varepsilon}$ is always positive, the non-negativity constraint for P is always respected. The model so far described is the classic RW. A possible variant allows for conditional variance.[4] The RW can be rewritten as

$$\ln\left(P_t\right) = \mu + \ln\left(P_{t-1}\right) + \sigma_t\, \varepsilon_t \tag{6.32}$$

where the time subscript indicates that the variance can change over time. We can also assume that the drift, instead of being constant, is conditional. The term μ would be replaced by μ_t.

J.P. Morgan's RiskMetrics assumes that log prices according to a RW with no drift and conditional variance.[5] Assuming a constant single-period drift equal to μ, we also have

$$E\left(P_t\right) = P_0\, e^{\mu T} \tag{6.33}$$

and

$$\mathrm{Var}\left(P_t\right) = P^2{}_0 \exp(2\mu T)\ [\exp(T\sigma^2) - 1] \tag{6.34}$$

indicating that the variance increases with time even if the drift is zero. In fact, if the drift is zero, the t-period ahead expected price is just the current price while the t-period ahead variance is given by $P^2{}_0\, [\exp(T\sigma^2) - 1]$.

Random Walk: Empirical Evidence

There are several possible approaches to test the random walk hypothesis. We can draw out three main approaches:

1. To test whether returns are independent and identically distributed (IID).
2. To test whether returns are independent.
3. To test whether returns are uncorrelated.

Notably, the joint hypothesis of noncorrelation and normality of asset returns implies statistical independence. The predictability of asset returns plays a key role for VaR models, especially when using simulation techniques such as Monte Carlo.

To study the predictability of asset returns, we used several time series, especially the two following ones:

1. Stock market series (daily log returns):
   MIBTEL—Italian Stock Market.
   NYSE composite index.
   DAX.
2. Foreign exchange time series:
   USD/DEM.
   USD/JPY.

We used two main types of test:

1. Nonparametric runs test.
2. Autocorrelation function and Ljung Box test.

The results are shown in Table 6.1. In four of the five cases, the run test demonstrated that the null hypothesis of independence of returns cannot be rejected at 5% confidence level. Only the return series for DAX shows some form of statistical dependence. To have a deeper look into the stochastic process generating the returns, we calculated the autocorrelation for lag 1 to 20 for the selected series. The LB statistics and the ACF are shown in Figures 6.1 through 6.5.

For all the selected series, we did not experience significant levels of autocorrelation at any lag, apart from first-order autocorrelation for the USD/JPY series. On average, all the series show very small autocorrelation confirming the known evidence that financial series of returns are usually only slightly autocorrelated.

CONTINUOUS STOCHASTIC PROCESSES

In a continuous-variable process, the underlying variable can take any value within a certain range, whereas in discrete-variable processes only certain discrete values are possible. In the real world, stock prices are restricted to discrete values and changes can be observed only when the exchange is open. Nevertheless, continuous processes prove to be a useful

TABLE 6.1   Results for Nonruns Test on Log Returns

	MIBTEL	DAX	NYSE	USD/DEM	USD/JPY
Expected runs	375.477	373.9093	375.9893	375.9333	375.9573
Actual runs	373	402	357	426	412
Reject independence	No	Yes	No	No	No

FIGURE 6.1 **Autocorrelation Function for MIBTEL**

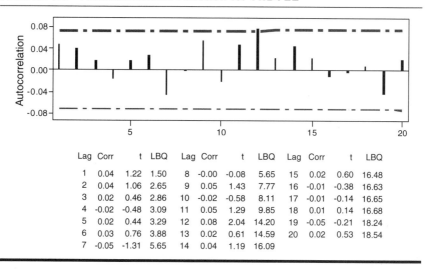

Lag	Corr	t	LBQ	Lag	Corr	t	LBQ	Lag	Corr	t	LBQ
1	0.04	1.22	1.50	8	-0.00	-0.08	5.65	15	0.02	0.60	16.48
2	0.04	1.06	2.65	9	0.05	1.43	7.77	16	-0.01	-0.38	16.63
3	0.02	0.46	2.86	10	-0.02	-0.58	8.11	17	-0.01	-0.14	16.65
4	-0.02	-0.48	3.09	11	0.05	1.29	9.85	18	0.01	0.14	16.68
5	0.02	0.44	3.29	12	0.08	2.04	14.20	19	-0.05	-0.21	18.24
6	0.03	0.76	3.88	13	0.02	0.61	14.59	20	0.02	0.53	18.54
7	-0.05	-1.31	5.65	14	0.04	1.19	16.09				

FIGURE 6.2 **Autocorrelation Function for DAX**

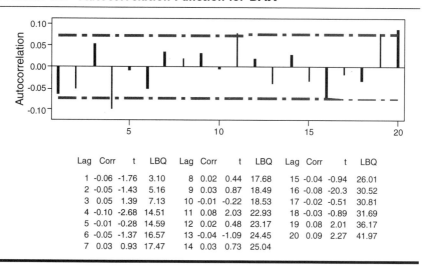

Lag	Corr	t	LBQ	Lag	Corr	t	LBQ	Lag	Corr	t	LBQ
1	-0.06	-1.76	3.10	8	0.02	0.44	17.68	15	-0.04	-0.94	26.01
2	-0.05	-1.43	5.16	9	0.03	0.87	18.49	16	-0.08	-20.3	30.52
3	0.05	1.39	7.13	10	-0.01	-0.22	18.53	17	-0.02	-0.51	30.81
4	-0.10	-2.68	14.51	11	0.08	2.03	22.93	18	-0.03	-0.89	31.69
5	-0.01	-0.28	14.59	12	0.02	0.48	23.17	19	0.08	2.01	36.17
6	-0.05	-1.37	16.57	13	-0.04	-1.09	24.45	20	0.09	2.27	41.97
7	0.03	0.93	17.47	14	0.03	0.73	25.04				

FIGURE 6.3   Autocorrelation Function for NYSE

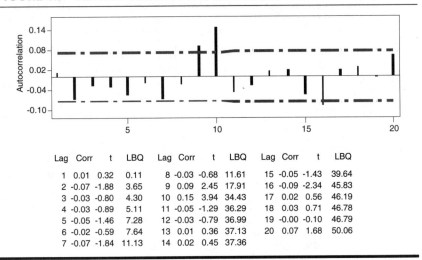

Lag	Corr	t	LBQ	Lag	Corr	t	LBQ	Lag	Corr	t	LBQ
1	0.01	0.32	0.11	8	-0.03	-0.68	11.61	15	-0.05	-1.43	39.64
2	-0.07	-1.88	3.65	9	0.09	2.45	17.91	16	-0.09	-2.34	45.83
3	-0.03	-0.80	4.30	10	0.15	3.94	34.43	17	0.02	0.56	46.19
4	-0.03	-0.89	5.11	11	-0.05	-1.29	36.29	18	0.03	0.71	46.78
5	-0.05	-1.46	7.28	12	-0.03	-0.79	36.99	19	-0.00	-0.10	46.79
6	-0.02	-0.59	7.64	13	0.01	0.36	37.13	20	0.07	1.68	50.06
7	-0.07	-1.84	11.13	14	0.02	0.45	37.36				

FIGURE 6.4   Autocorrelation Function for USD DEM

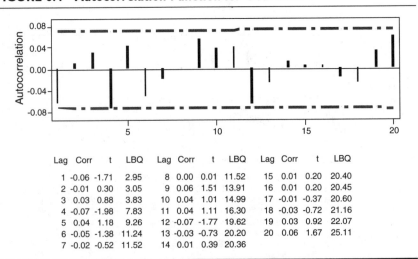

Lag	Corr	t	LBQ	Lag	Corr	t	LBQ	Lag	Corr	t	LBQ
1	-0.06	-1.71	2.95	8	0.00	0.01	11.52	15	0.01	0.20	20.40
2	-0.01	0.30	3.05	9	0.06	1.51	13.91	16	0.01	0.20	20.45
3	0.03	0.88	3.83	10	0.04	1.01	14.99	17	-0.01	-0.37	20.60
4	-0.07	-1.98	7.83	11	0.04	1.11	16.30	18	-0.03	-0.72	21.16
5	0.04	1.18	9.26	12	-0.07	-1.77	19.62	19	0.03	0.92	22.07
6	-0.05	-1.38	11.24	13	-0.03	-0.73	20.20	20	0.06	1.67	25.11
7	-0.02	-0.52	11.52	14	0.01	0.39	20.36				

FIGURE 6.5   Autocorrelation Function for USD YEN

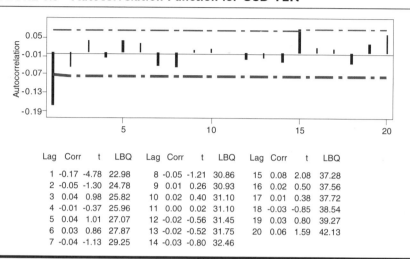

Lag	Corr	t	LBQ	Lag	Corr	t	LBQ	Lag	Corr	t	LBQ
1	-0.17	-4.78	22.98	8	-0.05	-1.21	30.86	15	0.08	2.08	37.28
2	-0.05	-1.30	24.78	9	0.01	0.26	30.93	16	0.02	0.50	37.56
3	0.04	0.98	25.82	10	0.02	0.40	31.10	17	0.01	0.38	37.72
4	-0.01	-0.37	25.96	11	0.00	0.02	31.10	18	-0.03	-0.85	38.54
5	0.04	1.01	27.07	12	-0.02	-0.56	31.45	19	0.03	0.80	39.27
6	0.03	0.86	27.87	13	-0.02	-0.52	31.75	20	0.06	1.59	42.13
7	-0.04	-1.13	29.25	14	-0.03	-0.80	32.46				

approximation for most purposes. Continuous processes also have some appealing properties. The most important is that continuous process can be treated with standard tools of stochastic calculus. A Markov process is a particular type of stochastic process where only the present value of a variable is relevant for predicting the future. The past history of the variable and the way in which the present value has emerged from the past are irrelevant. Remarkably, Markovian processes imply that the probability distribution of the price at any particular time depends only on the current stock price.

The Wiener Process

The Markov property of stock prices is consistent with the weak form of market efficiency. This states that the present price of a stock impounds all the information contained in a record of past prices.

Models of price behavior are usually expressed in terms of what is known as *Wiener process*. A Wiener process is a particular type of Markov process. In physics, it has been used to describe the motion of a particle subject to a large number of small molecular shocks and is often referred to as Brownian motion. The name comes from the Scottish physician Robert Brown. Suppose a given variable r (e.g., returns), follows a Brownian motion.

In this case, the following three properties apply:

1. $\Delta r = \varepsilon \Delta t$ where $\varepsilon \approx N(0,1)$.
2. Δr for two different (short) time intervals are statistically independent.
3. $E(\Delta r) = 0$, $\sigma(\Delta r) = \sqrt{\Delta t}$.

For a relatively long period, $T \ (= N\Delta t)$, the change in the value of the variable can be denoted by $r(T) - r(0) = \sum_j \varepsilon_j \sqrt{\Delta t}$. The difference between the initial value and the current value can be considered as the sum of the increases of r in small time intervals of length Δt. It follows that $E[r(T) - r(0)] = 0$ and $\sigma[r(T) - r(0)] = \sqrt{T}$.

The variance of the variable Δr increases proportionally with time. This property stems from that fact that the variances for a set of independent random variables are just the sum of the variances of each single variable. It follows that the standard deviation grows proportionally with the square root of time. This assumption plays a key role in VaR modeling, since the standard deviation can be scaled up to any time horizon just by multiplying it by the square root of time.

The Geometrical Brownian Motion

The Geometrical Brownian Motion (hereafter GBM) is, loosely speaking, the continuous counterpart of the discrete RW model examined earlier. We have also described a continuous process for describing stock price behavior, known as the Wiener process. A generalized Wiener process for stock prices can be expressed by

$$dS = a\,dt + b\,dz \qquad (6.35)$$

where dz is a standard Wiener process and a is a constant drift. For a small time interval, we can write

$$\Delta S = a\,\Delta t + b\,\varepsilon\sqrt{\Delta t} \qquad (6.36)$$

Thus ΔS has a normal distribution with mean equal to $a\Delta t$ and variance $b^2\Delta t$.

Generalized Wiener process cannot be used to describe stock price behavior since it fails to capture an important feature of stock prices. The return an investor requires is independent from the level of the stock price. A generalized Wiener process would imply that expected returns are constantly declining since the expected stock price change (assumed positive) is always the same as the stock price increases. This assumption must be replaced by the assumption that the percentage return is expected to be constant. Hence, the model for stock price would be

$$\frac{dS}{S} = \mu \; dt \quad \text{or} \quad dS = S \, \mu \; dt \tag{6.37}$$

For a short period, the model could be rewritten as $\Delta S = S \, \mu \, \Delta t$. In a risk-free world, the drift would be equal to the risk-free rate and no uncertainty about future stock prices would exist.

In the real world, the expected return is correlated with risk and stock prices exhibit volatility. To account for volatility, a stochastic term is added having

$$\frac{dS}{S} = \mu \; dt + \sigma \; dz \tag{6.38}$$

where dz follows a Wiener process. The expected instantaneous drift is μS and the instantaneous variance rate is $S^2 \sigma^2$. Notably, the variance is assumed to be constant for any level of S and any time. The model described by Equation 6.38 represents Geometrical Brownian Motion. For simulation purposes, the discrete version of the GBM is often used:

$$\frac{\Delta S}{S} = \mu \; \Delta t + \sigma \; \varepsilon \sqrt{\Delta t} \tag{6.39}$$

where $\varepsilon \approx N(0,1)$. $\Delta S/S$ is normally distributed with mean equal to $\mu \; \Delta t$ and standard deviation equal to $\sigma \sqrt{\Delta t}$. An application of the discrete version of GBM in the context of Monte Carlo simulation is provided in Chapter 16.

APPENDIX: ALTERNATIVE MODELS FOR STOCK PRICES

In Chapter 6, we analyzed the Geometrical Brownian Motion (GBM). GBM is the most common process used to model stock price behavior. The assumption that stock prices follow a GBM is a key assumption for the Black-Scholes option pricing formula. Stock prices are *assumed* to follow a GBM; different assumptions about stock prices' behavior would lead to different option pricing formulas. This aspect is important for VaR calculation too: different stochastic processes generate different price paths and different pricing formulas for derivative instruments. The choice of the stochastic process for stock prices becomes a crucial issue especially in the context of simulation models such as the Structured Monte Carlo (SMC).

In this appendix, we review the GBM in greater detail and briefly analyze alternative stochastic processes used to describe stock price paths.

The Arithmetic Brownian Motion

Equation A.6.1 defines the arithmetic Brownian motion

$$dS = \mu \, dt + \sigma \, dW_t \qquad\qquad (A.6.1)$$

where dW is a Wiener process with zero mean and variance proportional to time. Both the drift term μ and the diffusion term σ are unconditional: they do not depend on time, and they are constant. In the discrete form of Equation A.6.1, we substitute dS with ΔS.

Equation A.6.1 can be rearranged to explicitly derive current stock price:

$$S_t = S_{t-1} + \mu \, dt + \sigma \, dW_t \qquad\qquad (A.6.2)$$

The main characteristic of the arithmetic Brownian motion are:

- Stock price fluctuates around a straight line with slope μ.
- The size of σ determines the extent of fluctuations around this line. These fluctuations *do not* become larger and larger as time passes.
- It can be a good approximation if the behavior of stock prices is stable over time, if the trend is linear, and if variations do not get any larger.
- Finally, it assumes that stock prices show no jumps or discontinuities.

The Geometrical Brownian Motion

As we have seen, the standard model in financial theory is the GBM. Equation A.6.3 defines the GBM:

$$\frac{dS}{S} = \mu \, dt + \sigma \, dW_t \qquad\qquad (A.6.3)$$

where dW is a Wiener process with zero mean and variance proportional to time. Both the drift term μ and the diffusion term σ are unconditional: they do not depend on time, but they are *not* constant since they are "corrected" by the level of S.

Equation A.6.3 can be rearranged, giving Equation A.6.4:

$$dS_t = \mu\, S_t\, dt + \sigma\, S_t\, dW_t \qquad\qquad\qquad (A.6.4)$$

Hence, the drift and the diffusion coefficients both depend on the information that becomes available at time t. The drift and the standard deviation change proportionally with S_t. It also means that the drift and diffusion of percentage changes of S_t still are both time invariant.

The main characteristics of GBM are:

- While, in the case of ABM, prices fluctuate around a linear trend, this model gives prices fluctuating around an exponential trend. For most asset prices, the exponential trend is somewhat more realistic.
- The variance, on the other hand, increases in a way proportional to the square of S_t. In some cases, it can add too much variation to S_t.

A possible correction to the GBM, aimed at reducing the fluctuations induced by a diffusion term proportional to S_t is given by the "square root process." The square root process can be expressed by Equation A.6.5:

$$dS_t = \mu\, S_t\, dt + \sigma\, \sqrt{S_t\, dW_t} \qquad\qquad\qquad (A.6.5)$$

Here S_t still follows an exponential trend, while the standard deviation is made a function of the square root of S_t. It is an appropriate model if price volatility does not increase too much when S_t increases.

Mean Reverting Models

A model that has shown to be particularly useful in modeling asset prices is the mean reverting model. This model has been already encountered in Chapter 6 and is often used to model interest rate dynamics.

According to this model, as S_t falls below some "mean value," the term in the parentheses $(\mu - S_t)$ will become negative positive, making dS_t more likely to be positive. It means that S_t will eventually move to the mean value μ.

The mean reverting model is defined by Equation A.6.6.

$$d S_t = \lambda \left(\mu - S_t \right) dt + \sigma S_t \, dW_t \qquad\qquad\qquad\qquad \text{(A.6.6)}$$

Alternatively, the diffusion term may be dependent on the square root of S_t, as expressed in Equation A.6.7:

$$d S_t = \lambda \left(\mu - S_t \right) dt + \sigma \sqrt{S_t \, dW_t} \qquad\qquad\qquad\qquad \text{(A.6.7)}$$

Some characteristics of the mean reverting model should be mentioned:

- Although the mean reverting process has a trend, deviations around the trend are not completely random. In fact, the process can take an excursion away from the long-run trend, but it eventually reverts back.
- The length of the excursions depends on the parameter $\lambda > 0$. The smaller λ the longer the excursions will be. Thus asset prices may exhibit some kind of predictability. This behavior is inconsistent with market efficiency; nevertheless, mean reverting models for interest rates have proven to be quite successful.

EFFECTS ON VaR

The choice of the model to predict asset prices may have dramatic consequences on VaR. Suppose we want calculate the VaR at 95% and 90% probability level on a 10-day time horizon for a portfolio perfectly mirroring the NYSE Index. We estimated, for the period January 1, 1997, to May 22, 1998, the mean and standard deviation of absolute changes and log returns.

The results are:

Absolute changes:
Mean = 0.5085
Standard deviation = 4.7936

Log returns:
Mean = 0.0005
Standard deviation = 0.0043

Using the discrete approximations of ABM and GBM, we simulated 100 price paths for a 10-day time horizon. Then we took 5% and 10% of the simulated series on the tenth day.

The results are:

	VaR 90%	_VaR 95%_
ABM	19.05	25.02
GBM	9.85	12.90

What is impressive is the remarkable difference between the calculated VaRs when two different models are used. This fact should make the readers aware of the strict relationship is between the output calculated and the statistical assumptions underlying the calculations.

NOTES

1. A complete review of stochastic processes theory is beyond our scope. We just want to provide a brief introduction and describe the uses of stochastic processes in modeling assets' returns and prices. For a detailed analysis see, among others, D. Hamilton, _Time Series Analysis,_ Princeton, NJ: Princeton University Press, 1994; M. Priestley, _Spectral Analysis and Time Series,_ New York: Academic Press, 1982; C.W. Granger and P. Newbold, _Forecasting Economic Time Series,_ Academic Press, 2nd ed.

2. If the logarithm of prices follow a random-walk process, then log returns follow a white noise process.

In fact, if

$$\log (P_t) = \log (P_{t-1}) + E_t$$

then

$$\log (P_t) - \log (P_{t-1}) = E_t$$
$$\log (P_t / P_{t-1}) = E_t$$

3. See C.W. Granger and P. Newbold, _Forecasting Economic Time Series,_ Academic Press, 2nd ed, 1986.

4. See Chapter 8 for details.

5. Variance is modeled with an exponentially weighted moving average model.

7

Estimating and Forecasting Volatility

Accurate forecasting of volatility and correlation is a key issue for successful risk management and analysis. We can say that these forecasts are the backbone of any risk management system. Volatility provides essential data about the probability of achieving certain outcomes; and this is a key aspect for decisions about asset allocation and portfolio management in financial markets. Volatility is essential in pricing financial instruments such as options, while correlation and covariance are essential for pricing equities. Estimation and forecasting of volatility and correlation make up one of the cornerstones of quantitative financial analysis. In some cases (such as in some VaR models), these forecasts will be the only stochastic parameters in the model.

The chapter is organized as follows: three basic methodologies are reviewed (moving-average techniques, ARCH/GARCH techniques, and the implied-volatility technique); advantages and limitations of each technique for VaR purposes are outlined; and in the final paragraph, we use ARCH/GARCH techniques to model the volatility of actual time series.

THE CONCEPT OF VOLATILITY AND CORRELATION

The concept of volatility refers to the degree of dispersion of possible outcomes of a random variable. Assuming a random variable X is normally distributed, the volatility is usually represented by its standard deviation. The standard deviation is not the only possible measure of dispersion. For example, the mean absolute error could be used as well.

Nevertheless, standard deviation has two attractive properties:

1. Using standard calculus tools, we can calculate the derivatives of a squared function, whereas absolute values are much more complicated to deal with.
2. In the case of a normal pdf, standard deviation has a precise meaning in terms of probability of events to occur.

Therefore, the use of standard deviation to measure volatility is commonplace in financial economics.

In addition, assuming that outcomes are not serially correlated, the standard deviation is easily scalable. For example, if the standard deviation is measured on a daily basis, it can easily be annualized using Equation 7.1:

$$\sigma_y = \sigma_d \sqrt{250} \qquad\qquad (7.1)$$

assuming 250 working days per year.

In financial economics, volatility is measured as the standard deviation of returns rather than the standard deviation of prices, since returns can be assumed to be generated by a stationary process with a constant finite unconditional mean and variance. The finite variance implies that volatility is tied to a constant mean—it is mean reverting.

Prices, on the other hand, have infinite variance, in the sense that their variance grows with time. This fact stems directly from nonstationarity of prices, and it is a well-known property of random walk.[1]

Correlation involves two time series and is defined as the ratio of the covariance to the product of the standard deviations of the two series:

$$\rho_{x,y} = \frac{\text{Cov}(x, y)}{\sigma_x \sigma_y} \qquad\qquad (7.2)$$

Notably, if we take two series x and y, we expect not only the two series to be individually stationary, but also jointly stationary. In this case, the unconditional covariance between the two series will be a finite constant.

Of course, it is always possible to calculate correlation from sample data, but unconditional correlation is not measured unless the two series are jointly stationary. In such cases, calculated correlation jumps a lot over time—a clear sign of nonjoint stationarity.[2]

Correlation does not need to be annualized because it is already in a standardized form, ranging from −1 to +1. It measures short-term co-movements and has little to do with any long-term co-movements. For common trend analysis (e.g., in prices), techniques based on cointegration offer many advantages.[3]

MOVING-AVERAGE METHODS FOR ESTIMATING VOLATILITY

A moving average is an average taken over a rolling window of a fixed number of data points. Each time the window is rolled, a new point is added, and the oldest previous window is excluded; so the sample size remains constant. Moving-average techniques have been widely used in financial economics, especially for estimating prices and returns. They are relatively simple to use, through statistical packages and require much fewer statistical assumptions than the ones required by the more complex ARMA/ARIMA techniques.

To generate variance estimates using moving averages, it is customary to apply the average of squared returns r_t^2, or squared mean deviations of returns $(r_t - \mu_r)^2$, where μ_r is the mean of returns over the data window. Empirical research has shown that it is often better not to use mean deviations of returns, but to use squared returns instead.[4]

Equally Weighted Historic Moving Averages

Efficient markets imply that asset prices follow a random-walk process, but asset returns follow a stationary white-noise process. Returns are taken as inputs to volatility estimation and forecasting. The n-period historic estimate of variance at time T is based on an equally weighted moving average of the n past one-period squared returns. The squared root of this estimate is then converted into an annualized percentage to obtain the historic volatility. Annualization is obtained using Equation 7.1.

The equally weighted moving average is described by Equation 7.3:

$$E\left(\sigma_t^2\right) = \frac{\sum\limits_{T-n}^{T-1} r^2}{n} \tag{7.3}$$

Equation 7.3 is a short-term estimate of current volatility and can be used as a forecast over the next n days. The long-term volatility forecast is simply the unconditional mean of squared returns. The rationale for this is that financial volatility tends to come in clusters, with periods of relatively low volatility following more turbulent periods. Short-term forecasts should reflect this clustering, while long-term volatility should be unaffected by this behavior. Historic volatility is typically estimated with an averaging period equal to 30 or 60 days.

The equally weighted moving average has an inherent major drawback that has motivated a general shift in methodology toward exponentially weighted moving averages. This drawback is generally known as *ghost features* (or *echo effect*). This effect refers to the behavior of the MA when there is a jump in the market price (or there is an unusually large return, both positive or negative).

First, the equally weighted average of squared returns will jump up the very next day. The one large squared return will continue to keep volatility estimates high for the number of days included in the averaging window, whereas the true volatility will have long ago returned to normal levels. Second, exactly n days after the shock has occurred ($n = 30$ in a 30-day moving average; $n = 60$ in a 60-day moving-average), the volatility will abruptly decline as the day of the shock is excluded from the averaging window. In other words, what has been seen from the day of the event until that day is just a ghost of what happened n days before.

These ghost features are always going to be a problem when weighted averages are applied to financial market data. The existence of ghost features has led to more advanced averaging techniques.

Exponentially Weighted Moving Average

Ghost features emphasize the most important drawback of equally weighted averages: all past squared returns that enter into the average are equally important, however long ago. An exponentially weighted moving average (EWMA) places more weight on recent observations: this reduces the problematic of ghost features while capturing volatility clusters as well. The exponentially weighted moving average is the technique used in J.P. Morgan's RiskMetrics™. The EWMA variance estimate at time T, based on a time series of squared returns, is calculated through Equation 7.4:

$$E\left(\sigma_t^2\right) = (1 - \lambda)\sum_{T-n}^{\infty}\lambda^{i-1} r_{T-1}^2 \qquad (7.4)$$

since the sum $\lambda + \lambda^2 + \ldots + \lambda^n$ converges to $1/(1 - \lambda)$ as $n \to \infty$.

When using EWMA, past observations are now weighted by the "smoothing constant" λ, ranging from 0 to 1, so an observation n days ago is multiplied by λ^n, which can be a very small coefficient if n is large. As a consequence, extreme events have a smaller and smaller impact on variance estimates as they move further into the past.

EWMA is a standard statistical technique, but it has some limitations for forecasting. First, it is really only useful as a one-step-ahead forecast. Using daily squared returns, EWMA provides a useful series of one-day variance forecasts. One-day-ahead forecasts need to be continuously updated with actual data. Second, there is no optimal theoretical approach for estimating the smoothing constant λ. RiskMetrics forecasts of volatility are calculated using a constant λ equal to 0.94 for daily data, and equal to 0.97 for monthly data. These values have been chosen by minimizing the mean square error (MSE) over the smoothed series.

In addition, when the EWMA is applied not to single-day squared returns but to one-month averages of daily squared returns (as is the case for RiskMetrics) the ghost effect—present in the original moving-averaged series—will be augmented when using an EWMA technique, rather than being reduced.

A Comparison of Moving-Average Methods

To fully understand the problematic effects problems that moving-average methods can create in estimating and forecasting volatility, we simulated the effects of a large volatility shock and measured how it could impact the different historical moving-averages techniques.

We assumed that daily log returns follow a normal distribution, with a mean equal to 1% and standard deviation equal to 0.6%. Using Microsoft Minitab 10.1™, we drew out 140 random numbers simulating 140 daily returns, with a mean equal to 1% and a standard deviation equal to 0.6%. The first 40 simulated returns were used for starting up the forecasting technique. Therefore, the test was performed on the last 100 simulated observations.

To analyze the effect on volatility of a sudden and extremely large return, we simulated a positive 8σ event at the fifty-first observation, leading to a simulated return of about 6% ($1\% + 8 * 0.6\% \approx 6\%$).

Moving averages were calculated with a rolling window of 20 and 40 days. The effects are shown in Figure 7.1. The daily volatilities were annualized using the standard formula of Equation 7.1. Ghost features are evident: although the shock occurring at observation 51 was immediately reversed, its effects on the moving-average forecasts persisted up to about observation 71 in the MA20 series and up to about observation 91 in the MA40 series, and then rapidly dropped, with no regard to the current simulated volatility.

Figure 7.2 shows the behavior of an EWMA10 forecast with $\lambda = 0.94$.

EWMA provides a much smoother forecasted series than the original series. Notably, EWMA works particularly well if the original series is autocorrelated, since it gives more weight to the closest past observations

FIGURE 7.I   **Ghost Features on Simulated Time Series**

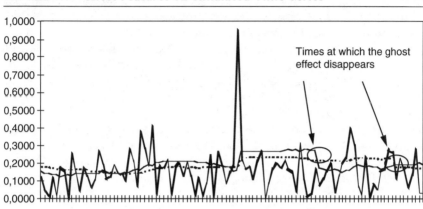

when forecasting current values. Paradoxically, if the original series is not autocorrelated, EWMA can provide even worse forecasts—in terms of MSE—than simple MA techniques.

From Figures 7.1 and 7.2, we can observe how EWMA very rapidly incorporates large volatility shocks, while the effects of these shocks smoothly decline over time until the moment when the shock exits from the sample on which the EWMA is calculated. The degree of persistence of the original shock in the forecasted series is determined by the "decay" factor λ. The closer λ is to 1, the more weight is given to past

FIGURE 7.2   **EWMA Forecasts**

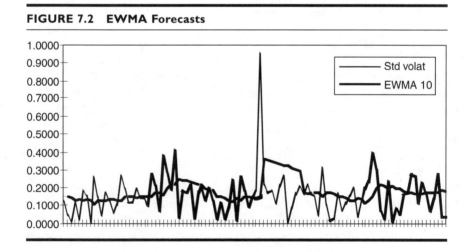

observations. In this case, the forecasted series will be very smooth. If actual returns vary in a very random fashion, a lower λ would be more appropriate, since a lower decay factor will produce a more volatile ("spiky") series of forecasts.

Although EWMA overcomes many problems encountered with the equally weighted moving-average, it suffers from many limitations. First, different classes of assets may show different values of the decay factor minimizing the MSE of forecasts. The use of a unique decay factor for all classes of assets can be misleading. Second, the decay factor can significantly change over time. The use of a constant decay factor could be inappropriate. A possible solution would be to frequently review the decay factor on the basis of actual data (e.g., selecting the value that minimizes the MSE of forecasts over the sample period) instead of choosing this decay factor "x-ante." Such an approach would be highly sensitive to the sample data chosen.

Covariances also can be estimated and forecasted using moving-average techniques. What is required is simply the substitution of r^2_t in Equations 7.3 and 7.4, with $rx_t\, ry_t$, where rx_t is the return on the series X at time t and ry_t is the return on the series y at time t. Joint stationarity is required for obtaining reliable results.

AUTOREGRESSIVE CONDITIONAL HETEROSKEDASTICITY MODELS

Conditional and Unconditional Volatility

The techniques previously reviewed have been developed to handle the empirical evidence that volatility may change over time. If a series is stationary, it will have a constant unconditional mean and variance. The unconditional mean is usually estimated using the sample mean, and the unconditional variance using the sample variance. The unconditional mean represents the long-term mean the series will tend to converge to in the long run. Stationary time series are, in fact, mean-reverting. The unconditional mean is the best estimate for very long time horizons. For short time horizons, we need a better technique.

If a time series is generated by a first-order autoregressive process $r_t = \alpha_0 + \alpha_1\, r_{t-1}$, and α_1 is < 1, the series itself has an unconditional mean equal to $\alpha_0/(1 - \alpha_1)$. Nevertheless, the one-period-ahead conditional mean is given by $E(r_t) = a_0 + a_1\, r_{t-1}$, where a_0 is the estimate of α_0 and a_1 is the estimate of α_1, obtained using ordinary least square (OLS) or ML. The estimate at time t is "conditional" in the sense that it depends on the set of information available at time t. This set, obviously, contains all past returns. The conditional mean at time t is often denoted by $E(r_t|\Omega_{t-1})$, where Ω_{t-1} represents the information set at time $t-1$. While the unconditional mean can be easily estimated as the sample mean over the whole time period, the conditional mean needs a model to be specified. Obviously, different models will yield different conditional mean estimates.

The same approach applies to variance. The unconditional variance is just the sample variance. On the other hand, the conditional variance needs a model to be specified. A lot of empirical research has been devoted to the analysis and specification of conditional variance models. The specification of the model yielding the conditional variance is a crucial assumption since it determines how past information is processed to generate conditional forecasts of variance.

Autoregressive Conditional Heteroskedasticity

The most common approach to model conditional variance is given by Autoregressive Conditional Heteroskedasticity models, also known as ARCH. As noted earlier, if log returns are generated by a white noise process, the conditional mean of returns is generated by just a constant-plus-error model. The errors are assumed to be normally distributed and uncorrelated at any lag, and therefore the variance-covariance matrix of errors is simply given by

$$V(\varepsilon) = \sigma^2_\varepsilon I \tag{7.5}$$

ARCH models assume that the error term ε_t is conditionally normally distributed with a mean equal to zero and a variance equal to σ^2_t, where σ^2_t is not constant but is allowed to change over time according to a specified model. The assumption of conditional normality is consistent with a leptokurtic[5] distribution of unconditional returns because a changing conditional variance allows for more outliers or unusually large observations.[6]

The original model of autoregressive conditional heteroskedasticity was introduced in 1982 by Robert Engle. An ARCH(p) model can be expressed by Equation 7.6:

$$\left(\sigma^2_t\right) = \alpha_0 + \alpha_1\varepsilon^2_{t-1} + \alpha_2\varepsilon^2_{t-2} + \ldots + \alpha_p\varepsilon^2_{t-p} + \varepsilon_t \tag{7.6}$$

where, to ensure that the variance is always positive, $\alpha_0 > 0$ and $\alpha_1, \alpha_2, \ldots, \alpha_p \geq 0$. The models capture the conditional heteroskedasticity of financial returns by using a moving average of past squared returns: if a major market movement in either direction occurred m periods ago (with

$m \leq p$), the squared error would be large and—assuming α_m is > 0—the effect would be an increase of today's conditional variance. This means that we would be more likely to have a large market move today, in either direction. Mandelbrot's intuition that large returns are likely to be followed by large returns in either direction is what we call conditional heteroskedasticity. Notably, although an ARCH is an acronym that stands for autoregressive conditional heteroskedasticity, the ARCH model is really a moving average of past squared errors. If we assume that the unconditional mean of returns is zero, Equation 7.6 can be rewritten as

$$E\left(\sigma^2_t\right) = \alpha_0 + \alpha_1 \, r^2_{t-1} + \alpha_2 \, r^2_{t-2} + \ldots + \alpha_p \, r^2_{t-p} + \varepsilon_t \tag{7.7}$$

Generalized Autoregressive Conditional Heteroskedasticity

Bollerslev has provided the generalization of Engle's ARCH model adding an autoregressive term to the moving averages of squared errors. This yields the Generalized Autoregressive Conditional Heteroskedasticity class of models, also known as GARCH. A GARCH(p,q) model is described by Equation 7.8

$$\begin{aligned} E\left(\sigma^2_t\right) &= \alpha_0 + \alpha_1 \, \sigma^2_{t-1} + \alpha_2 \, \sigma^2_{t-2} + \ldots + \alpha_p \, \sigma^2_{t-p} \\ &+ \beta_1 \varepsilon^2_{t-1} + \beta_2 \varepsilon^2_{t-2} + \ldots + \beta_q \varepsilon^2_{t-q} + \varepsilon_t \end{aligned} \tag{7.8}$$

The parsimonious GARCH(1,1) model, which has just one lagged squared error and one autoregressive term, is sufficient for most purposes since it has infinite memory. There is an interesting parallel with ARIMA class models: an ARIMA(1,1) is, in effect, an extremely parsimonious model with infinite memory. The GARCH(1,1) is defined by Equation 7.9:

$$E\left(\sigma^2_t\right) = \alpha_0 + \alpha_1 \, \sigma^2_{t-1} + \beta_1 \varepsilon^2_{t-1} + \varepsilon_t \tag{7.9}$$

By recursive substitution, we can see that a GARCH(1,1) is equivalent to an infinite ARCH process. The unconditional variance is given by

$$\begin{aligned} E\left(\sigma^2_t\right) &= \alpha_0 + \alpha_1 \, E\left(\sigma_{t-1}^2\right) + \beta_1 E\left(\varepsilon^2_{t-1}\right) + E\left(\varepsilon_t\right) \\ \sigma^2 &= \alpha_0 + \alpha_1 \, \sigma^2 + \beta_1 \, \sigma^2 \\ \sigma^2 &= \frac{\alpha_0}{1 - \alpha_1 - \beta_1} \end{aligned} \tag{7.10}$$

For the unconditional variance to be positive, $\alpha_1 + \beta_1 \leq 1$. In the financial market, it is common to have GARCH lag coefficients in excess of 0.7, but error coefficients tend to be smaller. The economic interpretation is quite easy: large GARCH coefficients indicate that volatility dies out slowly—it is persistent. Large error coefficients would indicate that volatility reacts quickly to market movements and tends to be more spiky.[7]

Alternative GARCH models have been developed to account for behavior of volatility not explained by traditional ARCH-GARCH models. The most common are known as IGARCH, AGARCH, and EGARCH.

IGARCH (*Integrated* GARCH) models assume that $\alpha_1 + \beta_1 = 1$. The GARCH(1,1) can be then rewritten as

$$\sigma^2_t = \alpha_0 + \beta_1 \sigma_{t-1}^2 + (1 - \beta_1)\varepsilon^2_{t-1} + \varepsilon_t \tag{7.11}$$

Substituting β_1 with λ, and assuming α_0 to be zero, we obtain the exact formula for an infinite EWMA. In fact, Equation 7.11 can be rewritten as

$$\begin{aligned} \sigma^2_t &= (1 - \lambda)\varepsilon^2_{t-1} + \lambda \sigma_{t-1}^2 + \varepsilon_\tau \\ &\quad (1 - \lambda)\varepsilon^2_{t-1} + \lambda\left[(1 - \lambda)\varepsilon^2_{t-2} + \lambda(1 - \lambda)\varepsilon^2_{t-3} + \ldots\right] \\ &= (1 - \lambda) + \left(\lambda\varepsilon^2_{t-1} + \lambda^2\varepsilon^2_{t-2} + \ldots\right) \end{aligned} \tag{7.12}$$

This is a nonstationary model, since the unconditional variance does not exist.

Traditional GARCH models are not able to account for the skewness and the kurtosis of empirical financial returns. The kurtosis may be dealt with using a t-distributed error process rather than a normal one. Skewness may be accounted for by introducing an additional parameter $\zeta > 0$, which magnifies the effects on volatility of negative shocks and reduces the effects of positive shocks. This is appropriate when we expect more volatility following a market fall than following a market rise and is a common feature, especially for equities (this is also known as *leverage effect*).

The EGARCH (*Exponential GARCH*) model incorporates the natural logarithm of variance, rather than the variance itself, as the dependent variable. The RHS of the model can become negative, without creating problems for the LHS, which can be negative while maintaining the nonnegativity constraint of the variance. The EGARCH model is expressed by Equation 7.13:

$$\ln\left(\sigma^2_t\right) = \alpha_0 + \alpha_1 \left(\frac{|\varepsilon_{t-1}|}{\sigma_{t-1}}\right) + \beta_1 \sigma_{t-1}^{\;2} + \gamma\left(\frac{\varepsilon_{t-1}}{\sigma_{t-1}}\right) \qquad (7.13)$$

The EGARCH models maintain the asymmetric response to positive and negative large shocks.

Forecasting with GARCH

Once one of the GARCH models has been selected and the appropriate order for the autoregressive and the moving-average components chosen,[8] the parameters are estimated through a maximum-likelihood algorithm, although a recursive least-squares procedure can be used for ARCH models. GARCH can be used for two kinds of forecasts:

1. One-period-ahead forecasts, using a recursive algorithm.
2. Estimation of the term structure of volatility.

The one-period-ahead forecasting for the GARCH(1,1) model can be obtained directly from Equation 7.9:

$$E\left(\sigma^2_{t+1}\right) = \alpha_0 + \alpha_1 \, \sigma^2_t + b_1 \varepsilon^2_t \qquad (7.14)$$

where a_0, a_1, and b_1 indicate the estimated values for α_0, α_1, and β_1.

GARCH models allow for the construction of the term structure of volatility by using the estimated model. The j-step-ahead forecast of forward one-day variances is computed iteratively. We can also construct any forward volatility forecasts, such as a three-months' volatility starting six months from now. Assuming returns have no autocorrelation, the variance of h-day returns is given by summing the variance of h one-day-ahead forecasts. The obtained h-day volatility can be annualized multiplying it by $\sqrt{\Delta t}$.

$$E\left(\sigma^2_{t,h}\right) = \sum_{i=1}^{n} \sigma^2_{t+i} \qquad (7.15)$$

The term structure of volatility behaves in a mean-reverting fashion. The mean is the unconditional volatility given by Equation 7.10. The unconditional volatility is also called the *baseline* level, since it is the level of volatility the GARCH model will tend to converge to, from either above or below that level.

Forecasting Correlation with GARCH

GARCH can be used to estimate conditional covariance and correlations between two or more time series. In a bivariate (only two series are involved) GARCH, there will be three conditional variance equations, one for each conditional variance and one for the conditional covariance. This can be expressed by the system of Equations 7.16:

$$\sigma^2_{1,t} = \alpha_{1,0} + \alpha_{1,1}\sigma^2_{1,t-1} + b_1\varepsilon^2_{1,t-1}$$

$$\sigma^2_{2,t} = \alpha_{2,0} + \alpha_{2,1}\sigma^2_{2,t-1} + b_2\varepsilon^2_{1,t-1} \tag{7.16}$$

$$\sigma^2_{12,t} = \alpha_{12,0} + \alpha_{12,1}\sigma^2_{12,t-1} + b_{12}\varepsilon_{1,t-1}\varepsilon_{2,t-1}$$

where $\sigma_{12,t}$ is the conditional covariance, at time t, between series 1 and 2.

IMPLIED-VOLATILITY MODELS

Implied volatility is the volatility implicit in the prices of options. When an explicit analytic formula is available, the quoted prices of options can be used to estimate the volatility. It is a volatility forecast—not the estimate of current volatility. The forecast horizon is therefore given by the maturity of the option.

Implied volatilities can (sometimes) be used to calculate implied correlations, too. These volatilities and correlation forecasts differ from the other forecasts reviewed so far in this chapter. Although they are indirectly based on historical data, they use much more than the historical returns data considered so far.

Implied Volatility with the BS Formula

The Black-Scholes formula for the price of a call option, with strike price X and time to maturity T, on an underlying asset with current price S and t-period volatility σ, is

$$C = S\,N(d_1) - Xe^{-rt}N(d_2) \tag{7.17}$$

where r denotes the "risk-free" rate of interest and $N(.)$ is the cumulative normal distribution function.[9]

If C is known, then S, X, r, and T are also; and Equation 7.16 may be used instead to calculate the implied volatility of the asset. But, typically, there will be several options of different maturities and strikes on any one asset, and different options will give different answers for the same implied volatility. Formulas such as the BS formula cannot be analytically solved for the implied volatility, so an iterative algorithm must be used.

Iterative Algorithm for Implied Volatility[10]

There are two commonly followed methods to calculate implied volatility: the *Bisection* method and the *Newton-Raphson* method. The Bisection method starts with a low estimate of volatility and a high estimate of volatility, yielding—respectively—a lower and a higher price than the market price.

The next estimate is determined by an interpolation procedure:

$$\sigma_{est} = \sigma_{low} + \left(P - P_{low}\right) * \left(\frac{\sigma_{high} - \sigma_{low}}{P_{high} - P_{low}}\right)$$

(7.18)

If the estimated value is below (above) the actual option price, the procedure is repeated with the low (high) volatility and the estimated volatility. The procedure is iteratively repeated until the volatility price corresponds to the actual price of the option.

The Newton-Raphson method starts with a first (hopefully, reasonable) estimate of the volatility. The option price corresponding to the estimate of volatility is used to calculate the corresponding price. If $P_{est} \neq P$, the first estimate is adjusted using equation

$$\sigma_{est}(2) = \frac{\left(P - P_{est}\right)}{\dfrac{\delta C}{\delta \sigma_{est}(1)}}$$

(7.19)

where $\sigma_{est}(2)$ is the second iteration estimate of the volatility and $\sigma_{est}(1)$ is the first estimate. The process is repeated until the implied volatility yielding the market price is obtained.

The Volatility Smile and the Term Structure of Volatility

Two aspects of implied volatility deserve attention:

1. The volatility smile.
2. The term structure of volatility (an aspect already examined for GARCH estimates).

In general, at-the-money (ATM) options yield lower implied volatilities than out-the-money options (OTM) and, to a lesser extent, than in-the-money (ITM) option. This effect is the volatility *smile*. As implied volatilities for OTM options are larger than for ITM options, the *smile* is also skewed in favor of OTM options. This smile reflects a variety of factors, including:

- Adjustments for distributional assumptions underlying standard option pricing models.
- Directional assumptions regarding the movement in the underlying asset prices that are incorporated into the option volatility and price.
- Clientele effects and the demand for OTM options.
- Liquidity effects.[11]

One of the reasons for the volatility smile is the possible deviation of actual asset price movements from the assumed log normal distribution. In practice, the true stochastic process generating asset price changes seems to have the following characteristics:

- The market distribution of asset price changes appears to demonstrate *fat tails*[12] (statistically described as the leptokurtosis of the distribution). This type of distribution is characterized by larger price changes (in absolute values) than expected from a normal distribution.
- Fat tails are consistent with the presence of "jump" risk; that is, discontinuous changes or price movements causing a deviation from the assumption of a normal distribution. As described in Chapter 6, this is inconsistent with the random-walk hypothesis and with the assumption of the Black-Scholes (BS) option pricing model that asset prices follow a Geometrical Brownian Motion.

Therefore, the *assumed* pattern of price changes (or returns) would systematically underestimate the value of deep ITM and OTM options. Using a log normal distribution to model price behavior *systematically* underestimates the expected values that the option may take at maturity, in either tails of the distribution. The smile is particularly noticeable in the BS option-pricing model (most likely because of the inappropriate assumptions underlying the BS model) and tends to increase as the option approaches maturity: if a short-dated OTM option is to make any profit, a (relatively large) movement will have to occur in the underlying asset price. Hence, a much larger volatility must be implicit in its price. This effect is consistent with traders' behavior, which seeks to equate the premium received to the expected payout under the option incorporating the true asset price change distribution.

The directional assumptions regarding the movements of the underlying asset provide another reason for the structure of the implied volatility smile. The volatility smile (particularly the skew in its structure) thus seems to reflect the expectations about the direction of future price movements, which are incorporated in the option price and, hence, in the implied volatility. For example, if the US$/JPY is expected to decline from its current level of—let's say—110, then US$ puts/JPY calls may be more valuable, and US$ calls/JPY puts with a strike price at or above the spot rate may be correspondingly less valuable. This directional view may be reflected in the option price, which could be higher than it would be in the absence of this expectation, and so be reflected in the implied volatility. Volatility smile and the skew are also consistent with the inherent nature of log normal distributions, which have a natural skew to the right-hand tail, implying a higher probability of a rise than a fall in the asset price.

In addition, the market for options with different strike prices appears to exhibit significant biases in demand and supply. This effect is known as *clientele effect*. Usually OTM options are attracting vehicles for speculative demand, reflecting the following factors:

- The leverage (expressed as the asset price divided the option premium) of OTM options is higher.
- The purchase of the option entails a low absolute cash investment.

These factors dictate significant demand for these options. On the other hand, the supply for these options is constrained, since traders are reluctant to sell OTM options because of the difficulty of hedging or replicating these options in the event of a jump in the asset price (high gamma risk).

In contrast, different factors influence the position for ITM options. The dominating characteristic is that δ is close to 1, so that ITM options move closely with movements of the underlying asset prices. It means that ITM options can be used as a direct substitute for the asset itself. This characteristic makes ITM options attractive for traders who seek to synthesize positions in the asset at a lower cost. Obviously, these options have a limited supply because ITM options are likely to be exercised, requiring the seller to sell (in the case of a call option) or buy (in the case of a put option) the asset at a disvantageous price. For OTM and ITM options, therefore, the interaction between a limited supply and a large demand bids up the prices and, hence, implied volatilities above comparable volatilities for ATM options of the same maturity.

The combination of the preceding factors results in different liquidities of options with different strike prices for a given maturity. The implied volatility of ATM options reflects the higher liquidity of these options, due to the greater balance between demand and supply. ITM and OTM options are less frequently traded, and the imbalance between demand relative to supply is reflected in the higher implied volatilities. Notably, the volatility smile appears to diminish with maturity, reflecting the reduced impact of the factors identified.

The term *structure of volatility* refers to:

- The relationship between volatility and time to expiry of the option.
- The pattern of forward volatilities.

In general terms, implied volatility for an option with a shorter time-to-expiry is higher than the implied volatility for options with longer time-to-expiry. This is because asset price changes will have a proportionately larger impact on option value, incorporating a higher risk for the seller of the option that will have to be compensated for through higher premiums and higher implied volatilities. Thus, the elasticity of an option premium to the price of the underlying asset is higher for long time-to-expiry than for short time-to-expiry. This is true also in the BS framework, but the term structure of implied volatility indicates that options with shorter maturities are relatively overpriced compared with options that have longer maturities, all other things being equal. The relative higher premiums are required because options with a short time-to-expiry incorporate an higher risk, since negative asset price changes are more unlikely to be reversed before expiration for short maturities than for long maturities.

We have calculated the term structure of implied volatility for the call option on the MIB30 (the index for the Milan stock exchange including the first 30 securities in terms of daily trading volume). The current price is the value of the MIB30 on February 17, 1999. The strike price considered is equal to 35.000 for the following maturities: March 1999, April 1999, June 1999, and September 1999. The risk-free rate has been assumed to be equal to 3% per annum (p.a.).

The term structure of the implied volatility is represented in Figure 7.3.

The concept of forward volatility is analogous to the concept of forward asset prices such as forward interest rates. The forward volatility is calculated as the forward variance. The forward volatility can be considered as the expected spot volatility at a future time.

FIGURE 7.3   The Term Structure of Implied Volatility for the Call Option on the MIB30 (Strike Price=35.000) on February 17, 1999

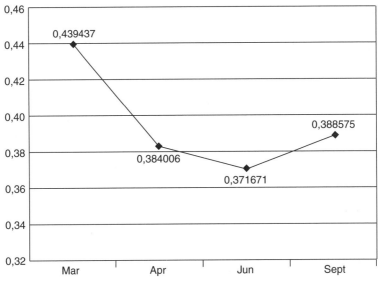

Assume that volatilities are trading as follows:

0.5 year (184 days) = 16.4% p.a.

1.0 year (365 days) = 15.25% p.a.

The forward volatility (the expected 181 days volatility in 184 days time) is given by:

$$\frac{\sqrt{365 * 0.1525^2 + 184 * 0.1640^2}}{365 - 184} = 0.1398 \text{ p.a.}$$

Limitations of the Implied Volatility

Moving averages and ARCH-GARCH models for estimating and forecasting volatility are based on the implicit assumption that the past allows for a sufficiently accurate forecasting of future behavior of volatility (*backward looking*). On the contrary, implied volatility is calculated from market data and, hence, is based on future expectations of market actors (*forward looking*). From this point of view, implied volatility could be a better predictor of volatility, being based on market expectations, not on historical data. In any event, two caveats are in order:

1. The pricing model used (for example, the BS model) should give reliable results and should actually be used by market actors. A volatility derived from a pricing model not adopted by market participants would not be representative of their expectations.
2. The market where the option is traded must be exempt of imperfections that can bias the actual price, such as shortages of demand forcing the current price to diverge from the price predicted by the model.

In addition, for use in risk management, implied volatility requires the following conditions to be satisfied:

- Options on the required asset must exist and be traded in a liquid, efficient, and organized exchange so that all the information required to calculate the implied volatility can be extracted.
- To have an estimate of volatility consistent with the desired time horizon, it would be necessary for the holding period to be equal to the time to expiry.

These limitations cause implied volatility not to be used for predicting variance in a risk management framework.

FORECASTING THE VARIANCE-COVARIANCE MATRIX FOR VaR CALCULATIONS

The current recommendation of the Basle committee (April 1995) is that 99% VaR (value at risk) measures be calculated over a holding period of 10 working days. The heart of any VaR model will be an accurate forecast of variances and covariances for the required holding period, whether the variance-covariance matrix or Monte Carlo simulation methodology is used.[13] J.P. Morgan's RiskMetrics™ uses an EWMA with a decay factor of 0.94 for daily data and 0.97 for monthly data. EWMA provides results very similar to GARCH(1,1) forecasting procedures reviewed in this chapter. Undoubtedly, GARCH provides the most complete forecasting techniques, but at the expense of a higher computational burden. When the holding period is longer than a few months, the simple unconditional variance-covariance matrix over a long and appropriate data period should be used, provided the series of squared returns is stationary (i.e., the unconditional variance exists). Although GARCH forecasts give increased accuracy over shorter time horizons, the computational problems inherent in attempting to estimate variance-covariance matrices of large dimensions are insurmountable. However, it is possible to use principal components analysis on the returns of all factors within a given risk category. This is not done—as is usually the case—necessarily to reduce dimensions, although some reduction in dimensionality will occur. Rather, the principal components will be orthogonal, so their unconditional correlations will be zero. An unconditional variance-covariance matrix of principal components is therefore diagonal, by definition.

Different models can be ranked according to how much better they perform according to a certain benchmark. Still, it is necessary to define some criterion on the basis of which we determine one model is better than another model. A possible approach[14] is to take the unconditional standard deviation over a very long data period as the benchmark against which to test different volatility-forecasting models: if a model cannot improve on this, there is no reason to use it.

However well a model fits in-sample (i.e., within the data period used to estimate the model parameters), the real test of its forecasting power is in out-of-sample (usually postsample) predictive tests. The standard econometric approach is to withhold a certain amount of data from the period used to estimate the model, and then forecasts made from the model are evaluated in some way.

In any event, we still encounter the problem of defining a criterion of fitness. The standard approach is to use the MSE to evaluate volatility and correlation forecasts, but this can be a problem. The root-mean-square error criterion comes from a normal likelihood function—minimizing the sum of the squared differences between the actual observations and the predicted means will maximize the normal likelihood when volatility is constant.[15] Unfortunately, although log returns are assumed to be normally distributed, their variance follows a distribution that, ex ante, is unknown. Therefore, a criterion based on maximum likelihood is impossible to apply.

Another reason that makes different forecasts of volatility difficult to compare is that they often refer to different time horizons. For example, historic volatility is usually used only for long-term forecasts, say of a month or more. Implied volatility, on the other hand, is difficult to compare with other forecasts because the maturity of its forecast is continually changing.

Whatever the forecasting procedure used, short-term volatility forecasts will be more accurate than long-term volatility forecasts. Unfortunately, this is the only definitive answer to the question of the relative effectiveness of different forecasting procedures.

CONDITIONAL HETEROSKEDASTICITY IN ACTUAL TIME SERIES

To test for the presence of conditional heteroskedasticity of log returns, we computed squared log returns. The test for the presence of conditional heteroskedasticity is based on the analysis of the autocorrelation function of squared returns. The selected series are MIBTEL, DAX, NYSE composite, CAC, USD/DEM, LIT/USD, and USD/YEN.

The first step is to test for the presence of heteroskedasticity of returns. This step is easily accomplished by running the regression

$$u^2{}_t = c_0 + c_1 u^2{}_{t-1} + c_2 u^2{}_{t-2} + \ldots + c_p u^2{}_{t-p} + \varepsilon \tag{7.20}$$

where u represents the series of estimated squared residuals of the least squares estimation of the model to which the u's adhere. One then calculates an ordinary F test for the hypothesis that c_1 through c_p are zero. Thus, for any regression model estimated using time series data, it is very easy to test the null hypothesis of homoskedasticity against the alternative that errors follow an ARCH(p) process.

In practice, a GARCH model with very few parameters often performs as well as an ARCH model with many parameters. In particular, a model that often works very well is the GARCH(1,1) model. Identification and estimation are more complicated for GARCH models than for pure ARCH models. The problem is essentially the same as estimating a moving-average model or an ARMA model with a moving-average component. Fortunately, in most cases, a GARCH(1,1) model "looks like"[16] an ARCH(2) model.

An appropriate test for GARCH(1,1) errors is simply to regress the squared residuals on a constant term as well as on the squared residuals lagged once and twice. In general, identification procedures for ARCH/GARCH models are basically the same used for AR/ARMA models.

In this section, we estimated a GARCH(1,1) for each series selected. To test for the presence of heteroskedasticity, we performed a simple ordinary least square (OLS) of returns against a constant. The estimated residuals have been squared, and their auto correlation function (ACF) and partial auto correlation function (PACF) inspected. All the series of squared returns showed high levels of correlation, indicating the presence of conditional heteroskedasticity. We estimated the GARCH(1,1) model because—having an infinite memory—this is, in fact, sufficient for most purposes. The results are provided in Table 7.1.

For all the estimated models, the GARCH lag coefficient is greater than 0.7, ranging from about 0.72 (DEM/USD) to 0.96 (CAC). It indicates that, for all the series, volatility is persistent and adjusts slowly to market

TABLE 7.1 Results of GARCH(1,1) Model Estimation for the Selected Series

	Constant	GARCH Error	GARCH Lag
MIBTEL	0.1580 (3.60)	0.1345 (5.77)	0.7721 (18.82)
DAX	0.5077 (4.93)	0.0989 (6.34)	0.8594 (39.22)
NY NYSE	0.1538 (4.09)	0.1281 (11.93)	0.8527 (59.14)
CAC	0.0099 (1.57)	0.0301 (4.08)	0.9630 (93.88)
DEM/USD	0.0611 (2.67)	0.0823 (4.48)	0.7168 (8.49)
LIT/USD	0.0048 (3.51)	0.0768 (7.94)	0.9090 (69.70)
YEN/USD	—	—	—

changes. We could not estimate the model for YEN/USD series, since the GARCH error coefficient was outside its boundary condition, suggesting a possible nonstationarity of the process generating the squared residuals.

NOTES

1. See Chapter 6.

2. See C. Alexander, "Volatility and Correlation Forecasting," in *Handbook of Financial Risk Management,* New York: Wiley, 1996, 233–260.

3. Loosely speaking, two series are cointegrated if they have a common long-term trend.

4. See C. Alexander, "Estimating and Forecasting Volatility and Correlation" in S. Das, *Risk Management and Financial Derivatives,* New York: McGraw-Hill, 1998, 337–354.

5. See Chapter 8 for further details.

6. This is the assumption used in J.P. Morgan's RiskMetrics™.

7. See C. Alexander, "Volatility and Correlation Forecasting."

8. This process is known as "identification" and follows the same steps used to determine the appropriate order in an ARIMA model. This process starts from the analysis of the auto correlation function (ACF) and partial auto correlation function (PACF) of squared returns.

9. See Chapter 12 for further details on the pricing of options.

10. See S. Das, "Estimating Volatility," in *Risk Management and Financial Derivatives,* 322.

11. See Das, *ibid.,* page 329.

12. See Chapters 6 and 8 for further details.

13. See Chapters 13 to 16 on VaR models for further details.

14. See C. Alexander, "Volatility and Correlation Forecasting," 255.

15. In fact, if residuals are homoskedastic, OLS regression is totally equivalent to ML estimation.

16. See R. Davidson and J. McKinnon, *Estimation and Inference in Econometrics,* New York: Oxford University Press, 1993, 557–560.

8

The Distribution
of Returns

In this chapter, we explore the distribution of log returns. The assumption of unconditional normality—common to almost all financial theory—is critically reviewed making evident that log returns are not (unconditionally) normally distributed and that there is a need for models able to account for the well-known phenomenon of "fat tails." Two alternative approaches are shown. The first is based on the use of known leptokurtic distributions, such as the t-distribution. These distributions have fatter tails than the normal distribution and are much better suited for modeling financial returns. Unfortunately, they do not have many of the desirable properties of the normal distribution (stability under summation, equivalence of noncorrelation and statistical independence, just to mention the most important ones). Finally, the RiskMetrics™ approach is reviewed. This approach assumes that the one-period-ahead conditional distribution is normal but is generated by a mixture of n different normal distributions with different means and variances. Although the sum of n normally distributed random variables is a normally distributed random variable, the unconditional distribution of returns generated by a mixed-normal process is likely to be leptokurtic and possibly skewed, according to empirical evidence.

UNCONDITIONAL DISTRIBUTION

Financial theory has always assumed that log returns are normally distributed. This is one of the assumptions the Black-Scholes (BS) formula is based on. This implies that prices are lognormally distributed. A variable has a lognormal distribution if the natural logarithm of the variable is normally distributed. Log returns are defined as $r_t = \ln(P_t/P_{t-1}) = \ln(P_t) - \ln(P_{t-1})$. It follows that prices are lognormally distributed: since the linear combination of two normally distributed random variables is a normally distributed random variable, both $\ln(P_t)$ and $\ln(P_{t-1})$ are normally distributed; hence, prices are lognormally distributed.

In particular, normality of log returns implies

$$r_t = \ln\left(P_t\right) - \ln\left(P_0\right) \approx N\left[\left(\frac{\mu - \sigma^2}{2}\right)(T-t);\ \sigma\sqrt{T-t}\right] \tag{8.1}$$

where P_t is the asset price at a future time, and P_0 is the current asset price.[1]

A variable that has a lognormal distribution can take any value between zero and infinity. This property makes this distribution particularly useful for modeling prices that cannot take a value less than zero.[2] The standard deviation of log returns grows with the square root of time. This process, known as *scaling,* is based on the assumption that log returns are generated by a white noise process, and so are uncorrelated. In fact, the variance of two or more uncorrelated variables is nothing more than the sum of the single variables' variances. Assuming that the process is stationary and random variables occur at discrete time intervals, the cumulative variance after T periods of time, is equal to $\sigma^2 T$, where σ^2 is the single-period variance. Since we assume the process to be stationary at least up to order 2, σ is also the unconditional variance. The standard deviation is therefore equal to $\sigma\sqrt{T}$. Although log returns are often treated as if they were normally distributed, empirical evidence has shown that log returns have fatter tails than predicted by the normal distribution. This means that large events are more likely to occur than as predicted by the normal distribution. In addition, return distribution is often higher and narrower around the mean than with the normal distribution.

This characteristic is known as "thin waist" and, along with fat tails, is a characteristic of leptokurtic distribution. In addition, with empirical evidence, as shown in Chapters 6 and 7 (returns sometimes show a significant level of autocorrelation and squared returns often show significant autocorrelation), the failure of the normal distribution to accurately model returns is clearly demonstrated. Researchers have started looking for alternative modeling methods, which have evolved into two broad classes:

1. Unconditional distributions (different from the normal).
2. Conditional (time-dependent) distributions.

Models in the class of unconditional distribution of returns assume that returns are independent and that the return-generating process is linear, with parameters that are independent of past realization. The unconditional standard distribution has a mean μ and a standard deviation equal to σ. These parameters are assumed to be time independent, so there is no need for a time subscript. Other examples of unconditional distribution models include the finite variance leptokurtic distribution (such as the *t* distribution), mixed-diffusion-jump models, and the infinite-variance stable Paretian distributions. Conditional distributions of returns have been examined in earlier chapters and arise from the evidence that refutes the independently and identically distributed assumption. Models in this category, such as GARCH models, treat volatility[3] as a time-dependent, persistent process.

UNCONDITIONAL NORMAL DISTRIBUTION

The easiest assumption is that log returns follow an unconditional normal distribution. This assumption is rejected by empirical evidence. To derive this evidence, we used the usual five series:

1. MIBTEL.
2. DAX.
3. NYSE composite.
4. USD/DEM exchange rates.
5. USD/JPY exchange rates.

The main statistics of the distributions of log returns for the selected financial series are shown in Table 8.1. The standardized skewness has been obtained by dividing the sample skewness by the

TABLE 8.1 Statistics of the Distribution of Log Returns for the Selected Series

	MIBTEL	DAX	NYSE	USD/DEM	USD/YEN
Mean	0.1199%	0.1310%	0.0927%	0.0321%	0.0666%
Std. deviance	1.2490%	1.1652%	0.8227%	0.5697%	0.8642%
Std. skewness	−1.5914	−9.1129	−10.0939	−0.4007	5.4190
Std. kurtosis	15.1669	31.8695	49.8943	14.5639	112.3349
Observations	750	750	750	750	750

skewness-asymptotic standard deviation equal to $\sqrt{6/N}$, where N is the number of observations. The standardized excess kurtosis has been obtained by dividing the sample excess kurtosis by its asymptotic standard deviation, equal to $\sqrt{24/N}$.

All the distributions show significant levels of kurtosis. This means that all unconditional distributions have fatter tails than the normal distribution, while three of the five series also show significant levels of skewness.

To appreciate the importance of fat tails, we have estimated the VaR at three different probability levels, using a parametric approach, based on the normal distribution. The VaR is computed with observed percentiles. Results are shown in Table 8.2. In other words, we assumed that the actual series of returns provides a good approximation of the actual distribution of returns.

At 95%, VaR calculated with a parametric approach overestimates the actual VaR. This is quite interesting and can be partially explained by the strong negative skewness that some series show. This may mean that large returns tend to occur on the right tail rather than on the left tail, so they are ignored. The evidence at 97.5% is mixed. In two cases out of five, parametric VaR overcomes simulation VaR. At 99%, parametric VaR underestimates simulation VaR in all the cases. Although results at 95% are surprising, the overall result is that the more unlikely we consider the event to be, the more inappropriate the parametric VaR becomes if the distribution of returns is leptokurtic. In fact, with leptokurtic distributions, the probability of large events is much higher than predicted by the normal distribution. Many methods have been developed to deal with this

TABLE 8.2 Comparison between Parametric and Simulation VaR for Fat Tails Distributions

	VaR 95%		VaR 97.5%		VaR 99%	
	Param (%)	Simu (%)	Param (%)	Simu (%)	Param (%)	Simu (%)
MIBTEL	−1.94	−1.74	−2.33	−2.23	−2.79	−3.09
DAX	−1.79	−1.77	−2.15	−2.44	−2.58	−5.67
NYSE	−1.26	−1.15	−1.52	−1.65	−1.82	−2.31
USD/DEM	−0.91	−0.93	−1.08	−1.22	−1.30	−1.49
USD/YEN	−1.36	−0.99	−1.63	−1.46	−1.95	−2.32

kind of problem. A possible approach is to use known leptokurtic distributions to approximate the distribution of log returns.

LEPTOKURTIC DISTRIBUTION AND RETURNS

To understand how known leptokurtic distributions can be used in estimating VaR, we used the same five series of log returns. This time, however, we assumed that returns are distributed according to a known leptokurtic distribution. We arbitrarily chose a t-distribution with 10 degrees of freedom. Compared with the normal distribution, this shows much fatter tails. Obviously, we can no longer assume that—let's say—5% of the distribution is on the left of -1.65σ. Leptokurtic distributions—compared with the normal distribution—are thinner around the mean and have fatter (higher, if we consider the distance from the X-axis) tails.[4] This means that by starting the integration of a pdf from $-\infty$, a value of 0.05 is reached sooner than for a normal distribution. In fact, for a t-distribution with 10 degrees of freedom, the critical values for the 95%, 97.5%, and 99% probability levels are 2.23σ, 2.63σ, and 3.17σ, respectively. We have compared the parametric VaR (this time, with a t-distribution with 10 degrees of freedom) and the simulation VaR for the series under examination. Results are shown in Table 8.3.

Parametric VaR has been made more prudent using a leptokurtic distribution. At a 99% probability level, the simulation VaR overcomes the parametric VaR in only one case out of five. The choice of a t-distribution with 10 degrees of freedom is totally arbitrary, but it serves the purpose of demonstrating how predictions can be more accurate if the hypothesis of normality is relaxed, allowing for distributions that are fatter in the tails.

TABLE 8.3   Comparison between t-Distributed Parametric and Simulation VaR

	VaR 95%		VaR 97.5%		VaR 99%	
	Param (%)	Simu (%)	Param (%)	Simu (%)	Param (%)	Simu (%)
MIBTEL	−2.67	−1.74	−3.18	−2.23	−3.84	−3.09
DAX	−2.47	−1.77	−2.95	−2.44	−3.56	−5.67
NYSE	−1.74	−1.15	−2.08	−1.65	−2.52	−2.31
USD/DEM	−1.24	−0.93	−1.47	−1.22	−1.77	−1.49
USD/YEN	−1.86	−0.99	−2.21	−1.46	−2.67	−2.32

MIXED DISTRIBUTION

Another possible approach, used by J.P. Morgan's RiskMetrics, is to allow the one-period-ahead distribution of returns to not only be conditional (e.g., variance is forecasted using an EWMA technique) but also to be generated by a mix of (usually normal) distributions, with different means and variances. A possible approach could be to assume that returns are generated alternatively by two distributions. Returns are generated by the one or the other pdf (probability density function) with a prespecified probability. The resulting pdf would be:

$$r_t \approx p_1 N(\mu_1, \sigma_1) + (1 - p_1) N(\mu_2, \sigma_2) \qquad (8.2)$$

The rationale for this approach is that we can assume returns to be affected by two kinds of factors: structural factors, represented by the most likely distribution; and random factors, represented by the less likely but more dispersed distribution. For example, we can assume $\mu_1 = 0$, $\sigma_1 = 0.01$, $\mu_2 = 0$, $\sigma_2 = 0.04$, and $p_1 = 0.95$. Using Microsoft Minitab 10.1™, we drew out 950 random numbers from distribution 1 and 50 numbers from distribution 2. Results are shown in Table 8.4

The effects are clear. Although data taken from each individual distribution are normally distributed with the specified standard deviation, the unconditional distribution is not only negatively skewed, but also highly leptokurtic. This confirms the idea that unconditional leptokurtosis may be due to conditional normal distribution occurring on the basis of a mixed-normal process.

The RiskMetrics approach is only slightly different. Returns are assumed to be generated by

$$r_t = n_t + \pi \beta_t \qquad (8.3)$$

TABLE 8.4 Mixed Normal Distribution and Its Effect on Tails

	Full Distribution	N1	N2
Mean	−0.045%	−0.016%	−0.602%
Std. deviation	1.347%	1.022%	4.056%
Skewness	−12.676	−0.767	−0.979
Kurtosis	62.453	0.213	−0.364

where n_t and β_t are normally distributed random variables with different means and variances and π is a boolean variable, assuming a value of 1 with probability $p1$ and a value of 0 with probability $p2$.

J.P. Morgan estimates[5] that mixed-normal methodology definitively overcomes unconditional estimates of the distribution of returns and allows for a much more accurate estimation of VaR. A Bayesian technique for estimating the required parameter of Equation 8.3 is also provided.

NOTES

1. See J. Hull, *Options, Futures and Other Derivatives,* Englewood Cliffs, NJ: Prentice Hall, 1997, 228-229.

2. See Chapter 5.

3. And also the mean, as in the case of ARIMA models.

4. In any case, for being a pdf, a function must have an integral from $-\infty$ to $+\infty$ equal to 1.

5. P. Zangari, "An Improved Methodology for Measuring VaR," *RiskMetrics Monitor,* 2nd quarter, 1996.

9

Fractal Distributions and Applications to VaR

I n this chapter, we briefly review an alternative approach to modeling
financial risk and return.[1] This approach is based on a particular set
of distributions, called Pareto-stable distributions, or fractal distributions. A full coverage of the theory of fractal would require an entire en-
cyclopedia. Even if we should limit to the applications in economics and
finance, we would require an entire dissertation. We limit our analysis to
a very specific field: fractal statistics and its impact on VaR.

But, what is a fractal? There is no precise answer. A fractal is better explained on the basis of its property than by a precise definition. The word
"fractal" comes from the Latin word *fractum* (from the verb *frangere*,
which means "to divide"). A fractal is something that can be indefinitively
divided while keeping its properties. It is a scale-invariant. Conversely, it
can indefinitively be summed while retaining its properties. Classical examples are mammalian lunge and pine trees. A second characteristic is the
coexistence of local randomness and global determinism. A classical example is the Sierpinsky triangle or "Chaos Game."[2] Even if a fractal system
evolves randomly on a local scale, the global result is deterministic. In time
series analysis, this implies long-range dependence, long-run quasi-deter-
ministic trends, and cycles superimposed to short-term random processes.

This brief review of fractal distributions provides an analysis of their
properties in the context of VaR. Finally, the effects of fractal distribution
on the well-known diversification effect predicted by portfolio theory are
reviewed, and the consequences for VaR computation are analyzed.

STABLE DISTRIBUTIONS AND THEIR PROPERTIES

We have stated several times that the normal distribution is not adequate to
describe market returns. In Chapter 8, we reviewed two main alternatives:

unconditional leptokurtic distributions (such as the t-distribution) and conditional mixed distributions. In this section we explore a new alternative: the possibility that assets' returns are distributed according to a Pareto-stable distribution different from the normal. The central limit theorem (CLT) states that the liner combination of n independent random variables with finite mean and variance is a normally distributed random variable. It is the theorem on which most of modern statistics is based; philosophically, it is the ultimate imposition of order to disorder. Unfortunately, the central limit theorem does not always hold. Pareto, for example, found out that the income distribution was lognormally distributed for 97% of the population, whereas for the remaining 3% the tail was much fatter than expected. The point is that there are some distributions, discovered by Pareto and deeply analyzed by Levy, for which the CLT does not hold. In particular, there are instances where amplification occurs at extreme values. This occurrence will often cause a long-tailed distribution.

Stable Pareto-Levy's distributions have desirable properties that make them particularly consistent with observed market behavior. However, these same characteristics make the usefulness of stable distributions questionable. The main properties of the stable distributions are:

- *Invariance under addition.* For portfolio theory, the normal distribution had this very desirable characteristic. The sum of IID random variables is a normally distributed random variable. When fractal distributions with the same characteristic exponent[3] are added, the result is a fractal distribution with the same characteristic exponent of the adding distributions. This property is often called *stability.*
- *Self-similarity.* If the characteristic exponent is the same, it is possible to rescale the distribution by changing just one of its parameters, but the probability remains the same at all scales. In other words, the distribution is indefinitively divisible, when just changing a scaling factor. To make a parallel with fractal geometry, we know that if we sum n fractal shapes, we obtain a greater fractal shape with the same characteristic. Apart from the scale (it is greater), it has exactly the same properties as its components. Each component can be divided indefinitively into smaller components that have the same properties apart from being smaller. The normal distribution, for example, retains the same properties even for changes in scale.

Notably, we have not mentioned fat tails as a characteristic feature of fractal distributions. To define tails as fat, we need a benchmark, usually provided by the normal distribution itself. We have seen that the normal distribution has exactly the same properties characterizing the fractal distribution. The normal distribution is both self-similar and stable under addition. As we will see, the normal distribution is a degenerate fractal distribution that shares most—but not all—the properties of fractal distributions. It is the threshold distribution between the fractal and the nonfractal distributions but is itself a fractal distribution. Instead of being the expression of a general rule of order, it is nothing else than a special case in the class of fractal distributions. Stability under addition is in no way related to the CLT. Stability occurs for any small number of normal distributions (and, as described, for any number of fractal distributions) added, while the CLT is valid only for a large number of distributions with finite mean and variance.

Returning to fat tails, we can say that all fractal distributions[4] have fatter tails than the normal. Nevertheless, many nonfractal distributions have fatter tails than the normal (i.e., are leptokurtic). For example, the t-distribution is a nonfractal leptokurtic distribution. In fact, it is neither stable nor self-similar. When n t-distributed random variables are added ($n \rightarrow \infty$), the resulting random variable will be normally distributed.

Notwithstanding this, the fat tails of fractal distributions have some interesting features. If we assume log returns to be generated from a fractal distribution instead of the standard normal distribution, we encounter much more large values than we could expect even from a leptokurtic nonfractal distribution. Extreme values are encountered with a non-negligible probability, contrary to the normal distribution.

The consequence is that prices can abruptly change. These are the so-called price jumps or discontinuities. Standard financial theory (e.g., the Black-Scholes formula for option pricing) is based on the assumption that prices are continuous (i.e., loosely speaking, there are no price jumps). Price jumps are excluded if returns are generated by a normal distribution. On the other hand, price jumps are characteristic of all those processes generated by fractal distributions, apart from the normal distribution. The normal distribution is more compact than fractal distributions so extremely large values are unlikely to actually occur, thus preventing the possibility of price jumps. Fat tails and discontinuities are typical of all the fractal distribution apart from the normal. Being a threshold distribution, some of its fractal properties degenerate or are lost, even if it can be highly desirable from a statistical viewpoint. Some of these characteristics, although statistically difficult to treat, explain market behavior very well. Discontinuities are due to a typical characteristic of fractal distributions (but not of the normal distribution): infinite variance. We return later to this point.

FORMAL PROPERTIES OF FRACTAL DISTRIBUTIONS

We have only the closed forms of two fractal distribution: the normal and the Cauchy distribution.[5] The closed form of the Cauchy distribution is

$$f(x) = \left(\frac{1}{\Pi}\right)\left[\frac{\gamma}{\gamma^2 + (x - \delta)}\right] \tag{9.1}$$

where δ is a location parameter while γ is a scale parameter indicating the dispersion of the distribution. For the normal distribution, δ is the mean while γ is a multiple of the standard deviation. In general, a fractal distribution depends on four parameters: δ, γ, α, and β. β indicates the skewness of the distribution and ranges from -1 to $+1$. If $\beta = +1$ the distribution is positively skewed and only the left tail exists. The opposite is true if $\beta = -1$. If $\beta = 0$, the distribution is symmetrical around the location parameter. The most important parameter is α. It is called the "characteristic exponent" and determines the peakness at δ and the fatness of tails. It ranges from 0 (> 0) to 2 (≤ 2) and characterizes fractal distributions. When $\alpha = 2$, the distribution is normal with finite mean and variance equal to $2\gamma^2$. However, when $1 < \alpha < 2$, the second moment (the population variance) becomes infinite or undefined. When $0 < \alpha \leq 1$, the first moment, too (the mean), becomes infinite. Notably, all moments higher than the second also will be infinite. Sample estimates of variance and kurtosis will not converge as the sample size increases but will tend to increase indefinitively.

The existence of infinite variance explains the existence of discontinuities. In capital markets, it happens when panics break out, and fear breeds fear amplifying the bearish/bullish sentiment causing discontinuities. The normal distribution, on the other hand, has a finite variance so it is less dispersed than all other fractal distributions. This rules out discontinuities.

We can now better appreciate the basic properties of fractal distributions. The characteristic exponent is helpful in explaining the additivity property of fractal distributions. If n random variables fractally distributed all with location equal to 1 and characteristic exponent equal to, let's say, 1.75 are added, the resulting random variable will have a mean equal to $1*n$ and characteristic exponent equal to 1.75.

If all the adding random variables are normally distributed ($\alpha = 2$), the resulting distribution will be normally distributed as well. In this case, not only the mean but also the variance will be finite and equal to $1^2*n = 1*n$.

It is now clear that the so beloved additivity property of the normal distribution is not a kind of magic peculiar only to the normal distribution that represents the final order superimposed to apparent chaos, but it is a property belonging to an entire class of distributions where the normal is a special rather than a general case. This explains why the CLT does not apply to fractal distributions: if we add n Cauchy-distributed random variables, we will obtain a Cauchy-distributed random variable, not a normally distributed random variable, even if $n \to \infty$.

The normal and the Cauchy distribution are two special cases of fractal distributions. When $\alpha = 2$ and $\beta = 0$, we have a normal distribution with mean equal to δ and variance equal to $2^*\gamma^2$; when $\alpha = 1$ and $\beta = 0$, we have the Cauchy distribution, which has both infinite mean and variance. In this case, δ is just the median and γ is the semi-interquartile range. Fractal distributions are usually studied when δ is equal to 0 and $\gamma = 1$. In this case, we have the *reduced forms* of fractal distributions: the standardized normal distribution is nothing but a special case of reduced fractal distributions.

There are many problems with fractal distributions. One of the greatest problems is that they do not have closed-form solutions apart from those for the normal and the Cauchy distribution. The probability density function cannot be solved for explicitly. Fortunately, research has been performed to derive numerically the probability density function or the probability cumulative density function for fractal distributions with different values of α, usually from 0.25 to 2 with increments of 0.25. The technique used is based on the definition of distribution given by a weighted average of the normal and the Cauchy distribution. Cumulative distribution tables for reduced distributions for different values of α can be found in Peters,[6] which also provides many other details about the estimation of probability cumulative density functions for distributions other than the normal and the Cauchy. The reduced distribution is obtained by defining u as the difference between x and δ (the location parameter) divided by the scale parameter γ. Since the scale parameter γ is equal to $\sigma / \sqrt{2}$ for the normal distribution, $F(z)$ is slightly different than $F(u, \alpha = 2)$. It follows that

$$u = \sqrt{2^*z} \tag{9.2}$$

Using the cumulative distribution tables provided by Peters,[7] we can see that $F(u = 2, \alpha = 2) = 0.9104$. It means that the probability of u being greater than 2 is 0.0896, much greater than $1 - F(z = 2) = 0.0228$. For a value of z of 2, the corresponding value of u is $2^* \sqrt{2} \approx 2.8$. Not casually, $1 - F(u = 2.8, \alpha = 2) = 0.9761$ is equal to 0.0239, very close to the expected value of 0.0228. This will be very useful when analyzing the impact on fractal distributions on VaR calculation.

The second property of fractal distribution is self-similarity. We use this property any time we perform an hypothesis testing. Since it would be too tedious to have tabulated any possible combination of mean and variance for the normal distribution, we standardize the actual distribution and use the standardized normal distribution function. This can be done only because the normal distribution is self-similar (i.e., it is scale invariant). Once we adjust the original distribution for a scale parameter (the standard deviation that is just a multiple of the fractal scale parameter γ) the properties of the distribution are retained: 5% of the probability mass will lie on the left of $\mu + 1.65\sigma$ for every μ and σ.

We do not have the equivalent of the CLT theorem for fractal distributions. It means that we do not know what will be the characteristic exponent of a distribution resulting from the sum of n distributions with different αs.

We can now turn to analyze the effect of fractal distributions on VaR.

EFFECTS ON THE CALCULATION OF VaR

All fractal distributions but the normal have three interesting characteristics: they have fat tails, they generate discontinuities, they generate series that have a long memory. The effects of these properties on VaR will be analyzed. In this paragraph we concentrate on the effect of fat tails.

Assume we have a single asset, whose 1-day expected returns are generated by two fractal distributions, the normal and the Cauchy. For the sake of simplicity, we used the reduced form with $\delta = 0$ and $\gamma = 1$. Using Microsoft Minitab 10.1™, we generate two series of 10,000 random numbers from a normal distribution with mean equal to zero and tandard deviation equal to $1/\sqrt{2} \approx 0.7071$. We calculated VaR for the two distributions using the sample percentiles. The results are summarized in Table 9.1.

If returns are generated by a Cauchy distribution, VaR computed assuming normality (e.g., applying the standard rule -1.65σ for a 95% probability level that would yield an estimated VaR of -1.17, very close to the observed VaR of -1.18) can significantly underestimate true VaR. At 99% probability level, the true VaR assuming returns are Cauchy-distributed would be about 15 times larger than the VaR computed assuming normality. This can be seen by looking at the number of observations in our simulation exceeding different values of u. Results are shown in Table 9.2.

TABLE 9.1   Comparison of VaR for the Normal and the Cauchy Distribution

	95%	97.5%	99%
Normal	−1.19	−1.40	−1.64
Cauchy	−6.41	−12.00	−28.80
Normal	98.82	98.61	98.37
Cauchy	93.80	88.69	74.97
VaR Normal	1.18	1.39	1.63
VaR Cauchy	6.20	11.31	25.03

Figure 9.1 depicts the left tails of the Cauchy and the normal distribution for different values of u. The normal distribution declines much faster than the Cauchy, which has much fatter tails.

Finally, using the tables of fractiles (percentiles of fractal distributions, see Table 9.3), we can appreciate how the characteristic exponent α can dramatically change the probability mass of the distribution and hence VaR.[8]

TABLE 9.2   Comparison between the Normal and the Cauchy for Different Values of u

u	Normal	Cauchy	Percent Normal	Percent Cauchy
1.0	1,518	2,475	15.18	24.75
1.2	1,099	2,185	10.99	21.85
1.4	744	1,967	7.44	19.67
1.6	500	1,768	5.00	17.68
1.8	336	1,616	3.36	16.16
2.0	224	1,450	2.24	14.50
2.2	130	1,352	1.30	13.52
2.4	86	1,263	0.86	12.63
2.6	46	1,182	0.46	11.82
2.8	27	1,105	0.27	11.05
3.0	14	1,027	0.14	10.27
3.2	8	962	0.08	9.62
3.4	4	903	0.04	9.03

FIGURE 9.1   Left Tails of the Normal and the Cauchy Distributions

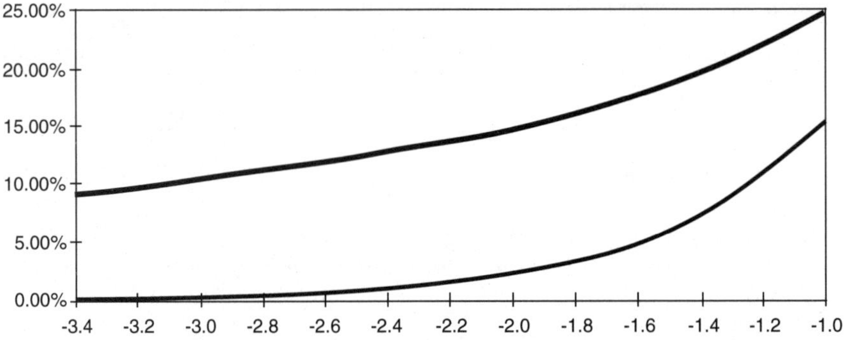

THE NOAH EFFECT

Another interesting feature of fractal distributions is that they allow for discontinuities—large and abrupt price changes (or, equivalently, extreme returns)—that conform more to the real behavior of financial market than the pattern predicted by the normal distributions. This effect has been referred to several ways but the most colorful term is "Noah effect" recalling the biblical deluge. Another name for this feature is "infinite variance syndrome." Although the words deluge and syndrome are best suited for negative situations, discontinuities can be both disasters and rallies. In this chapter, we are dealing with symmetrical distributions only ($\beta = 0$). The normal and the Cauchy are symmetrical distributions. Nevertheless, it is possible to use asymmetrical fractal distribution to account for the fact that negative discontinuities (deluges) seem to be more frequent than positive discontinuities. To provide an example of such an effect, we took the first 500 random numbers of the set of 10,000 numbers previously selected and constructed two simulated time series,

TABLE 9.3   Comparison of Fractiles for Different Values of Alpha

α (%)	1.00	1.50	1.80	1.95	2.00
95	6.314	3.053	2.505	2.363	2.327
97.5	12.706	4.485	3.160	2.846	2.772
99	31.820	7.737	4.291	3.461	3.290
99.5	63.657	54.337	18.290	3.947	3.643

assuming that log returns were generated by a normal distribution and by a weighted average of the normal distribution and the Cauchy distribution. In other words, denoting with ε_t the normally distributed random numbers and with χ_t the random numbers selected from the Cauchy distribution, the two series were generated assuming that $P_t = P_{t-1}\exp(\varepsilon_t)$ for the normal series and that $P_t = P_{t-1}\exp(0.75\varepsilon_t + 0.25\,\chi_t)$ for the infinite variance series. The weighted average should produce a distribution of returns with a characteristic exponent of about 1.75 to avoid the very abrupt discontinuities of the Cauchy distribution that would have made any comparison impossible. The two series are shown in Figure 9.2. As can be seen, there are some points where the weighted time series jumps, passing abruptly from one level to another. The normal series, on the other hand, is much smoother and continuous. Incorporating fractal distribution into forecasting models would also help predict extreme changes in market factors not accounted for from the standard normality assumption, making simulations much more realistic.

The infinite volatility property deserves more attention. When we deal with fractal distributions, we assume they are unconditional distributions. On the other hand, a mixed process having conditional normal distribution with different variance could explain fat tails as well and is the most plausible alternative to fractal distributions. Conditional variance can be designed through the well-known ARCH-GARCH models examined in Chapter 7. It is possible that these phenomena (infinite unconditional variance and finite conditional variance) coexist. We recall that an IGARCH(1,1) model is a model where the coefficients of the squared error and of the autoregressive term are constrained so that their sum is 1. The unconditional variance then becomes infinite, although the

FIGURE 9.2 Comparison of Two Simulated Time Series ($\alpha = 2$ and $\alpha \approx 1.75$)

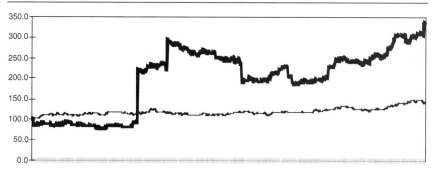

conditional variance is not. Since the approach of conditional variance modeled with ARCH/GARCH models is the greatest challenge to the use of fractal distributions, this observation gives a useful inside toward a reconciliation of the two approaches. We also checked for the presence of discontinuities in the time series we have so far used as our benchmark. We considered a discontinuity in the time series of returns to be any return exceeding in absolute value 4σ. According to the normal distribution, values below -4σ or above $+4\sigma$ should occur with a relative frequency of 0.0063% or 1 time out of 15,873. Our series all have a length of 750 daily log returns. Values exceeding 4σ in absolute values were found two times for the MIBTEL, two times for the DAX, four times for the USD/DEM series, and four times for the USD/YEN series.

Although this analysis cannot be considered conclusive, there are clear signs that there can be discontinuities in some of the most important economic time series; hence the use of fractal distributions can be extremely fruitful.

THE JOSEPH EFFECT

A third feature of fractal distributions is their capability to generate time series that show long-range dependence. We provide here only some remarks since—although in the theory of fractal analysis—it plays a large role, it is the least interesting for our purposes. Long-range dependent time series exhibit an unusually high degree of persistence, meaning that observations in the remote past are not trivially correlated with observation in the distant future, even if the time span increases. This is a common phenomenon in natural sciences such as hydrology, meteorology, and geophysics. This phenomenon creates long-range trends and very long cycles. Its name recalls Joseph's prophecy of seven years of plenty followed by seven years of famine. Not casually, the most important statistical tool to detect long-range dependence—the rescaled range—has been developed by the British hydrologist Hurst studying long-term storage capacity of reservoirs on the Nile river! In the frequency domain, such series would exhibit power at the lowest frequencies: they would show cycles with very long periods. Peters[9] showed that economic and financial time series show a cycle of about 4 to 5 years. Long-range dependence cannot be easily analyzed with standard statistical tools, but requires different tools. Although it is an extremely interesting subject, long-range dependence is not relevant for VaR purposes since the time horizons we are usually interested in are much shorter. We are interested in short-range markovian dependence, which can be treated with standard statistical tools described in earlier chapters.

MODERN PORTFOLIO THEORY AND FRACTAL DISTRIBUTIONS

Modern portfolio theory (MPT) by H. Markowitz is still a milestone of the theory of financial markets. MPT demonstrates that portfolio selection can be analyzed through mean-variance optimization if we assume assets' expected returns to be normally distributed. For a portfolio, the expected return is merely the weighted average of the expected returns of the individual stocks in the portfolio. Individual stock risk was the standard deviation of the stock return, or σ. However, the risk of a portfolio was more than just the risk of the individual stocks added together. To evaluate the risk of a portfolio, it became important to know that the two stocks could be correlated. If there was positive correlation, then the risk of two stocks added together would be lower than the sum of the risk of the two. If there was negative correlation, then the risk of the two stocks added together could even drop to zero! They would *diversify* one another. In the original formulation, which is widely used, the expected return and risk are calculated for each combination of all the stocks in the portfolio. The portfolio with the highest expected return for a given level of risk was called an *efficient* portfolio. The collection of all the efficient portfolios was called the *efficient frontier.* Optimizing mean return versus variance gave rise to the term *mean/variance efficiency,* or optimization. In this way, Markowitz quantified how portfolios could be rationally constructed and how diversification reduced risk.

All VaR methodologies apart from historical simulation rely—more or less explicitly—on MPT and on the concept of correlation. VaR for a diversified portfolio is less than just the simple sum of undiversified VaRs of every single asset, unless all assets are perfectly correlated. In this last case, undiversified and diversified VaR coincide.

Using fractal distributions, we have two problems: (1) variance and (2) correlation coefficient.

The obvious problem deals with variance. In the mean/variance environment, variance is the measure of a stock's and portfolio's risk. Fractal distributions do not have a variance to optimize. A more difficult problem deals with the correlation coefficient, ρ. In the stable family, there is no comparable concept, except in the special case of the normal distribution.

Some of the greatest financial economists, such as Fama, Roll, and Miller, have tried to adapt MPT to incorporate Pareto-stable distributions. They have assumed that assets' expected returns were distributed according to Pareto-stable distributions with a characteristic exponent equal to 1.70. This was not much of an advance compared to Markowitz's assumed characteristic exponent of 2! A detailed analysis of their works is beyond our scope. The interesting part relies in the conclusion. They found out that, as long as the characteristic exponent is greater than 1, diversification is retained, although the effects of diversification decline as α declines to 1. When $\alpha = 1$ (assets' expected returns are Cauchy-distributed) diversification does not take place. If $\alpha < 1$ diversification is reversed: adding assets to a portfolio will increase rather than decrease total risk. The result, although surprising, is logical: the importance of fat tails (i.e., large events) becomes greater as the characteristic exponent declines. When $\alpha < 1$, large events become so frequent that they tend to reinforce each other rather than to diversify each other.

We provide a simple numerical example. We simulated three portfolios made up of two assets each. The assets' return are assumed to be normally distributed, Cauchy distributed, and distributed according to an equally weighted average of the normal and the Cauchy distribution. The resulting distribution should have approximately a characteristic exponent of 1.5.

To measure risk, we needed a nonparametric measure of dispersion. We used the difference between 95% and 5%. We used these values to be sure to account for large values. Using Microsoft Minitab 10.1, we generated two series of 100 normally distributed and two series of Cauchy distributed returns. Then, we computed the equally weighted mixed distribution. Finally, we computed the returns for the three equally weighted portfolios. According to previous works, diversification should take place for the normally distributed portfolio and for the mixed-distribution portfolio. For the Cauchy distributed portfolio, we should see no diversification effect. Diversification should be greater for the normal distribution than for the mixed ($\alpha = 1.5$) distribution. Results are shown in Tables 9.4 and 9.5.

Our simulation was consistent with fractal-adjusted MPT. Risk reduction takes place both for the portfolio of normally distributed assets and for the portfolio of mixed-distribution assets ($\alpha = 1.5$). Risk reduction is much more significant in the case of normality. On the other hand, risk increases if assets are normally distributed. This is not consistent with previous results where risk is stable for $\alpha = 1$ and grows only for $\alpha < 1$. It may be due to the arbitrarily chosen measure of risk. Nevertheless, on the

TABLE 9.4   Simulated Risk for Individual Assets (risk in % form)

	Normal	Cauchy	Alpha = 1.5
Asset 1	3,4899	8,6000	5,6498
Asset 2	3,4683	11,7000	5,1556

TABLE 9.5   Effects on Diversification for Different Values of α (risk in % form)

	Ptf-Normal	Pt-Cauchy	Ptf-Mixed
Undiversified	3,4791	10,1500	5,4027
Diversified	2,6739	13,7500	4,8410
Risk reduction	−23%	35%	−10%

whole, diversification reduces and even reverses as fractal distributions have a lower value of α.

The consequences for VaR are extremely interesting. If returns are generated by a Cauchy distribution (or by a distribution with α < 1), diversification does not pay and hence VaR for a diversified portfolio is even greater than just the simple sum of undiversified VaR. Evidence from Peters has shown that the characteristic exponent for financial time series ranges from about 1.42 to about 1.70.[10] This means that the diversification effect could be less intense than predicted by standard normal portfolio theory. The managerial consequences are important. For example, it would be necessary to set aside more reserves or to allocate more capital than expected under the normality assumption. It is an interesting field of research that should receive more attention.

The adaptation of traditional MPT provided by Fama and Roll did not become popular because it was too complicated compared to the standard Gaussian case. At that time, indeed, there was not enough conclusive evidence to show that the markets were not Gaussian. In any case, a major problem lies in the value of α itself. The adaptation assumes that all of the securities in the portfolio have the same value of α. This is necessary because the sum of stable Paretian variables with the same characteristic exponent, α, will result in a new distribution that still has the same characteristic exponent, α. This is the additive property discussed earlier. There is no equivalent of the CLT for fractal distributions. Until such a theorem is demonstrated, mathematical complexity and incomplete endowment of statistical tools make extensive use of fractal distributions in finance almost impossible.

CONCLUSION

In this chapter we have reviewed fractal distributions and how they can influence the calculation of VaR. Fractal distributions have several desirable characteristics:

- Additivity.
- Self-similarity.
- Fat tails.

The first two characteristics define fractal distributions, and are common to any fractal distribution, including the normal distribution. Fat tails characterize all fractal distributions (excluding the normal), but also some nonfractal distributions. Their appeal stems from the fact that empirical distributions from financial markets do have fat tails. They also have characteristics that make them difficult to use in financial modeling:

- Discontinuities.
- Infinite variance.

These are problems only from a statistical viewpoint since they well describe the actual behavior of financial markets.

Although popular in the 1960s and early 1970s, stable distributions are less used today. They have fallen out of favor partly because they make theoretical modeling difficult (finance theory always requires a finite second moment to estimate risk) and because empirical evidence is controversial. Sample estimates of the variance often tend to converge rather than becoming infinite when sample size increases. In addition, since they are stable, they require that both short-term distributions and long-term distributions are non-normal. In practice, evidence of non-normality is much stronger for short-term distributions rather than for long-term distributions.[11]

Efforts should be made to gain a deeper knowledge of fractal distributions so we can create more realistic financial models relaxing the need to justify the use of tools based on the assumption of normality rather than on the ground of empirical evidence.

APPENDIX: ESTIMATION AND FORECASTING WHEN RETURNS ARE NOT NORMALLY DISTRIBUTED

In the previous chapters, we have seen that asset returns are often non-normally distributed. Standard econometric theory is based on the assumption of normality; therefore, financial data pose a great challenge to the statistical and econometric tools commonly used in estimation and forecasting. In this appendix, we review some of the most common techniques used to cope with the phenomenon of non-normality in financial data. Empirical evidence is used to compare the predictive power of each of these techniques.

The Standard Approach

Financial literature often refers to regression as a simple and straightforward way to estimate financial models. *Regression* almost always means "ordinary least squares," or OLS. Most of the time, the assumptions required for OLS to provide optimal estimates of coefficients in linear models are forgotten, and the implications of departures from the basic assumptions are neglected. Since the assumptions required for OLS to provide optimal estimates are rarely met, the analyst should pay attention both to the technique of estimation used and to the interpretation of results.

Econometric techniques are mainly used in equity valuation, since standard calculus techniques are well suited for fixed-income security pricing, whereas stochastic calculus is needed—and sufficient—for option pricing.

On the contrary, the models most commonly used for equity valuation—the Capital Asset Pricing Model (CAPM) and the APT—are linear models, the parameters of which can be easily estimated using econometric techniques. In the rest of this appendix, we refer to the market model (i.e., the model used to estimate CAPM's beta).

The market model can be expressed by Equation A.9.1:

$$E\left(R_j\right) = a_j + b_j R_m + e_{t,j} \tag{A.9.1}$$

where $E(R_j)$ is asset-j's expected return and R_m is the market return.

OLS can be effectively used if

$$E(e_j) = 0$$

$E(e_{t'j}; e_{t-k'j}) = 0$ if $k \neq 0$ (i.e., no autocorrelation among residuals exists, at any lag) and is equal to σ^2_{ej} when $k = 0$ (for any t, implying homoskedasticity).

In addition, the market model requires the residuals for security-j to be uncorrelated with the residuals of any other security in the portfolio.

Neither the market model nor OLS requires the residuals to be normally distributed, although it is a very desirable property.

If residuals are also normally distributed, the OLS technique not only is BLU (best linear unbiased) but is also optimal; i.e., it has the smallest possible variance of errors (this property of estimators is often called "efficiency"). In this special case, the OLS estimators attain the Cramer-Rao lower bound and are also equivalent to the maximum likelihood estimators (ML).

If residuals are not normally distributed, some of the properties of the normal-OLS are lost. We should distinguish the case when the distribution of residuals has a finite variance (leptokurtic-Gaussian distributions, such as the t-distribution with more than 2 degrees of freedom, the Laplace distribution, and so on) from the case when this distribution has an infinite variance (e.g., the Cauchy distribution or the t-distribution with 1 degree of freedom[12]). Finite-variance leptokurtic distributions were discussed in Chapter 8; infinite-variance distributions, in Chapter 9.

In the finite-variance case, the OLS estimator loses some of the properties it has with normally distributed residuals. The main differences are summarized in Table 9A.1.

TABLE 9A.1   OLS-Estimator's Properties when Residuals Are Not Normally Distributed (finite variance)

OLS If Residuals Are Normally Distributed	OLS If Residuals Are Not Normally Distributed (but Still Finite Variance)
The OLS estimator of coefficients is not only unbiased, but has minimum variance within the class of *all* unbiased estimators. It is also consistent.	The OLS estimator of coefficients is unbiased minimum variance from within the class of *linear* estimators. It is also consistent.
The variance estimator $s^2/(T-K)$ is unbiased minimum variance from within the class of *all* unbiased estimators. It is also consistent.	The variance estimator $s^2/(T-k)$ is unbiased and consistent. $s^2/(T-k)$
Estimators of coefficients and variance are asymptotically efficient.	Estimators of coefficients and variance are no longer efficient or even asymptotically efficient. In general, if the distribution of residual is known, ML can be used. It is highly nonlinear but, under certain regularity conditions, is asymptotically efficient. If the distribution of residuals is not known, a robust estimator should be used. In this case, depending on the true distribution, such an estimator may be more asymptotically efficient than the OLS estimator.
T-tests and F-tests are valid in finite samples, since coefficients are normally distributed and $(T-K)s^2/\sigma^2$ is distributed as a $X^2(T-k)$	T-tests and F-tests are no longer valid in finite samples, since coefficients are not normally distributed and $(T-K)s^2/\sigma^2$ is not distributed as a $X^2(T-k)$. These tests do have an asymptotic justification, although they may have a reduced power against certain departures from normality.

The consequences are much greater in the case of infinite-variance distributions. Given that such distributions may be good representations of many data series—especially financial data series—it is natural to wonder why we should assume the residuals to be normally distributed, and what the consequences are for the OLS estimator of this kind of departure from normality.

For a given continuous random-variable X, the variance is given by:

$$G_x^2 = \int x^2 f(x) dx$$

(A.9.2)

For the variance to be finite, this integral must converge. Infinite variance distributions arise when $f(X)$ does not approach to zero sufficiently quickly to "compensate for" the increment in X^2. That is why distributions with infinite variance have fat tails; as a consequence, outliers will be relatively frequent. This is the mathematical rationale for the Noah effect seen in Chapter 9.

Because OLS minimizes the sum of squared deviations, it places more weight on outliers, and their presence can lead to estimates that are extremely sensitive. Thus, in repeated samples, OLS estimates will vary more than in the finite-variance case. If the variance does not exist, it is impossible to have reliable estimates of the variance itself. The obtained number will have no meaning. In addition, the same concept of "minimum variance" estimator vanishes. The first consequence is that t-tests and F-tests on coefficients are definitively meaningless.

If the error distribution has an infinite mean too (as in the case of a Cauchy distribution), the OLS estimator cannot even be unbiased, because its mean will not exist. The possibility of non-normal disturbances in general, and infinite-variance disturbances in particular, has led to the development of an alternative estimation technique that places less weight on outliers than least squares.

Next we examine two aspects:

1. How to detect for non-normality.
2. Robust estimation technique.

Tests for Detecting Non-Normality of Residuals

The literature on testing for normality of residuals is vast. In practice, analysts are used to test the third and the fourth moment. This means testing for skewness and excess kurtosis. For a normal distribution with variance σ^2, the third central moment, which determines skewness, is zero, while the fourth central moment, which determines kurtosis, is $3\sigma^4$.

If the third central moment is different from zero, the distribution is skewed. If the fourth central moment is larger than $3\sigma^4$, the distribution is leptokurtic (i.e., it is thinner than the normal distribution around the mean, while it has fatter tails); if the fourth central moment is smaller than $3\sigma^4$, the distribution is platykurtic (i.e., it is fatter than the normal distribution around the mean, while it has thinner tails). In practice, residuals are frequently leptokurtic and rarely platykurtic.

A large number of tests for normality are based on how far estimates of the third and the fourth moments, μ_3 and μ_4, deviate from 0 and $3s^2$, where s^2 is an estimate of σ^2. We used this approach to test for normality of returns in Chapter 5. We also know from Chapter 5 that both $\mu_3/\sqrt{(6/T)}$ and $(\mu_4 - 3)/\sqrt{(24/T)}$ are asymptotically normally distributed with a zero mean and a unit variance. Therefore, each of their squares will be asymptotically distributed as a $\chi^2(1)$. Since it can be demonstrated that the two tests are independent, their sum will be asymptotically distributed as a $\chi^2(2)$. This test was suggested by Jarque and Bera,[13] and thus is known as the Jarque-Bera test. The Jarque-Bera test is able to detect departures from normality due to skewness or to lepto/platykurtosis, since the null hypothesis is that the third central moment is zero *and* the excess kurtosis is zero.

Estimation When Residuals Are Not Normal

Since the distribution of residuals is not known in advance, it would be desirable to have estimation procedures that produce estimates of parameters that are insensitive to the true distribution of residuals. These estimators are called "robust" estimators and, although less efficient than the OLS estimator when errors are normally distributed, they can be considerably more efficient than the OLS estimators for non-normal errors.

This is an important issue in risk management since financial models, as a consequence of the leptokurtosis of returns, tend to produce non-normal residuals. After all, if we regress returns against a constant term, the residuals that we would have obtained are nothing else than the deviations of returns from their mean.

If the distribution of residuals has an infinite variance, the OLS estimator provides poor estimates of the parameters, since it aims at minimizing something that is actually infinite. A possible alternative approach is to choose a different criterion for estimating the parameters. For example, one could choose to minimize not the sum of squared errors, but the sum of absolute errors instead. If the true distribution of errors has an infinite variance, this estimator is still valid. If the true distribution of errors is leptokurtic, this estimator gives less weight to outliers than the OLS estimator, thus providing more stable and reliable estimates. This estimator is often referred to as LAD (Least Absolute Estimator).

The LAD estimator is optimal (and is equal to the ML estimator, which has the usual asymptotic properties) when the disturbances follow a two-tailed exponential distribution with density function:

$$f(e_t) = \left(\frac{1}{2\lambda}\right)\exp\left(-\frac{|e_t|}{\lambda}\right) \tag{A.9.3}$$

where λ^2 is the variance of the distribution. This distribution is also called Laplace distribution and the LAD estimator is called Laplace estimator (or L1), as opposed to the Gauss-estimator (or L2), which is the standard OLS estimator. When compared to the normal distribution, the Laplace distribution has fatter tails, but it still has a finite variance. The L1 estimator is also more efficient then the OLS estimator when the distribution of residual is so fat-tailed that the median is superior to the mean as an estimation of location. As shown in Chapter 9, this is the case for the Cauchy distribution (the mean does not even exist), but also for the Laplace distribution and for many other distributions where outliers are prevalent.

Estimation and Forecasting with Non-Normal Errors

Robust estimators for financial risk management should provide not only better estimates but also better forecasts than the OLS estimator. We compared three estimators using real data from the Italian stock market. We chose eight major stocks and formed an equally weighted portfolio.

The selected stocks, and their respective industrial sectors, are:

Alleanza Assicurazioni	Insurance
Banca Commerciale Italiana	Banking
Credito Italiano	Banking
ENI	Oil and Gas
INA	Insurance
Mediaset	Entertainment and Media
Montedison	Chemicals
Telecom Italia	Telecommunications

The whole sample consists of 349 observations from January 1, 1997, to May 26, 1998. We estimated the market model using three different estimators:

1. The OLS estimator.
2. The GARCH–ML estimator.
3. The LAD estimator.

We first divided the whole sample into two subsamples of equal size; the first subsample was for estimating the coefficients, the second subsample for assessing the predictive power of each estimator. Then, we performed a preliminary test for the structural stability of the market model.

The Chow test revealed that the null hypothesis of structural stability could be rejected at 95% probability level. The value of the test was 3.31061, with a p-value of 0.038. The lack of structural stability made these subsamples not significant for our purposes.

We divided the whole sample into four subsamples of approximately equal size; we called them sample 1, 2, 3, and 4, respectively. Sample 1 and sample 3 were used to estimate the market model, while sample 2 and sample 4 were used to compare the predictive power of each estimator. The underlying rationale was the assumption of no structural shift occurring between sample 1 and 2, and between sample 3 and 4.

The Chow test between sample 1 and sample 2 was 0.710154 (p-value = 0.402) while the Chow test between sample 3 and sample 4 was 0.519232 (p-value = 0.596). These values indicated that no shift occurred between samples 1 and 2, and between samples 3 and 4. The results of the estimations are shown in Table 9A.2.

TABLE 9A.2   Results of the Estimations (samples 1 and 3)

	Sample 1	Sample 3
Ordinary Least Squares		
R^2- adjusted	74.0621%	87.0465%
Durbin-Watson	1.78410 (p-value < 0.177)	2.33808 (p-value < 0.952)
Jarque-Bera	17.1101 (p-value = 0.000)	0.135490 (p-value = 0.934)
Log likelihood	311.621	330.197
Alpha	0.000281742 (t-stat = 0.38)	0.00127091 (t-stat = 2.05)
Beta	0.824842 (t-stat = 15.7023)	0.866880 (t-stat = 24.1998)
ARCH-GARCH		
ARCH(1) – F-test	0.361691 (p-value = 0.549)	0.0006592 (p-value = 0.980)
ARCH(2) – F-test	1.58389 (p-value = 0.211)	0.390895 (p-value = 0.678)
Least Absolute Deviation		
R^2- adjusted	74.0621%	87.0465%
Durbin-Watson	1.53929	2.33483
Log likelihood	312.853	326.281
Alpha	−0.000912708 (t-stat = −1.67)	0.00135243 (t-stat = 2.78)
Beta	0.705573 (t-stat = 18.13)	0.865133 (t-stat = 30.739)

TABLE 9A.3 Predictive Power of OLS and LAD Estimators (sample 2)

Prediction Error in Sample 2 Estimates of Sample 1	OLS (%)	LAD (%)
MSE	0.6426	0.6325
MAE	0.4845	0.4772

Table 9A.2 shows three main issues:

1. In both the samples, there is no evidence of ARCH/GARCH; therefore, in both cases, OLS seems an appropriate technique to estimate the coefficients of the market model.
2. There is a strong evidence of non-normality of residuals in sample 3 but not in sample 1.
3. When residuals are not normally distributed (sample 1), there is a significant difference between the OLS-estimate and the LAD-estimate of the beta coefficient.

We used the estimates of sample 1 and sample 3 to predict portfolio returns in sample 2 and sample 4, respectively. The predictive power of OLS and LAD estimators has been tested using the mean square error (MSE) and the mean absolute error (MAE). The results are shown in Tables 9A.3 and 9A.4.

The results show that the OLS estimator (slightly) outperforms the LAD estimator when residuals are normally distributed. When residuals are not normally distributed, the LAD estimator has a stronger predictive capacity than the LAD estimator. Therefore, in the case of departure of residuals from the hypothesis of normality, estimation techniques alternative to the OLS should be used.

TABLE 9A.4 Predictive Power of OLS and LAD Estimators (sample 4)

Prediction Error in Sample 4 Estimates of Sample 3	OLS (%)	LAD (%)
MSE	0.7642	0.7647
MAE	0.5688	0.5700

NOTES

1. This chapter is based upon the literature available on fractals in finance. Among the most important: E. Peters, 1991, and 1994; B. Mandelbrot, *Fractals and Scaling in Finance,* Springer-Verlag, 1997; "The Gaussian distribution" is often called "normal," because of the widespread opinion that it sets a universally applicable "norm." In the case of the phenomene studied throughout my life and described in this book, this opinion is unwarranted. In this case, randomness is lightly non-Gaussian, but it is no longer possible to describe it as "pathological," "improper," or "abnormal." Mandelbrot, 1997, p. 119; R. Trippi, Oreos and Non-linear Dynamics in the Financial Markets, Irwin, 1995.

2. Peters, *Fractal Market Analysis: Applying Chaos Theory to Investment and Economics,* John Wiley & Sons, 1994, 11.

3. We will see later in the this chapter what it exactly means. It is a measure of the fatness of the tails and can range from 0 to 2. If it is 2, we have the normal distribution. As long as it decreases to zero, the tails become more and more fat.

4. Apart from the normal itself.

5. This is a misfortune. Neither the normal nor the Cauchy can properly describe assets' returns for two opposite reasons. What we need is a fractal distribution intermediate between the two previously mentioned, if possible closer to the normal than to the Cauchy. This point is made clear later.

6. See Peters, *Fractal Market Analysis: Applying Chaos Theory to Investment and Economics,* John Wiley & Sons, 1994, Appendix C.

7. *Ibid.,* 290–291.

8. *Ibid.,* 292–293.

9. E. Peters, *Chaos and Order in the Capital Markets: A New View of Cycles, Prices, and Market Volatility,* John Wiley & Sons, 1996.

10. *Ibid.,* Chapter 8.

11. See J. Campbell, A. Lo, and A. MacKinlay, *The Econometrics of Financial Markets,* Princeton, NJ: Princeton University Press, 1997, Chapter 1.

12. The t-distribution with 1 degree of freedom has both an infinite mean and an infinite variance: it is the Cauchy distribution. The t-distribution with 2 degrees of freedom has a finite mean but an infinite variance (we could say that the characteristic exponent is greater than 1 but lower than 2). With 3 or more degrees of freedom, the t-distribution is still a leptokurtic distribution but has a finite mean and variance.

13. Jarque, C., and A.K. Bera, (1980), "Efficient tests for normality hetroscedasticity and serial independence of regression residuals," *Economic Letters, 6* 255–259.

10

Fixed-Income Mapping

C hapters 10 through 12 are devoted to the analysis of pricing methods for financial assets. After having analyzed the statistical background needed to model asset returns and risk and calculate VaR, we must now look more closely at the financial foundations of VaR, which relies heavily on financial theory and on the pricing formulas that have been identified for pricing financial assets.

In this chapter, we analyze the pricing of fixed-income securities, in particular:

- The concept of yield-to-maturity and yield curve.
- The use of duration and convexity for bond pricing.
- The RiskMetrics approach and bond decomposition (cash-flow mapping).
- Techniques to account for "roll down" and "pull-to-par phenomena."

Chapters 11 and 12 are devoted, respectively, to equity pricing and derivative pricing.

BOND PRICING USING YIELD TO MATURITY

Defining Yield to Maturity

To understand how pricing of fixed-income securities works and how it can be used for VaR calculation, we start with the analysis of a single, fixed-income bond. A fixed-income bond is an asset that generates a predefined stream of payments at scheduled times. Since payments are fixed, any change of the prevailing interest rate in the market will affect the price of the bond. Fixed-income bonds are exposed to market risk in the form of interest-rate risk. Bonds denominated in a foreign currency are subject to currency risk, too. Unless differently specified, we refer to bonds denominated in the domestic currency.

The price of a bond—as with any security—equals the present value of its expected cash flows. For fixed-income bonds—with no call provision—cash flows are exactly known in advance and, at any point in time, the price can be defined as

$$P = \frac{\Sigma_t\, C_t}{(1+y)^t} \tag{10.1}$$

where t is the number of periods to maturity, C_t is the cash flow a time t, and y is the yield-to-maturity for this bond.

Equation 10.1 is general enough to include coupon bonds, as well as zero-coupon bonds. In the first case, there will be intermediate cash flows before maturity equal to coupon payments, and the last payment is the principal repayment. In the second case, we will have only one payment at maturity. In the case of sinking funds, intermediate cash flow will include not only interest but also a portion of the principal, according to an amortization schedule.

Without any further assumptions, Equation 10.1 is a mere tautology. Equation 10.1 can be used to decide whether to buy the bond or not, provided a cutoff discount factor is chosen ex-ante. Alternatively, we can define as yield to maturity (*YTM*) the rate of return that equates the present values of future cash flows to the actual price of the bond. In other words, *YTM* is the internal rate of return (IRR) of the bond, as it suffers all the limitations that IRR has in the context of investment decisions.

The *YTM* is not equal to the coupon rate, since it depends on the actual price and on the structure of payments (existence of sinking funds). For bonds where the principal is repaid at maturity as a lump sum and are quoted at par (actual price is equal to 100), *YTM* coincides with coupon rate.

Bond Pricing Using YTM

A fixed-income bond is subject to interest-rate risk since prevailing *YTM* in the market can change, affecting the price of the bond itself. For example, the *YTM* of a 5-year bond with an annual coupon of 5%, quoted at par, is 5% (see Table 10.1).

The sum of present values—the price—is, not surprisingly, equal to par. If the prevailing *YTM* for bonds of the same class (maturity, credit risk, liquidity) becomes, let's say, 7%, the price of the bond will decline to equalize the *YTM* of the bond to the prevailing *YTM* in the market.

TABLE 10.1 Examples of Price Calculation of a Fixed-Income 5% Coupon Rate

Time	t	Cash Flows	Discount @ YTM = 0.05	Present Value
1-year coupon	1	5	1.0500	4.7619
2-year coupon	2	5	1.1025	4.5351
3-year coupon	3	5	1.1576	4.3192
4-year coupon	4	5	1.2155	4.1135
5-year coupon	5	5	1.2763	3.9176
Principal	5	100	1.2763	78.3526
Sum of present values				100.0000

The equalization is obtained through a fall of the actual price of the bond.

Table 10.2 calculates the new price of the 5-year, 5% annual coupon, bond that will result from a growth to 7% in the prevailing *YTM* for the class of bonds it belongs to. The price of the bond falls by 8.2% or 820 basis points. On the other hand, if the prevailing *YTM* falls to 3%, the price of the bond will rise to 109.1594 (9.15%, or 915 basis points).

Problems of Yield to Maturity. The Price-Yield Relationship

The *YTM* (as the IRR) relies on two basic assumptions:

1. The bond is held to maturity.
2. Interim cash flows can be reinvested at the computed *YTM*.

TABLE 10.2 Examples of Price Change when YTM Goes to 7%

Time	t	Cash Flows	Discount @ YTM = 0.07	Present Value
1-year coupon	1	5	1.0700	4.6729
2-year coupon	2	5	1.1449	4.3672
3-year coupon	3	5	1.2250	4.0815
4-year coupon	4	5	1.3108	3.8145
5-year coupon	5	5	1.4026	3.5649
Principal	5	100	1.4026	71.2986
Sum of present values				91.7996

Both these assumptions are extremely simplifying. Call provisions can force the bondholder to give up the bond before maturity. Call options are exercised if the prevailing *YTM* is lower than the coupon rate, making new issues less expensive for the borrowers. It also means that it is not possible for the bondholder to reinvest the obtained cash flows at the previously computed—or promised—*YTM*. The actual (ex-post) *YTM* will result lower than expected.

The preceding example shows that the price-yield relationship is not linear. In fact, when the *YTM* falls by 2%, the price rises by 915 basis points; but when the *YTM* rises by 2%, the price falls by 820 basis points, suggesting that the price-yield relationship is convex. In other words, when the *YTM* falls by a given number of basis points, the price rises more than it would fall if the *YTM* should rise by the same number of basis points. This property, known as convexity, plays a crucial role in bond pricing. Remarkably, this convexity is true only if there are no call provisions in the indenture. For callable bonds the price-yield relationship can be really different. Starting from yield y^* (for simplicity, close to the par value yield), if interest rates increase (*YTMs*), the value of the call option declines because, at market interest rates substantially above the coupon rate, it is unlikely the issuer will want to call the issue. Therefore, the relationship will be close to that of noncallable bonds.

On the other hand, if market interest rates fall below y^*, the probability increases that the issuer will exercise the call; hence, the value of the call option increases, and the relationship of callable bonds will show a negative convexity. With the callable bond, when rates decline, the price increases at a lower rate and eventually does not change at all. Call provisions add to the market risk of a bond, when compared to the market risk of a noncallable bond.[1]

Calculating VaR Using the *YTM* Approach

The *YTM* approach can be useful in calculating the price risk and, hence, the Value at Risk, for a portfolio composed of fixed-income securities. Suppose that our portfolio is made up of only a 5-year, 5% coupon government bond. The actual price of the bond is 100, implying that the prevailing *YTM* for default-risk-free bonds maturing in 5 years is 5%. The actual market value of the portfolio is supposed to be US$100.

Suppose that:

- The chosen time horizon is 1 year.
- The historical volatility of *YTM* for 5-year government bonds over a 1-year time horizon is 1%.
- Expected *YTMs* are normally distributed with zero mean and $\sigma = 1\%$.

Then the worst possible outcome at 95% confidence level is given by

$$\text{worst } YTM = \text{actual } YTM + (1.65 * \text{volatility})$$
$$= 5\% + 1.65 * 1 = 6.65\%$$

(10.2)

If the *YTM* is equal to 6.65%, the price of the bond falls to 93.1708. The value at risk for the portfolio under examination is then US$(100 − 93.1708) = US$6.83.

This approach can be easily extended to portfolios made up of more than one bond. For example, suppose that, in addition to the previous bond, we also hold in our portfolio a 2-year, 3% coupon government bond. The prevailing *YTM* for 10-year government bonds is 4%, making the actual price equal to 98.11. The market value of this second bond is assumed to be $98.11. Suppose that the 1-year volatility of 2-year *YTM* has been estimated as equal to 1.2%.

The worst *YTM* over a 1-year time horizon, and with a 95% probability level, is:

$$\text{worst } YTM = 4\% + (1.65 * 1.2\%) = 5.98\%$$

(10.3)

The price of the bond, with a prevailing *YTM* equal to 5.98%, would be 94.54. The VaR then is US$(98.11 − 94.54) = US$3.57.

The undiversified VaR of the US$198.11 portfolio is equal to US$(6.83 + 3.57) = US$10.4.

As shown in Chapter 4, correlation plays a great role in assessing a portfolio's VaR. The mere sum of single bonds' VaR implies that the correlation between 5-year *YTM* and 2-year *YTM* is equal to 1.

Common sense and empirical evidence suggest that *YTM*s at different maturities are strongly correlated. Suppose the correlation between 2-year *YTM* and 5-year *YTM* to be equal to 0.95.

The portfolio VaR would be:

$$\text{portfolio VaR} = \sqrt{[6.83^\wedge 2 + 3.57^\wedge 2 + 2 * (6.83 * 3.57 * 0.95)]}$$
$$= \text{US\$}10.28$$

(10.4)

The gain from diversification would then be US$0.12.

THE YIELD CURVE

Defining the Yield Curve

The term structure of interest rates (or yield curve) is a static function that relates the term to maturity to the yield to maturity for a sample of bonds at a given point in time. Thus, it represents a cross-section of yields for a category of bonds that are comparable in all respects but maturity. It is possible to construct different yield curve for Treasury bonds, government-agency issues, municipal bonds, AAA corporate bonds, and so on.[2]

The traditional representation of the term structure is based on par-yield bonds; that is, using yield to maturity of bonds with a coupon close, or equal, to their *YTM*.[3] That is why it is often referred to as the *par-yield curve*. It is possible to take the most recently issued 2-year, 5-year, and 7-year notes and 30-year bonds to infer the yield curve from 2 to 30 years. This method, however, selects fairly liquid bonds and thus reflects prevailing market conditions, ignoring outstanding bonds.

An alternative approach is to fit a yield curve through the yields of all outstanding issues. In the following section we analyze in detail how the yield curve can be modeled and used for prediction.

The Shape of the Yield Curve

The relevant issue here is that the yield curve is not static but changes frequently. Also, the slope of the curve can change dramatically over time. Although a rising shape is the most common shape, it is not unusual for the yield curve to have a different shape.

The most common shapes the yield curve takes are:

- *Rising shape. YTMs* with shorter maturities are lower than *YTMs* with longer maturities.
- *Declining shape. YTMs* with shorter maturities are higher than *YTMs* with longer maturities. This prevails in the case of very high short-term *YTMs*.
- *Flat shape. YTMs* are approximately equal at all maturities. This rarely exists.
- *Humped shape. YTMs* with intermediate maturities are higher than *YTMs* with short maturities, and *YTMs* with long maturities are below *YTMs* with short maturities. This prevails when high rates are expected to decline to more normal long-term rates.

Since the yield curve is dynamic, we can distinguish three relevant kinds of movements:

1. *Shifts.* When, following a shock, the whole yield curve moves upward or downward in a parallel fashion.
2. *Twists.* When the yield curve reacts differently to a shock at different maturities (e.g., 1-year *YTM* rises by 1.5% while 3-year *YTM*

by 1%, or the reverse). The graphical effect is that the curve rotates as a consequence of the different sensitivities of *YTM*s at different maturities.

3. *Butterflies*. When the yield curve, reacting to a shock, changes its convexity.

Although shifts are rare, pricing techniques based on *YTM* (and duration) often assume changes of *YTM*s to be the consequence of a shift, rather than a twist or a butterfly, in the yield curve.

Term-Structure Theories

Although, in theory, any shape of the yield curve is acceptable, empirical evidence suggests that the yield curve is definitively upward biased. This is theoretically justified on the basis of the *liquidity-preference hypothesis,* which states that long-term securities should provide higher returns than short-term obligations because investors in short maturity obligations are willing to sacrifice some yields to avoid the price volatility of long-maturity bonds.[4] The preference for short-term obligations stems from the fact that these can be easily converted into predictable amounts of cash should unforeseen events occur. This theory states that the yield curve should slope upward and that any other shape should be viewed as a temporary aberration. This is as an extension of the *expectation theory,* which states that any long-term *YTM* simply represents the geometric mean of current and future 1-year *YTM*s expected to prevail over the maturity of the issue. Expectation theory allows the yield curve to take any shape and explains this in terms of expectation of future *YTM*s. If the yield curve is declining, *YTM*s are expected to decline in the future. If the yield curve is rising, *YTM*s are expected to rise. Although this provides insight into what is implied in the yield curve, it is not able to explain the upward bias found in practice.

If we introduce a liquidity premium into the expectation theory to compensate investors for added uncertainty in the long run, we introduce an upward bias in the yield curve that can be reversed only if expectation about future declines of *YTM*s completely offsets the liquidity premium.

A third theory, the segmented-market hypothesis, states that yields at any maturity segment are simply determined by supply and demand within that maturity segment, irrespective of what the yields for different maturity segments are. This theory, apart from the fact that it fails to explain the upward bias of the yield curve, is not able to encompass the high level of correlation that is usually found for *YTM*s at different maturities.

Yield Curve and Bond Pricing

Bond-pricing techniques, based on *YTM,* use a single-discount factor for all the cash flows generated by the bond itself to assess its price. Although this approach is limited, and the cash-flow-based approach is aimed at overcoming this limitation, it is a simple and useful approximation to estimate bond-price changes due to changes in the prevailing interest rates.

The choice of the *YTM* plays a crucial role. If the yield curve is flat, there exists only one *YTM* prevailing in the market, so the choice is obligatory. If the yield curve is not flat, we have different *YTM*s prevailing in the market for different maturities. If the yield curve moves, the choice of the *YTM* is crucial for calculating the new price and, hence, the VaR for the bond or for a portfolio of bonds.

In general, one should choose the new *YTM* corresponding to the maturity of the bond to price. For example, to calculate the price change of a newly issued 5-year bond, due to a change of prevailing *YTM*s over a 1-year time horizon, one should estimate what the prevailing 4-year *YTM* will be 1 year from now.

THE DURATION APPROACH

Toward a Better Measure of Interest Rate Sensitivity

Although appealing, bond-pricing techniques based on *YTM* rely on nonlinear calculations to assess the price changes due to changes in the prevailing *YTM*s. In addition, they give no suggestion about what trading strategies should be undertaken if a portfolio manager wants to maximize exposure to interest-rate risk or minimize it. Obviously, the longer the maturity and the higher the coupon rate, the higher the sensitivity to changes of *YTM*s.

A measure of the interest rate sensitivity of the price of a bond is encompassed in its duration. Duration is a composite measure that considers both coupon and maturity, defining in a single number the price risk of a bond due to interest rate changes. In other words, duration measures the sensitivity of a bond price to changes in *YTM*s. This is why duration is such a valuable tool for risk management.

Macauley Duration and Modified Duration

Back in 1938, Macauley showed that the duration of a bond was a more appropriate measure of time characteristics than the term-to-maturity of the bond because duration considers both the repayment of capital at maturity and the size and timing of coupon payments prior to final maturity.[5]

Macauley duration is defined by the equation

$$D = \frac{\Sigma_t \left[\dfrac{t\, C_t}{(1+YTM)^t} \right]}{\left[\dfrac{C_t}{(1+YTM)^t} \right]} = \frac{\Sigma_t \left[\dfrac{t\, C_t}{(1+YTM)^t} \right]}{P} \qquad (10.5)$$

The denominator in this equation is the price of a bond, as defined by Equation 10.1. The numerator is the present value of all cash flows weighted according to the time to cash receipt.

The main characteristics of Macauley duration are:[6]

- Duration of a bond with coupon payments is always less than the maturity. Duration of a zero-coupon bond is equal to maturity.
- There is an inverse relationship between coupon and duration; the larger the coupon, the shorter the duration because more of the total cash flow comes back in the form of interest payments.
- There is a positive relationship between duration and term to maturity: all other things being equal, the longer the maturity the longer the duration.
- There is an inverse relationship between *YTM* and duration. In fact, from Equation 10.2 we can see that, all other things being equal, the numerator is reduced and, hence, so is the duration.
- Sinking funds and call provisions dramatically reduce duration. Call provisions make the estimation of duration difficult.

Duration can be used to estimate price changes of a bond as a consequence of a change of the *YTM*. To estimate the link between duration and bond price changes, we can take the first derivative of Equation 10.1:

$$\frac{dP}{dYTM} = \left[\frac{-1}{(1+YTM)} \right] * \Sigma_t \left[\frac{t\, C_t}{(1+YTM)^t} \right] \qquad (10.6)$$

Multiplying both the sides of Equation 10.3 by $1/P$, we have

$$\left(\frac{dP}{P} \right)\left(\frac{1}{dYTM} \right) = \left(\frac{1}{P} \right)\left[\frac{-1}{(1+YTM)} \right] \Sigma_t \left[\frac{t\, C_t}{(1+YTM)^t} \right]$$

$$\left(\frac{dP}{P} \right)\left(\frac{1}{dYTM} \right) = \frac{-D}{(1+YTM)} = D^* \qquad (10.7)$$

The right-hand side of Equation 10.7 is called *modified duration* and was introduced by Redington in 1952. It measures the percentage price

TABLE 10.3   Computation of Duration for a 5-Year, 5% Annual Coupon Bond

Time	t	Cash Flows	Discount @ YTM = 0.05	Present Value	Weighted CFs
1-year coupon	1	5	1.0500	4.7619	4.7619
2-year coupon	2	5	1.1025	4.5351	9.0703
3-year coupon	3	5	1.1576	4.3192	12.9576
4-year coupon	4	5	1.2155	4.1135	16.4540
5-year coupon	5	5	1.2763	3.9176	19.5882
Principal	5	100	1.2763	78.3526	391.7631
Sum				100.0000	454.5951

change of a bond, given a change of the *YTM*. Tables 10.3 and 10.4 show the calculation of the modified duration for a 5-year, 5% annual coupon bond. Duration is equal to 4.54 years, while modified duration is equal to −4.33 years.

Rearranging Equation 10.7, we have:

$$dP = P * dYTM * D^* \tag{10.8}$$

where the price change is a linear function of the change of the *YTM*.

Recall that a rise of 2% of the *YTM* lowers the price by 820 basis points. Using Equation 10.8, the expected price change is equal to

$$dP = P * dYTM * D^* = 100 * 0.02 * -4.33 = -8.66 \tag{10.9}$$

or −866 basis points. The forecasted price is 100 − 8.66 = 91.34, as compared to 91.8 calculated by Equation 10.1. On the other hand, if *YTM* falls to 3%, Equation 10.5 predicts a price fall equal to:

$$dP = P * dYTM * D^* = 100 * (-0.02) * 4.33 = +8.66 \tag{10.10}$$

TABLE 10.4   YTM, Coupon, Duration, and Modified Duration

YTM	5.00%
Coupon rate	5.00%
Modified duration	−4.33
Duration	4.55

The forecasted price is then 100 + 8.66 = 108.66, compared to 109.16 calculated by Equation 10.1.

The price changes predicted by the modified duration are only approximations of the price changes that would actually occur as a reaction to the changes of *YTMs*. Although its simplicity is appealing, the modified duration approach suffers three main drawbacks:

1. It approximates linearly the price-yield relationship while, as we have seen, this relationship is actually nonlinear (convex). Price changes predicted by Equation 10.5 are greater when the prevailing *YTM* rises and lower when the prevailing *YTM* falls than predicted by Equation 10.1.
2. It provides a good approximation for small changes of the prevailing *YTM*. When changes of the *YTM* are significant, the convexity of the price-yield relationship makes this approximation less and less precise.
3. Changes of *YTM* are produced by shifts of the yield curve. Neither twists nor butterflies are compatible with the duration approach to measure bond-price risk. In addition, since each cash flow is discounted at the same rate, Macauley's duration—and, similarly, modified duration—requires the yield curve to be flat. These joint assumptions—about the shape and the dynamics of the yield curve—are highly unrealistic.[7] More complex, multifactor duration models have been developed to account for twists of the yield curve, but empirical evidence shows that they do not perform better than the basic model of Equation 10.5.[8]

Notwithstanding these drawbacks, duration is still valuable because it has two desirable properties: it can be used to translate yield volatility into price volatility easily, and it can be easily handled for portfolios of bonds.

Rearranging Equation 10.7, we obtain Equation 10.11:

$$\frac{dP}{P} = -D^* * d(1 + YTM) \tag{10.11}$$

The percentage change of prices can be obtained as a linear relation with the change in the prevailing *YTM*.

Therefore, we have:

$$\sigma\left(\frac{dP}{P}\right) = D^* * \sigma[\,d(1 + YTM)\,] \tag{10.12}$$

For example, a 10-year zero-coupon *YTM* is 8%, with an annual volatility of changes of *YTM*s equal to 0.94%. The correspondent price volatility is equal to

$$\sigma\left(\frac{dP}{P}\right) = \frac{10}{1.08} * 0.94 = 8.70\%^9 \tag{10.13}$$

In addition, since duration is a measure of linear exposure, the duration of a portfolio of bonds is simply the weighted average of the durations of individual bonds. This makes duration particularly appealing since it provides a unique measure of interest rate exposure for the whole portfolio. Calculations of VaR are thus highly simplified. The required assumption is that the yield curve is flat—the same across all maturities—since the same yield changes are used for the whole portfolio. If this were not the case, portfolio duration would approximate the portfolio interest rate sensitivity. Nevertheless, duration provides a useful measure of interest rate sensitivity in risk management practice.

Duration and VaR

The appeal of duration for VaR purposes is easy to understand. In Chapter 4, we have examined the importance of delta parameters as a parsimonious way to analyze security price risk. Delta parameters define a linear relationship between an asset's expected price change and the expected market-factor change.

In the context of fixed-income securities, modified duration is the natural candidate for being the delta parameter linking expected price changes of a fixed-income bond, or portfolio of bonds, to expected changes in interest rates. Nevertheless, price risk can be much more accurately measured if, besides duration, we consider a quadratic term able to better mimic the convexity of the price-yield relationship. In the context of VaR, assuming the terminology used in option pricing theory, these parameters are called *gamma* parameters. We examine a gamma parameter for fixed-income securities in the next section.

CONVEXITY

Defining Convexity

The convexity approximation is a quadratic term introduced to correct the approximation provided by duration alone. From the previous section, we know that the duration model tends to overestimate price declines and underestimate price increases, when compared to the actual price-yield relationship.

Modified duration can be expressed as $(dP/dYTM)/P$. The term $dP/dYTM$ is the slope of the line tangent to the price-yield curve at a given yield. For small changes in yields, this tangent line gives a good estimation of the actual price changes. For a given change in YTM, in both directions, the duration approach forecasts symmetrical price changes, while the curvilinear price-yield relationship does not predict a symmetrical price change in response to a symmetrical change in interest rates.

Convexity is a measure of the curvature of the price-yield relationship. Since duration is the slope of the curve at a given yield, convexity indicates changes in duration. Mathematically, it is the second derivative of price, with respect to YTM. It is a measure of how much a bond's price-yield curve deviates from its linear approximation of that curve. For non-callable bonds, convexity is always a positive number, implying that the price-yield curve lies above the straight-line approximation. In general, there is an inverse relationship between coupon (and yield) and convexity. In other words, convexity is higher for zero-coupon bonds than for high coupon-yield bonds. In addition, there is a direct relationship between maturity and convexity.[10]

From a mathematical point of view, the adjustment term for convexity is nothing but the second term of a Taylor series, used to approximate a complex polynomial. In particular:

$$\text{Price change due to convexity} = \tfrac{1}{2} * \text{convexity} * \text{price} * dYTM^2 \quad (10.14)$$

Convexity is defined as

$$\text{convexity} = \frac{\left(\dfrac{d^2P}{d^2YTM}\right)}{P} \quad (10.15)$$

Taking the second derivative of Equation 10.1, we have

$$\frac{dP}{dYTM} = \left[\frac{-1}{(1+YTM)^2}\right]\Sigma_t\left[\frac{(t^2+t)C_t}{(1+YTM)^t}\right] \quad (10.16)$$

We can now use Equation 10.15 to have a better approximation of the price change:

$$\text{convexity effect} = 0.5 * \text{price} * \text{convexity} * (dYTM)^2 \quad (10.17)$$

Calculating Convexity

Suppose we are long a 5-year, 5% annual coupon government bond and we want to calculate the price change resulting from a change in the prevailing YTM, using the convexity adjustment.

The computation of convexity is shown in Tables 10.5 and 10.6. If we assume that the prevailing YTM rises to 7%, the convexity effect is equal to

$$\text{convexity effect} = 0.5*100*26.3894*0.004 = 0.4813 \qquad (10.18)$$

or 48 basis points.

The price change is given by

$$\text{price change} = \text{duration effect} + \text{convexity effect} \qquad (10.19)$$

$$\text{price change} = -8.66 + 0.48 = -8.18 \qquad (10.20)$$

or 818 basis points.

The estimated price change is then

$$\text{new price} = 100 - 8.18 = 91.82 \qquad (10.21)$$

much closer to the 91.8 predicted by the discount model of Equation 10.1. On the other hand, if YTM falls to 3%, the expected price change is

$$\text{price change} = 8.66 + 0.48 = 9.14 \qquad (10.22)$$

TABLE 10.5 Computation of Convexity for a 5-Year, 5% Annual Coupon Bond Quoted at Par

Time	t	Cash Flows	Discount @ YTM = 0.05	Present Value	Weighted Cash Flows	$(t^2+t)*$ Present Value
1-year coupon	1	5	1.0500	4.7619	4.7619	9.5238
2-year coupon	2	5	1.1025	4.5351	9.0703	27.2109
3-year coupon	3	5	1.1576	4.3192	12.9576	51.8303
4-year coupon	4	5	1.2155	4.1135	16.4540	82.2702
5-year coupon	5	5	1.2763	3.9176	19.5882	117.5289
Principal	5	100	1.2763	78.3526	391.7631	2350.5785
Sum				100.0000	454.5951	2638.9426

TABLE 10.6   Calculation of Duration, Modified Duration, and Convexity for a 5-Year, 5% Annual Coupon Bond Quoted at Par

YTM	5.00%
Coupon rate	5.00%
Modified duration	−4.33
Duration	4.55
Convexity	26.3894

and the forecasted new price of the bond is

$$\text{price change} = 100 + 9.14 = 109.14 \qquad (10.23)$$

again, much closer to the price computed by Equation 10.1 equal to 109.16.

Some concluding remarks about convexity and its implications for VaR calculations are called for. First, convexity greatly improves the accuracy of the price-change forecasts. In both cases (decline and increase of the prevailing *YTM*), the difference in the price computed with the discount model falls from 50 to only 2 basis points. This is a valuable advantage over the modified-duration approach.

Another appealing feature of convexity is that, as was the case for duration, the convexity of a portfolio of fixed-income instruments can be derived from a simple weighted average of the components of portfolio convexity.[11] This greatly simplifies the calculations needed for huge portfolios of fixed-income securities.

In terms of VaR, price risk assessment is greatly improved over the modified-duration approach and, hence, VaR is much more accurately estimated. The duration-convexity approach can be generalized for VaR purposes. In general, the pricing of many financial instruments requires a quadratic approximation—one which is not linear. Delta models can be greatly improved by adding a quadratic approximation.

This introduction has given life to delta-gamma models, where gamma parameters represent the sensitivity to a squared change of market factor. Generalizing, once we have estimated the maximum rise of *YTM* over a given time horizon and probability level (let's call it ΔYTM_{VaR}), the VaR for a portfolio of fixed-income bonds can be easily calculated as:

$$VaR = \text{Actual Market Value of the Portfolio} + \delta * \Delta YTM_{VaR}$$
$$+ \frac{1}{2} * \gamma * \left(\Delta YTM_{VaR} \right)^2$$

where δ is the portfolio modified duration, and γ is the portfolio convexity.

THE CASH-FLOW APPROACH

Why a Cash-Flow Approach?

If the yield curve were flat and movements were only in parallel (shifts), the duration-convexity approach would definitively be appropriate for assessing the price risk of a portfolio of fixed-income securities. Unfortunately, the yield curve neither is flat nor moves only in a parallel fashion.

Although the duration-convexity approach still provides a valuable approximation of the price risk of a portfolio of fixed-income securities, a more general approach is needed if we want a better approximation, especially in those cases where the yield curve differs remarkably from the assumptions required for the duration-convexity approach. Thus far, we have used a yield valuation model, which assumes that we discount all cash flows by a common yield, reflecting the overall required rate of return.

This is a more general approach that can be used to evaluate almost every kind of security, provided we know—or, we can estimate—the appropriate discount factor. Equation 10.1 then becomes:

$$P = \frac{\sum_t C_t}{(1 + y)^t} \qquad\qquad (10.24)$$

where the discount rate is not a unique rate but varies across maturities. This approach, called the "cash-flow" approach, has been used by J.P. Morgan's software RiskMetrics™ for the valuation of interest-rate-sensitive instruments.

Bond Decomposition

Any bond can be decomposed into its component cash flows. These cash flows must then be discounted with an appropriate discount factor to provide the present value (i.e., the price) of the bond itself. Table 10.7 shows the calculation of the price of a 5-year, 5% annual coupon bond

TABLE 10.7   Calculation of a Bond Price Using Different Discount Factors

Time	t	Cash Flows	Discount Rate (%)	Discount Factor	Present Value
1-year coupon	1	5	4.0	1.0400	4.8077
2-year coupon	2	5	4.5	1.0920	4.5786
3-year coupon	3	5	5.0	1.1576	4.3192
4-year coupon	4	5	5.5	1.2388	4.0361
5-year coupon	5	5	5.5	1.3070	3.8257
Principal	5	100	5.5	1.3070	76.5134
Sum					98.0807

using different discount rates, rather than a unique discount rate as in the yield valuation model.

This model is much more flexible than the yield-valuation model. First, we are allowed to have different discount rates at different maturities. The discount-rate curve (the equivalent of the previous yield curve) can have any shape. In this case, it has a rising shape. Given this discount-rate curve, the price of the bond is 98.08.

What happens if the discount-rate curve changes? Suppose it moves upward but not in a parallel fashion. For example, short-term discount rates move up more than long-term discount rates. Table 10.8 shows the calculation of the new bond price.

The new bond price is 94.92. In other words, the original bond is decomposed into its fundamental components and treated as a portfolio of 5 zero-coupon bonds with different maturities, with a principal equal to the interest payments (5) for the first four bonds and equal to the principal

TABLE 10.8   Calculation of New Bond Price

Time	t	Cash Flows	Discount Rate (%)	Discount Factor	Present Value
1-year coupon	1	5	5.0	1.0500	4.7619
2-year coupon	2	5	5.5	1.1130	4.4923
3-year coupon	3	5	6.0	1.1910	4.1981
4-year coupon	4	5	6.25	1.2744	3.9233
5-year coupon	5	5	6.25	1.3541	3.6925
Principal	5	100	6.25	1.3541	73.8508
Sum					94.9189

plus the last interest payment (105) for the last one. What we need to apply this technique is the complete set of zero-coupon discount rates for all the maturities needed. This subject is examined in greater detail later. Let us now examine the differences between the yield-valuation model and the cash-flow approach.

If the market price of the bond is 98.02, the computed YTM is 5.45% (slightly more than it would be if the market price were 100; i.e., 5%). If the market price falls to 94.92, the computed YTM is 6.21%. Suppose that a new issue of the same class of bond is priced at 94.92. The prevailing YTM is then changed from 5.45% to 6.21%. The modified duration, at an YTM equal to 5.45%, is 4.54 years.

Applying the duration approach, the estimated new price would be

$$\text{new price} = 98.02 - 4.54 * 98.02 * (0.0621 - 0.0545)$$
$$= 98.02 - 3.38 = 94.64 \tag{10.25}$$

We can improve our estimate using the duration-convexity approach, as explained in Equation 10.26:

$$\text{new price} = 98.02 - 3.45 + \frac{1}{2} * 23.65 * 98.02 * (0.0076)^{\wedge 2}$$
$$= 98.02 - 3.38 + 0.67 = 95.31 \tag{10.26}$$

The computation of duration and convexity is shown in Table 10.9.

TABLE 10.9 Computation of Duration and Convexity, Using the Computed YTM

Time	t	Cash Flow	Discount Rate (%)	Discount Factor	Present Value	Prsent Value @ YTM	$(t^2+t)*$ Cash Flow/ Discount
Market price		−98.08					
1-year coupon	1	5.00	4.0	1.0400	4.8077	4.7416	9.6154
2-year coupon	2	5.00	4.5	1.0920	4.5786	8.9932	27.4719
3-year coupon	3	5.00	5.0	1.1576	4.3192	12.7928	51.8303
4-year coupon	4	5.00	5.50	1.2388	4.0361	16.1756	80.7217
5-year coupon	5	105.00	5.50	1.3070	80.3391	402.6681	2410.1732
Sum					98.0807	445.3713	2579.8124
YTM	5.45%						
Modified duration	4.54						
Convexity	23.65						

Since we have a rising zero-coupon yield curve, discounting all the cash flows with a single rate (intermediate between the highest and the lowest in the curve) will tend to overestimate the price of the bond when compared with the more appropriate technique of discounting each single cash flow by its zero-coupon curve. A crucial role is played by the zero-coupon yield curve, or spot-rate curve. Unfortunately, it is not easy to estimate.

Estimating the Spot-Rate Curve

The spot rate is defined as the discount rate for a cash flow at a given maturity. As long as zero-coupon bonds are issued for different maturities, it is possible to derive the spot-rate curve by simply observing zero-coupon bond prices in the market and calculating the discount rate that equals the market value of the principal at a given maturity. Zero-coupon bonds are issued almost exclusively by governments and, most important, only for a limited range of maturities.[12]

The most used technique to derive the spot rate curve is to use existing coupon bonds to calculate spot rates. This technique is called *bootstrapping*. It is assumed that the value of the Treasury coupon security should be equal to the value of a package of zero-coupon securities that duplicate the coupon bond's cash flow. What is needed is to have a set of outstanding coupon bonds covering virtually all the possible maturities. Suppose we observe, from outstanding zero-coupon bonds, the spot rates shown in Table 10.10.

Suppose we observe a 3-year, 5% coupon bond quoted at 98.5. We want to use this bond to estimate the 3-year spot rates. The price of the bond should equal the present value of the three cash flows, each discounted at the appropriate spot rate. Hence:

$$P = \left(\frac{5}{1.04}\right) + \left(\frac{5}{1.05^2}\right) + \left[\frac{105}{(1+x)^3}\right] = 98.5 \tag{10.27}$$

TABLE 10.10   Spot Rates Observed in the Market

Maturity	Spot Rate (%)
1-year	4.00
2-year	5.00

where x is the 3-year spot rate. Rearranging Equation 10.27, we have

$$98.5 = 4.81 + 4.53 + \left[\frac{105}{(1+x)^3} \right]$$

$$89.16 = \left[\frac{105}{(1+x)^3} \right] \qquad (10.28)$$

$$x = \sqrt[3]{\left(\frac{105}{89.16} \right)} - 1 = 5.6\%$$

So, we can add the 3-year spot rate to our spot-rate curve in Table 10.10. This process can continue recursively until all the spot rates for the desired maturities have been estimated.

Another approach for estimating spot rates beyond the maturities covered by zero-coupon issues is to use fixed rates of interest + rate swaps (IRS). Swaps usually have maturities up to 2 or 3 years and can be helpful in filling the gap for maturities where the correspondent spot rates are not available.

ESTIMATING THE YIELD/SPOT-RATE CURVE THROUGH ECONOMETRIC TECHNIQUES

When spot rates are available for only a limited number of maturities and bootstrapping is not possible, a feasible approach is to estimate the term structure (yield curve or spot-rate curve) with econometric techniques. A deep analysis of the econometric techniques used to estimate the term structure is beyond our scope. We provide a simple example and show how this approach can be used for cash-flow mapping.

The standard approach is to use at least a second-order model to take into account the convexity of the yield curve. A third-order equation is able to account for more complex shapes of the yield/spot-rate curve. We are going to estimate the yield curve for the Italian government security market for a sample of 59 fixed-income bonds (BTP).

The chosen model is a third-order equation of the form:

$$YTM = a0 + a1 * t + a2 * t^{\wedge 2} + a3 * t^{\wedge 2} + a4 * t^{\wedge 3} \qquad (10.29)$$

where t is the number of years for the maturity.

The regression equation is

$$\text{Yield} = \underset{(71.96)}{5.00} \quad \underset{(-3.48)}{-0.124t} \quad \underset{(3.95)}{+0.0182t^{^\wedge 2}} \quad \underset{(-3.72)}{-0.000460t^{^\wedge 3}}$$

R-sq $= 45$

The R-squared is quite low, also thanks to the lack of data among maturities from 9 to 26 years. Nevertheless, using a regression equation like 10.29, it is possible to estimate the *YTMs* for any maturity in the sample. For example, the estimated 9-month *YTM* can be estimated as:

$$9\text{-month } YTM = 5.00 - 0.125 * (0.75) + 0.0182 * (0.75^{^\wedge 2})$$
$$-0.000460 * (0.75^{^\wedge}) = 4.81$$

The same approach can be used with spot rates from outstanding zero-coupon bonds. Alternatively, it is possible to choose different functional forms for Equation 10.26 to achieve a better fit.[13]

MAPPING OF CASH FLOWS

What Is Cash-Flow Mapping?

When using the cash-flow approach for pricing fixed-income securities, cash-flow mapping is a crucial step. We have seen how difficult the estimation of the spot rate for maturities over 12 months can be. On the other hand, a portfolio of fixed-income securities would generate a high number of cash flows occurring at any future date. For an exact pricing, one would need the spot-rate curve for any maturity—from 1 month to 30 years. To use this approach for calculating the Value at Risk, the standard deviation of the spot rate for any maturity and the correlation between each pair of maturities must be estimated. Without any constraint, cash flow occurring up to 30 years from now would require the estimation of about 60 million parameters—10,950 variances and (10,950 * 10,949/2) covariances—corresponding to daily spot-rate variances and covariances between each pair of daily spot rates.

What is needed is to allocate cash flows to predefined maturities (RiskMetrics defines 15 standard maturities) called vertices. With 15 vertices, only 120 parameters (15 variances and 105 covariances) must be estimated. If a cash flow coincides exactly with a single vertex, the cash flow is easily allocated. If it does not, it must be split between the immediately preceding and following vertices. This procedure is called *mapping* and plays a special role in the context of Value at Risk.

The Process of Mapping

The process of mapping is summarized in Figure 10.1.

   The first step consists of estimating the cash flows for all the interest-rate-sensitive positions (zero-coupon bonds, fixed-rate bills/notes/bonds, floating-rate notes, interest rate swaps, forward-rate agreements). In the second step, cash flows are allocated to the vertices using the techniques described in the following subsection. In the third step, the term structure (spot-rate curve) is estimated using one of the techniques described earlier. Then, the present values for all the cash flows allocated to each vertex are computed using the spot rates estimated in the previous step. In the fifth step, the volatility (standard deviation of prices) for each vertex is estimated. Finally, the VaR is computed, using one of the methods described in the next section.

FIGURE 10.1   The Process of Mapping for Interest-Rate Sensitive Positions

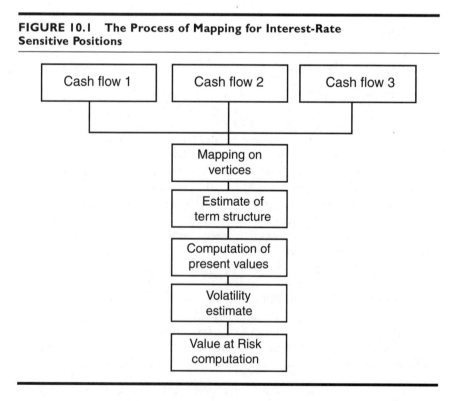

Allocating Cash Flows to Vertices

When cash flows do not coincide with any of the benchmark vertices, they must be allocated to predefined vertices.

Two methods can be used. The first, used by RiskMetrics (hence, referred to as the RiskMetrics approach), weights the two fractions of the cash flows to preserve (1) the market value, (2) the market risk, and (3) the sign of the original set of cash flows.

A common practice used, to date, throughout the financial industry has been to follow two standard rules when allocating cash flows between vertices:

1. Maintain present value.
2. Maintain duration.

To show how the RiskMetrics approach works, we will use a simple example.[14] Assume a given portfolio yields a positive cash flow 6 years from now. The closest standard (also called benchmarks) vertices are 5 years and 7 years. Hence, the 6-year cash flow must be allocated to the two standard vertices. The data needed are provided in Table 10.11.

The procedure runs as follows:

Step 1. The 6-year yield is calculated as a linear interpolation between the 5-year and the 7-year yields. Since the maturity of the cash flow is equidistant from the benchmark vertices, the 6-year yield can be calculated as a simple average of the 5-year and 7-year yields:

6-yr yield $= 0.5 * 6.605 + 0.5 * 6.745 = 6.675\%$

Step 2. Calculate the actual cash-flow present value (assumed the actual cash flow is equal to 1):

$$PV_{6-yr} = \frac{1}{1.0675} = 0.9374$$

TABLE 10.11   Data for Cash-Flow Mapping Using the RiskMetrics Approach

	Spot Rate	Price Volatility	5yr.–7yr. Bond-Return Correlation
5-year	6.605	0.35	0.9975
7-year	6.745	0.49	

Step 3. Calculate the actual price-return volatility of the actual cash flow:

$$\sigma_{6-yr} = 0.5 * \sigma_{5-yr} + 0.5 * \sigma_{7-yr} = 0.5 * 0.35 + 0.5 * 0.49 = 0.42$$

Step 4. The weights allocated to each vertex are determined by the following equation:

$$\text{Var(6-yr)} = w\,\text{Var(5-yr)} + (1-w)\,\text{Var(6-yr)}$$
$$+ w(1-w)\rho(5,7)\,\text{Var(5-yr)}\,\text{Var(7-yr)}$$

where w is the weight allocated to the 5-year vertex and $1-w$ the weight allocated to the 7-year vertex.

Conceptually, we are trying to build a portfolio made of two assets, yielding one cash flow—the first part after 5 years, the second after 7 years—that has the same risk as the original cash flow, occurring at year 6 (condition 2). The equation in Step 4 is a second-order equation, where the unknown variable is w.

The equation provides the solutions for $w = 5.999$ and $w = 0.489$. The first solution is disqualified since it violates condition 3. In simpler words, it would mean substituting positive cash flow at year 6 with a much greater positive cash flow in year 5 and a greater (but smaller, in absolute size, than the cash flow at year 5) negative cash flow at year 7. Therefore, we take the second solution. The present value of the original cash flow (0.9374) is allocated to the two vertices according to the solution of the equation in Step 4. Therefore 0.4655 is allocated to the 5-year vertex and 0.4717 to the 7-year vertex.

The original cash flow of 1 occurring at year 6, with an estimated present value of 0.9374, has been mapped into two different "virtual" cash flows occurring at year 5 and year 7, which have the same sign, risk, and present value of the original cash flow.

ACCOUNTING FOR "PULL TO PAR" AND "ROLL DOWN"[15]

Suppose we have a portfolio made up of a zero-coupon bond maturing in 1 year and providing a cash flow of $100,000. The spot-rate curve is described in Table 10.12. Daily volatility of the zero-coupon bond is equal to 0.05%.

The price of this bond is just the present value of the cash flow:

$$\frac{\$100,000}{1.09} = \$91,743$$

TABLE 10.12   Theoretical Spot-Rate Curve

Time	Percentile
1 month	5.00
2 months	5.50
3 months	6.00
6 months	7.00
1 year	9.00

The 1-year VaR at the 95% probability level is given by

$$VaR = \$91,743*1.65*0.0005*\sqrt{365} = \$1,446$$

This approach is clearly not correct since it overestimates the risk of the position. In fact, at maturity, regardless of the volatility and the level of spot rate, the price of the bond will be equal to the cash flow (its par value i.e., $100,000) and the VaR is zero.

The point is that the price of a bond reverts to its par value as maturity approaches. This deterministic trend effect is called the *pull-to-par* effect. In addition, convergence to par implies that the volatility of price declines as maturity approaches. This effect is known as *roll-down*. For short time periods, Equation 10.30 provides a reasonable approximation. This is not true if the time horizon is long.

Short Time-Horizons

Let's calculate the VaR for the previous bond for a time horizon of 15 days. Applying Equation 10.30, the VaR for the bond is $293. Symmetrically, the maximum probable gain is $293, corresponding to a price of $92,036.

Let's calculate the PV 15 days later. Now the maturity is 350 days. The appropriate spot rate for 1 year 15 days can be computed through linear interpolation between the 6-month and 1-year spot rates. In our example, it is equal to 8.83%.

Hence, the price of the bond is equal to $91,884. VaR still provides a reasonable approximation, since the maximum probable gain corresponds to a price bigger than the one expected if the price is calculated 15 days later.

Long Time Horizons

The situation changes if we consider a time horizon of 6 months. The VaR is $1,015, and the maximum probable gain corresponds to a price of $92,759. If spot rates do not change, the PV—the price—after 180 days is $93,458, higher even than the price corresponding to the most optimistic situation. Standard VaR clearly overestimates risk.

The Solution

If we want to correct this problem, we have to take into account both the deterministic drift and the reduction in price volatility as the time horizon approaches maturity. In the preceding example, we should:

- Calculate the price, as we would have done for a bond maturing 6 months from now, with the appropriate discount rate (accounting for pull to par).
- Take, as the appropriate volatility, the volatility of a 6-month zero-coupon bond (accounting for roll down).

If spot rates do not change, the expected price is $93,458, and the VaR is $1,034. The maximum probable loss corresponds to a virtual price of $92,426, still higher than the actual price of $91,743. Hence, the VaR adjusted for pull-to-par and roll-down effects is zero.

NOTES

1. F. Reilly and K. Brown, *Investment Analysis and Portfolio Management,* Hinsdale, IL: Dryden Press, 5th ed., 1997, 577.

2. *Ibid.,* 549.

3. P. Jorion, *Value at Risk: The New Benchmark for Controlling Derivatives Risk,* New York: McGraw-Hill, 1997, 105.

4. Reilly and Brown, *Investment Analysis and Portfolio Management,* 5th ed., 558.

5. *Ibid.,* 564.

6. *Ibid.,* 566.

7. Jorion, *Value at Risk: The New Benchmark for Controlling Derivatives Risk,* New York: McGraw-Hill, 1997, 123.

8. B. Solnik, *International Investments,* Reading, MA: Addison Wesley, 3rd ed., 1996, 323.

9. The duration of a zero-coupon bond is equal to its term to maturity; P. Jorion, *Value at Risk: The New Benchmark for Controlling Derivatives Risk,* New York: McGraw-Hill, 1997, 122.

10. Reilly and Brown, *Investment Analysis and Portfolio Management,* Hinsdale, IL: Dryden Press, 5th ed., 1997, 573.

11. For example, in Italy, where a huge market for government securities exists given the large government deficit, zero-coupon securities are issued only up to 12 months, while fixed-rate coupon bonds have maturities ranging up to 10 years. Recently, 30-year fixed-rate coupon bonds have been issued.

12. BTP or Buoni Pluriennali del Tesoro. These are fixed-income coupon notes/bonds with maturities ranging from 1 to 30 years.

13. For a review of the econometric techniques currently used for estimating the yield or the spot-rate curve, see P. Jorion, *Value at Risk: The New Benchmark for Controlling Derivatives Risk,* New York: McGraw-Hill, 1997.

14. This is the example provided by J.P. Morgan, *RiskMetrics Technical Documentation,* Chapter 6, 118, 1996.

15. This section is based on "Accounting for 'Pull to Par' and 'Roll Down' for RiskMetrics Cash Flows," *RiskMetrics Monitor,* 3rd quarter, 1996.

11

Equity Pricing

The object of this chapter is to illustrate how Value at Risk (VaR) can be calculated for equities. Two models are used for explaining equity returns: the traditional Capital Asset Pricing Model (CAPM) and the multifactor Arbitrage Pricing Theory (APT). The need for models describing stock returns in terms of market factors stems from the necessity of having a few risk factors useful for pricing a stock. The alternative approach—calculating a single stock's expected return, variance, and covariances with all other stocks and other financial instruments in the portfolio—would not be feasible for computational reasons. The last section illustrates, with an example from the Italian stock market, how VaR can be used with both CAPM and APT.

THE STANDARD APPROACH TO EQUITY PRICING: THE CAPITAL ASSET PRICING MODEL

The standard approach to equity pricing is given by the cornerstone Capital Asset Pricing Model, which is directly derived from the modern portfolio theory that Harry Markowitz developed in the 1950s. The CAPM, in its original formulation, states:

$$R_p = R_f + \beta_p * \left(R_m - R_f \right) \tag{11.1}$$

where R_p is the one-period return of a given security or portfolio, R_f is the risk-free rate of return, R_m is the one-period return of the market portfolio, and β_p is the standardized measure of systematic risk. Mathematically, β_p can be defined as

$$\beta_p = \frac{\mathrm{Cov}\left(R_m, R_p \right)}{\sigma^2_p} \tag{11.2}$$

Equation 11.1 has the remarkable advantage, for our purposes, of providing an easy way to estimate the expected one-period rate of return of a given stock or portfolio of stocks in terms of the risk-free rate plus a risk premium. The risk premium is determined by the systematic risk of the portfolio β_p and by the prevailing market-risk premium $(R_m - R_f)$.

The line that describes the relationship between the one-period rate of return of a stock or portfolio of stocks and β_p is the *security market line* (SML). In equilibrium, all stocks or portfolios of stocks should lie on the SML. This means that all stocks or portfolios of stocks should be priced so that their estimated rate of returns are consistent with their level of systematic risk (and nothing else). In an efficient market in equilibrium, no stocks/portfolios of stock should be plotted off the SML because all stocks should provide holding-period returns equal to their required rate of return.

Before examining how the CAPM can be used in the context of VaR, we should point out the six assumptions on which the CAPM is based:

1. There exists a risk-free rate at which investors can borrow and lend.
2. All investors have homogeneous expectations.
3. All investors have the same one-period time horizon, such as 1 month, 6 months, or 1 year.
4. No taxes or transaction costs are involved in buying and selling assets.
5. There is no inflation or changes in interest rates, or inflation is fully anticipated.
6. Capital markets are in equilibrium.

It is often claimed[1] that, although these assumptions are unrealistic, CAPM is nevertheless a useful tool for equity pricing—even in the real world. First, many of the assumptions can be relaxed without disrupting the model. Second, a theory should never be judged on the basis of its assumptions, but rather on how well it explains and helps us in predicting stock-return behavior in the real world. This is the most relevant observation for using CAPM for VaR purposes. The computation of VaR requires a model that provides us a reasonable approximation of expected stock returns; otherwise, no assessment of future gains and/or losses is possible. In the next section we show how the CAPM can be used in the context of VaR.

USING CAPM FOR VaR

The simplicity of Equation 11.1 makes it particularly suited for VaR purposes. Suppose we have a portfolio made up of only one stock, called stock A, and we want to calculate the VaR of this portfolio over a 1-month time horizon. From Equation 11.1, it is easy to realize that R_m is the market factor, while β_A is the delta factor. We are assuming that 1-month expected market returns are normally distributed with a 3% mean and a 3% standard deviation. Beta is assumed to be 0.9, and the risk-free rate is equal to 0.5%. Assuming a 95% probability level, the VaR for this stock is given by

$$\text{Expected return} = 0.5 + 0.9 * (2 - 1.65 * 0.5)$$
$$= 0.5 - 1.755 = 1.255\% \tag{11.3}$$

If the initial price is assumed to be \$20, the VaR is equal to

$$\text{VaR} = ABS(20 * -1.255\%) = \$0.351 \tag{11.4}$$

CAPM is particularly appealing for calculating VaR for two reasons:

1. *Linearity.* Unlike convexity, this property allows the expected returns on the portfolio to be normally distributed if expected market returns are normally distributed.
2. *Additivity.* Like the duration for bonds, the beta of a portfolio is the weighted average of the betas of individual stocks that make up the portfolio.

The systematic risk input for individual stocks or portfolios is derived from a regression model, referred to as the *characteristic line* of the market portfolio. The characteristic line is defined as:

$$R_p = \alpha_p + \beta_p * R_m + \varepsilon \tag{11.5}$$

and is obtained regressing the historical returns against the market returns of the stock/portfolio under examination.

PROBLEMS IN ESTIMATING THE CAPM

Although it seems an easy model to work with, the CAPM presents many problems when researchers try to estimate its parameters. This is a key step for defining the VaR for a portfolio of equities.

When computing the characteristic line, three caveats are in order:

1. The choice of the time interval.
2. The choice of the market portfolio.
3. The stability of beta.

The *time interval* is very important for beta estimation. Since there are no theoretical preferences for time intervals, every analyst can use the time interval he or she thinks to be the most appropriate for his or her purpose. Betas for the same stock calculated for different time intervals (e.g., using weekly or monthly data) can be different; this explains the differences between the Value Line betas (which use 260 weekly observations) and the Merrill Lynch betas (which use 60 monthly observations). Research has also shown that size affects betas for short time periods: large firms tend to have a larger beta for shorter time horizons, while small firms tend to have smaller beta.

A *market portfolio* of all existing risky assets is not directly observable, so a proxy must be used. Usually, the chosen proxies are stock market indexes such as—for the U.S. market—the NYSE composite index or the S&P 500. This approach is theoretically wrong, since these series contain only U.S. stocks. A true market portfolio should also contain U.S. bonds, non-U.S. stocks and bonds, real estate, coins, stamps, antiques, and any other marketable risky asset from around the world. In equilibrium, various assets should be held in the market portfolio in proportion to their market value. While the market portfolio is reasonable in theory, it is impossible to use when testing CAPM. At best, we hope the benchmark is highly correlated with the market portfolio. The problem arising from choosing a proxy for the market portfolio is often referred to as "benchmark error" and this has been especially stressed by Richard Roll.

The choice of an improper (which, in this context, simply means "uncorrelated"/low-correlated with the market portfolio) proxy can be misleading in two ways:

1. The computed beta would be an incorrect measure of the stock's systemic risk.
2. The SML would be wrong as well, since it would link the risk-free rate with an improperly specified market portfolio.

In general, the errors will tend to overestimate the performance of portfolio managers because the proxy used for the market portfolio is probably not as efficient as the true market portfolio; and so the slope of the SML would be underestimated. The beta itself would also be underestimated because the true market portfolio will have a lower variance due to greater diversification. Reilly and Akhtar[2] have shown that the more comprehensive the benchmark, the lower the correlation with the returns of major U.S. stocks. Nevertheless, the broader the portfolio, the lower the market portfolio variance (efficiency increases). In particular, when using the Brinson Global Stock Market Index

(GSMI)—a comprehensive index composed of global stocks and bonds—the variance effect dominates the covariance effect (i.e., the beta is higher than when computed using a U.S. stock market index such as the S&P 500).

The third problem regards the *stability* of beta. We would desire beta to be stable over time, although there is no theoretical reason to assume such a behavior. If the systematic risk of the stock increases, beta should increase as well. On the other hand, if the systematic risk decreases, beta should coherently decrease. Financing and operating decisions can, and actually do, change the sensitivity of a stock's returns to the market portfolio's returns. Therefore, the stability of beta over a long time horizon is more a hope than a theoretically sound outcome. Empirical works have demonstrated the following points about the stability of beta:

- Beta is not stable for individual stocks over short time periods (weeks). On the contrary, the stability of beta for portfolios of stocks increases dramatically.
- The stability of beta increases as the amount of data used in the calculations increases. Using monthly data, it is important to use at least 36 months. In this case also, beta is more stable for portfolios than for individual stocks.
- The stability of beta is a function of the trading volumes; the more a stock is traded, the more stable beta is.

For our purposes, what matters is whether the CAPM explains stock or portfolio returns. Regardless of the theoretical appeal and the degree of realism of the assumptions, we must have an operating instrument that allows us to make reliable forecasts over a given time horizon. A review of the vast literature regarding testing CAPM would be beyond the scope of this work. The main conclusions are:

- There is a positive, significant, linear relationship between individual stock/portfolio returns and market portfolio returns (or, at least, with the proxy's return usually being equal to the domestic stock market index).
- The intercept of the SML has been found to be generally higher than the risk-free rate.
- The systematic risk coefficient is not able to fully explain stock returns. Other variables—skewness of returns, size, financial leverage, and the book-to-market value ratio—have explanatory power for stock returns.

AN ALTERNATIVE APPROACH: THE ARBITRAGE PRICING THEORY

The CAPM, despite its appeal and apparent simplicity, has many draw-backs. First of all, empirical evidence is mixed about CAPM. The beta co-efficient is unstable for single securities or over short time horizons, and its relationship with market returns seems to be only one of the many pos-sible explanations for stock returns (in other words, the model is at least partially misspecified). In fact, other factors can be helpful in explaining a single stock's or a portfolio's returns.

An alternative pricing model was developed by Roll in 1976 and is known as arbitrage pricing theory (APT). APT originated for the reason that CAPM is not able to fully explain stock returns. Although CAPM has some explanatory power, several studies have shown that other variables (firm size, price-earnings ratio, book-to-market value ratio, leverage) have significant impact on stock returns, even greater than the impact of the market risk premium. The natural consequence is to define a pricing model encompassing several factors, rather than just one.

The arbitrage pricing theory also has the theoretical advantage of re-quiring far fewer assumptions than CAPM, which is an equilibrium model (i.e., describes the pricing of financial assets in equilibrium). APT is an arbitrage model: it only describes how returns should be defined and hy-pothesizes that any departure from the model would be wiped out by ar-bitrage. In particular, APT only requires that:

- Markets be perfectly competitive.
- Investors are rational, profit-maximizing agents.
- Stock returns conform to a K-factor stochastic model.

Formally, APT can be defined by Equation 11.5

$$R_p = \sum_{j=1}^{k} b_j * f_j \qquad\qquad (11.6)$$

where f_j are a set of k common factors which are supposed to explain stock returns and b_j are the reaction coefficients for each of the common factors.

Like the CAPM, the APT assumes that unique effects are independent and can be eliminated through diversification, so that the only relevant risk is captured by the specified risk factors used in the model. The most relevant problem with APT is that it does not specify what factors are to be used to explain asset/portfolio returns. This is considered an empirical issue. This is an important weakness from a theoretical point of view, since it provides neither a theoretical background nor any guidance for the selection of relevant risk factors. Paradoxically, while APT was born to provide better explanatory power than CAPM, it fails to specify the factors that determine asset/portfolio returns.

The most common approaches in selecting risk factors are:

- *The statistical approach.* Using factor analysis, the set of 3 to 5 factors that can best explain asset/portfolio return is chosen.
- *The macroeconomic approach.* A set of macroeconomic factors (expected inflation, current GDP, etc.) is used for estimating and predicting asset returns. The main problem is that macroeconomic data are available only monthly or quarterly, so it is impossible to use this approach with daily or weekly returns. This severely limits the number of observations available for estimation.
- *The firm-specific approach.* A mix of market indexes and firm-specific values (total asset volatility, P/E ratio, BV/MV ratio) are used for estimating and predicting asset returns.

The use of a multifactor model for calculating VaR is straightforward. Equation 11.6 can be rewritten, in terms of partial derivatives of the portfolio's returns, as a function of k market factors:

$$ dR_p = \frac{\partial R_p}{\partial f_1 df_1} + \frac{\partial R_p}{\partial f_2 df_2} + \ldots + \frac{\partial R_p}{\partial f_k df_k} \tag{11.7} $$

where $\partial R_p / \partial f_1 = b_1, \ldots, \partial R_p / \partial f_k = b_k$.

The estimated coefficients of the multifactor models are the delta coefficients for every single market factor. To calculate VaR, we can use the standard formula of Chapter 4:

$$ \text{VaR} = \alpha \sqrt{\delta' \Sigma \delta} \sqrt{\Delta t} \tag{11.8} $$

where Σ is the variance-covariance matrix of market-factor returns.

CALCULATING VaR FOR CAPM AND APT

In this section, we illustrate how VaR can be computed for equity, using two alternative models:

1. The standard CAPM.
2. A multifactor model (including a domestic stock market index and an industry index).

The equity chosen is FIAT and we used MIBTEL (the overall Milan Stock Exchange Index) and the index for the automotive and rubber industries. We used daily log returns for both the equity and the two indexes. The estimation period is from January 2, 1996, to May 25, 1998.

We first estimated the characteristic line for FIAT. The regression equation is FIAT = −0.000747 + 1.05 MIBTEL:

Coefficients	Estimates	Stdev	t-ratio	p
Constant	−0.0007466	0.0005776	−1.29	0.197
MIBTEL	1.05156	0.04369	24.07	0.000
R^2-adj	49%			
DW	1.70			

As expected, the FIAT β is not statistically different from 1[3], whereas it is clearly different from zero. The constant term is not significant.

To calculate the VaR, we need the standard deviation of market returns; and that is equal to 0.01314. The VaR at 95% probability level and a 1-day time horizon is equal to $1.65*0.01314*1.05*\sqrt{1} = 0.0228$. Since we have computed the VaR in terms of returns, we need to transform it into absolute values. If we assume that the initial capital invested in FIAT stocks was 10,000,000 ITL, the VaR is approximately[4] given by 10,000,000 * 0.0228 = 227,650 ITL.

We have also estimated the multifactor model for FIAT. The regression equation is: FIAT = −0.000695 + 0.633 MIBTEL + 0.555 AUTO.

Coefficients	Estimates	Stdev	t-ratio	p
Constant	−0.0006954	0.0004987	−1.39	0.164
MIBTEL	0.63255	0.04770	13.26	0.000
AUTO	0.55520	0.03871	14.34	0.000
R^2-adj	62%			
DW	2.39			

The variance-covariance matrix of market-factor returns is

	MIBTEL	AUTO
MIBTEL	0.00017258	0.00013025
AUTO	0.00013025	0.00026214

Hence the VaR (95% confidence level and 1-day time horizon) can be computed as $\text{VaR} = 1.65*\sqrt{\delta' \Sigma \delta}\sqrt{\Delta t} = 0.0256$.

Assuming an initial investment of 10,000,000 ITL, the VaR is given by 10,000,000 * 0.0256 ≈ 256,000 ITL.

Although strongly multicollinear (the correlation coefficient between market and industry returns is 0.612), the multifactor model provides a better explanation of asset returns (the adjusted R^2 grows from 49% to 62%) and the computation of VaR becomes more precise.

As a yardstick, we can calculate VaR for the portfolio of FIAT shares by calculating VaR directly from FIAT's historical data. If we assume FIAT's log returns to be normally distributed, using FIAT's standard deviation of returns, we can calculate VaR. VaR is equal to 1.65 * 0.01970 = 0.0325 and, hence, VaR ≈ 325,000 ITL in absolute terms.

As long as multifactor models incorporate market factors common to many instruments in the portfolio and are able to explain the behavior of asset returns significantly better than single-factor models (such as CAPM), they provide a much more accurate estimation of VaR than single-factor models.

NOTES

1. F. Reilly and K. Brown, *Investment Analysis and Portfolio Management,* Hinsdale, IL: Dryden Press, 5th ed.,1997, 279.

2. F. Reilly and A. Akhtar, "The Benchmark Error Problem with Global Capital Markets," *Journal of Portfolio Management,* 1995, 33–52.

3. In fact, $[(1.05 - 1)/0.05] < 1.96$, so β is not statistically different from 1.

4. This would have been the exact formula if the returns had been computed on a percentage basis. As shown in Chapter 5, daily log and percentage returns are very close, so the calculation shown is an accurate approximation of the VaR. The exact formula is given by $10,000,000 - (10,000,000*e^{-0.0228}) = 225,420$ ITL.

12

Derivative Pricing

D erivatives constitute the greatest challenge to VaR models. The challenge arises not from conceptual difficulties, but from the complex computational burden required to calculate the VaR for a portfolio with many derivatives.

Derivatives—and, here, we refer mainly to options—have two important characteristics:

- The relationship between the derivative's price and the underlying asset price is often highly nonlinear.
- The distribution of payoffs is not normal.

In addition, for some exotic derivatives, an exact closed-form solution does not exist. Traditional VaR models, based on the assumption of normality and linearity, can only poorly approximate the changes in derivative value in response to changes in market factors. Simulation models are able to fully capture only the nonlinearity of derivative payoffs; and simulation is also computationally intensive and data expensive.

In this chapter, we analyze three kinds of derivatives: linear derivatives (forwards, futures, and swaps), plain-vanilla options, and some exotic options. For options, the approximation provided by δ-normal models is often unsatisfactory, and simulation becomes the only accurate method to precisely estimate the VaR of nonlinear derivatives. In the last section, a mixed approach (therefore called "limited" simulation), is described.

FORWARDS

Futures (and forwards) are contracts that give the buyer (the seller) the obligation to buy (sell) a financial instrument, commodity, or index at a specified date in the future at an agreed price. Forwards and futures represent the simplest form of derivative instruments and are the easiest to treat in the context of VaR. For our purposes, futures and forwards are equivalent, so we will use the term *forward* to indicate both future and forward contracts.

The price of a forward is the price at which the transaction will be settled. Forwards do not have a specific price like options (the premium represents the price of the option) meaning that there is no price to pay to enter into a forward contract apart from the price agreed on. Once the price has been settled and the contract agreed on, the value of the contract may change as a consequence of changed market conditions. For VaR purposes, we are more interested in the current value of a forward held in the portfolio than in how the spot price of a forward is formed in the market. Nevertheless, since the spot price of a forward is a factor that affects the value of outstanding contracts, it is worth giving a brief look at the pricing of forward contracts.

Pricing a Forward Contract

The calculation of the spot price for a forward contract, under three different hypotheses, is shown in Table 12.1.

As an example, suppose that:

- An asset is currently traded at $90.
- The risk-free interest rate is 6.7%.
- The forward contract expires in 180 days.

TABLE 12.1   Formulas for Forward-Contract Pricing

	Price	Examples
Asset pays no dividend	$F_t = S_t (1 + r * dd/360)$	Metals, precious works, some commodities
Asset pays a constant income at an annual rate q	$F_t = S_t [1 + (r - q* dd/360)]$	Money market instruments, foreign exchange, equity indexes
Asset pays a lump sum	$F_t = S_t (1 + r * dd/360) - C_t$ $(1 + r * dd1/360)$	Bonds and equities

where F_t is the forward price
S_t is the spot price of the underlying asset
r is the annualized risk-free zero-coupon rate
dd are the days to expiration
$dd1$ are the days from the time of payment of the lump sum to expiration

If the asset pays no income, the forward price is given by

$$F_t = 90\left[1 + 0.067\left(\frac{180}{360}\right)\right] = 93.015$$

If the asset pays an income at 8% per annum on a constant basis

$$F_t = 90\left[1 + (0.067 - 0.08)\left(\frac{180}{360}\right)\right] = 89.415$$

If a lump payment of $4.5 is made at 89 days from expiration

$$F_t = 90\left[1 + 0.067\left(\frac{180}{360}\right)\right] - 4.5\left[1 + 0.067\left(\frac{89}{360}\right)\right] = 89.415$$

Valuation of a Forward Contract

In financial economics, the value of an instrument is given by the present value of all future cash flows. The present value generally represents a premium or discount to the face value of the asset. For forward contracts, the value at execution is zero. Once the price of the underlying asset has been agreed on, changes in market factors (such as interest rates) will lead to a change in the value of the contract. For the example given (assuming no income is paid on the asset), suppose that 30 days after the forward contract has been bought, the cash price of the security has dropped to $84.2 as a consequence of an interest rate growth to 8% per annum. The current forward price is then 84.2/[1 + 0.08 (150/360)] = 87.006.

The forward price—once agreed on—is fixed. At expiration, the value of the forward contract is given by the difference between the forward contract price and the current forward price. On the day of expiration, the contract would be 87.0067 − 93.015 = −6.0083. If this valuation occurs 150 days before expiration, the value of the contract is the present value of future expected cash flows: −6.0083/[1 + 0.008 (150/360)] = −5.81448.

RISK OF FORWARD CONTRACTS

Let us return to the pricing formula of a forward contract for an asset paying an income on a constant basis. The income price of the forward is given by the formula $F_t = S_t [1 + (r - q)^* dd/360)]$.

In general, the price of a forward contract is given by:

$$F_t = S_t\left[1 + (r - q) * \frac{dd}{360}\right] = f\left(S_t, r, q\right) \qquad (12.1)$$

For simplicity, we can transform Equation 12.1 using continuous compounding where $\upsilon = \ln(1 + q)$ and $\iota = \ln(1 + r)$ into Equation 12.2:

$$F_t = S_t e^{\iota\tau - \upsilon\tau} \qquad (12.2)$$

where τ is a fraction of a year or, equivalently,

$$F_t e^{-\iota\tau} = S_t e^{-\upsilon\tau} \qquad (12.3)$$

Once the forward price has been agreed on, the value of the forward contract is given by

$$ft = S_t e^{-\upsilon\tau} - K_t e^{-\iota\tau} \qquad (12.4)$$

where K_t is the fixed forward price.

Differentiating Equation 12.4 with respect to the various sources of risk to which the contract is exposed, we obtain:

$$df = \frac{\partial f}{\partial S} dS + \frac{\partial f}{\partial \iota} d\iota + \frac{\partial f}{\partial \upsilon} d\upsilon \qquad (12.5)$$

Risk arises from the exposure to each source of risk to which the contract is exposed. These sources include the underlying spot price, the risk-free interest rate, and the asset yield. We can rewrite Equation 12.4 as

$$df = \delta_S dS + \delta_\iota d\iota + \delta_\upsilon d\upsilon \qquad (12.6)$$

The forward contract can be viewed as a portfolio of exposures on risk factors. Its VaR is related to the volatilities and correlations of the various risk factors. VaR can be calculated as

$$\text{VaR} = \alpha\sqrt{\delta' \Sigma \delta} \qquad (12.7)$$

where δ is the vector of a portfolio's sensitivities to each market factor and Σ is the variance-covariance matrix of risk factors or, equivalently, as:

$$VaR = \alpha\sqrt{\chi'\Theta\chi} \tag{12.8}$$

where x is the vector of a portfolio's undiversified VaR with respect to each market factor and Θ is the correlation matrix of risk factors.

VaR FOR FORWARD CONTRACTS

The calculation of VaR for forward contracts involves two separate steps:

1. The decomposition of the risk into its fundamental factors.
2. The reconstruction of total risk from individual components.

In particular, Step 1 implies that the contract is synthetically replicated, and each replication is treated as a portfolio of different position. Only subsequently, through the variance-covariance or the correlation matrix, is the VaR for the whole portfolio of elementary positions calculated. An example for a foreign-exchange forward shows how this process of decomposition and recomposition works.[1] A forward contract to sell USD against CHF can be decomposed into three positions:

1. A borrowing of USD up to the amount needed to buy the desired quantity of CHF at the U.S. domestic rate (this is equivalent to issuing a zero-coupon bond denominated in USD at the U.S. domestic rate).
2. A spot sell of USD against CHF.
3. An investment in CHF at the Swiss domestic rate (this equivalent to buying a zero-coupon bond denominated in CHF at the Swiss domestic rate).

According to the interest rate parity theorem, the three positions replicate the desired forward contract exactly.[2] The term of the contract is 1 year, the U.S. rate is 6% per annum, the Swiss rate is 2% per annum, and the current exchange rate is 0.70 USD/CHF. The time horizon is 1 day and the probability level is 95%. We assume the daily price volatility to be 0.008 for the spot exchange rate, 0.004 for the CHF investment and 0.005 for the cost of USD borrowing. The amount of CHF to buy is 10,000 (USD 7,000). The VaR for each of the three components is:

1. $1.65 * 0.005 * 7,000 = USD\ 57.75$
2. $1.65 * 0.008 * 10,000 = USD\ 132$
3. $1.65 * 0.004 * 10,000 * 0.7 = USD\ 46.2$

The undiversified VaR is then USD 235.95. The VaR can be obtained by taking the square root of the quadratic form $\chi'\Theta\chi$, where $\chi' = [57.75, 132, 46.2]$ and the correlation matrix Θ is assumed to be:

	Spot Rate	*CH Rate*	*U.S. Rate*
Spot rate	1	−0.6	0.7
CH rate	−0.6	1	0.9
US rate	0.7	0.85	1

The VaR for the currency forward contract is USD 166.9.

VaR FOR SWAPS

Interest-rate swaps are broken down into two separate transactions. As discussed in Chapter 4, the fixed leg is treated as a position in a fixed-rate bond, while the floating-rate flows are treated as a position in a floating note. The risk of each set of cash flows can then be calculated independently. The fixed leg is valued as a bond. The floating leg will generally trade around the par value, with only the current option (fixed with reference to the last floating rate set) creating an interest-rate exposure that will need to be incorporated.[3]

Currency swaps are treated as two separate fixed-interest transactions in the respective currencies, with each security being broken down into the separate interest rate risk factors in the individual currency. The currency exposure is then incorporated, including the impact of correlation such as between the interest rate risk factors and the currency, when each fixed-interest bond is translated into the base reporting currency. Where one leg of the currency swap is on a floating-rate basis, the approach utilized is identical to that used for the floating-rate component of an interest rate swap.[4]

PLAIN-VANILLA OPTION PRICING

An option contract gives the owner the right (but not the obligation) to buy/sell a given financial instrument or commodity at a specified price at some time in the future (European option) or within a specified time (American option).

There are two basic types of options:

1. *Call option.* Gives the owner the right to buy the instrument/commodity.

2. *Put option.* Gives the owner the right to sell the instrument/commodity.

Notably, while the buyer of a call option has the right to buy at a specified price, the writer has the obligation to sell at the specified price, if requested. Conversely, while the buyer of the put has the right to sell at the specified price, the writer of the put has the obligation to buy at the specified price, if requested.

At expiration, the value of a call option is given by max(0; $S_t - X$), where S_t is the spot price at expiration and X is the strike (or exercise) price. The value of the put option at expiration is given by max(0; $X - S_t$).

Before expiration, the value (price) of an option depends on the probability it will end "in the money," and by what amount. Black and Scholes have derived a closed formula for European options for underlying assets paying no dividends. The well-known Black-Scholes (BS) formula for a call option is

$$C_t = S_t N(d_1) - Xe^{-rT} N(d_2)$$ (12.9)

where $d1 = \left[\ln(S_t / X) + (r + .5\sigma^2)T \right] / \sigma\sqrt{T}$, $d2 = d1 - \sigma\sqrt{T}$ and r is the risk-free rate.

The model is based on the following assumptions:

- The price of the underlying asset is continuous and follows a geometrical Brownian motion.
- The interest rate and variance are known and constant.
- Capital markets are perfect (no transaction costs or taxes or short sales allowed).

The most important assumption behind the model is that prices are continuous. This rules out discontinuities in the sample path, such as jumps, and mean reversion in the asset price (i.e., reversion to a fixed value). Therefore, the BS model is not strictly applicable to the fixed-income market where bond prices converge to face values. In practice, the BS formula provides a good approximation for options on medium- to long-term bonds, which mature much later than the option term, so that the mean reversion effect is small.

The key point in Black-Scholes's derivation is that a position in the option is strictly equivalent to a delta position in the underlying asset. Therefore, a portfolio combining the asset and the option in appropriate proportions is locally risk free (i.e., it is risk free for small movements in the spot price).

The BS formula can be adapted for pricing a put option:

$$P_t = S_t\left[N\left(d_1\right)-1\right] - Xe^{-rT}\left[1 - N\left(d_2\right)\right]$$ (12.10)

The economic interpretation of $N(d_1)$ and $N(d_2)$ deserves more attention. For every financial instrument, the price is equal to the present value of future expected cash flows. At expiration, the cash flow of a call option (for example) is given by MAX($0; S_t - X$). This cash flow needs to be discounted at present time. In a risk-neutral world with continuous compounding, the discount factor is given by e^{-rT}, where r is a risk-free rate.

Since the cash flow at maturity is not certain, it must be weighted with the probability that this cash flow will actually occur. It is uncertain whether this cash flow will occur and—provided it occurs—what amount it will be. The strike price X will be paid (and will be considered a negative component of the cash flow) if the spot price at maturity is higher than the strike price. $N(d_1)$ is the probability that the option will end in-the-money.

$Xe^{-rT}N(d_1)$ is the expected present value of the strike price. The amount of the cash flow depends also on the value the spot price will have at maturity, provided the option ends in-the-money. $S_t N(d_2)$ is the present value of the expected spot price at maturity, weighted by the probability that the option ends in-the-money.

These concepts are extremely helpful in explaining binary options.

DECOMPOSING AN OPTION INTO RISK FACTORS

The BS formula shows that the value of an option depends on five factors:

1. The spot price of the underlying asset.
2. The risk-free rate.
3. The volatility of the asset's returns.
4. The time-to-expiration of the option.
5. The strike price.

Since the strike price is fixed once the contract is agreed on, we can consider the first four factors only. We can use partial derivatives to analyze the changes in the option price. For simplicity, we refer our analysis to call options:

$$dC_t = \frac{\partial C_t}{\partial S_t}\,dS_t + \frac{\partial C_t}{\partial \sigma}\,d\sigma + \frac{\partial C_t}{\partial r}\,dr + \frac{\partial C_t}{\partial t}\,dt$$ (12.11)

The price of the option depends on the time-to-expiration, but in a deterministic fashion. Option-price sensitivities are indicated by a set of Greek letters, usually referred to as "the Greeks." A call option price change can be rewritten as:

$$dC_t = \delta\, dS_t + \lambda\, d\sigma + \rho\, dr + \theta\, dt \tag{12.12}$$

where $\delta = \partial C_t / \partial S_t$, λ[5] (also called vega or kappa) $= \partial C_t / \partial \sigma$, $\rho = \partial C_t / \partial r$ and $\theta = \partial C_t / \partial t$. It would be appealing to use the standard approach for calculating the VaR for an option once the risk has been mapped (i.e., after delta coefficients have been estimated). We recall from Chapter 4 that the VaR can be computed by the standard delta-normal formula $\alpha \sqrt{\delta' \Sigma \delta} \sqrt{\Delta t}$, where δ' is the vector of option price sensitivities (δ, λ, ρ, θ) and Σ is the variance-covariance matrix of market-factor changes. Although this approach can be used—and is actually used—for optionalized portfolios, it may lead to serious errors in the estimates of option-price changes. To understand how this can happen, we must give a closer look at each of the Greeks and understand how they affect the price of an option.

USING THE GREEKS: DELTA

The first—and most important—option-price sensitivity coefficient is called *delta*. It is the first derivative of an option's price to a change in the price of the underlying asset (hereafter *spot price*). Notably, it is the archetype of delta coefficients in the context of VaR. The δ for a call option is always positive; for a put option it is always negative. The economic interpretation of δ is straightforward. If $\delta = 0.5$, a spot-price change of 1 will cause a change in the option value of 0.5. If the spot-price change is infinitesimal, δ would give an exact option-price change. If the spot-price change is more than infinitesimal, the price change provided by δ is only approximate. Since option prices are extremely dependent on spot prices, spot prices are the key determinant of the price of options. It would be tempting to assume that risk factors other than spot prices are negligible so that VaR for an option could be computed from the following formula: $\text{VaR} = \alpha \sigma_s \sqrt{\Delta t}$.

The assumptions needed to justify such an approach are highly unrealistic. An important point of weakness is that we should assume δ to be constant for any level of the spot price; we must assume the relationship between option price and spot price to be linear. On the contrary, this relationship is highly nonlinear and, therefore, VaR could be different for the same spot-price change if the starting price is different. In fact, taking the first derivative of the BS formula to the spot price, we have

$$\frac{\partial C_t}{\partial S_t} = N\left(d_1\right) = \delta \qquad (12.13)$$

where $N(\ )$ is a normal cumulative density function and d_1 depends on the spot price itself. Keeping all other risk factors constant, $\delta = f(S_t)$; and this function is represented by an S-shaped curve ranging from zero to one (as S_t approaches infinity). This behavior can be well explained in the context of the BS framework. The BS formula includes the probability distribution of spot prices to account for possible changes from the current time up to expiration. So, even if the spot price is lower than the strike price, the price of a call option will be more than its intrinsic value since it incorporates the possibility that, at expiration, the spot price will be greater than the strike price.

If the spot price is significantly lower than the strike price, it is extremely unlikely that a change in the spot price will cause the spot price to be higher than the strike price at expiration; so any small changes will not be reflected in the option price ($\delta = 0$). If the spot price is significantly higher than the strike price, it is extremely unlikely that a change will cause the spot price to be lower than the strike price at expiration; so δ is equal to one, or close to one. In other words, any change in the spot price will be fully reflected in the option price. When the spot price is close to the strike price, δ is highly unstable and changes very rapidly in response to a change in the spot price.

The coefficient δ has another important interpretation. It is the inverse of the hedge ratio, so it can be used for hedging purposes. For example, if $\delta = 0.5$ it means that a $\Delta S = 1$ will cause a ΔC[6] approximately equal to 0.5. A portfolio made up of one long stock and two short calls will be locally hedged against changes in the spot price. A continuously rebalanced portfolio (i.e., always delta-hedged) should yield the risk-free rate. This is an important assumption behind the BS model. Obviously, even a δ-hedged portfolio cannot be considered immunized against spot-price risk if ΔS is large since, in this case, the nonlinearity of the relationship between spot price and call price will lead to a large underestimation error.[7]

To illustrate this effect, we have simulated the effect on a δ-hedged portfolio of a change in the spot price. The initial situation is described in Table 12.2.

Since δ is equal to 0.67, the portfolio is made up of two long stocks and three short calls. The initial value is 183.6355. Since the portfolio is δ-hedged, we expect that changes in the spot price will not cause changes in the value of the portfolio.

TABLE 12.2   Initial Situation for a δ-Hedged Portfolio

Strike	100 d1	0.432
Spot	100 d2	0.352
Volatility (year)	0.08 Price	5.45
Risk free (year)	0.04 Delta	0.67
Expiration (year)	1 Portfolio	183.6355

For example, if ΔS is equal to 0.5, the value of the portfolio remains almost unchanged (Table 12.3).

A 1-year volatility of 0.08 corresponds to a 1-day volatility of $0.08\sqrt{(1/250)} = 0.017889$, or 1.79%. A 2σ positive return—an infrequent, but not a rare event—will cause the value of the portfolio to fall to 182.55 (Table 12.4).

When the spot price rises, the price of the call grows more than expected, since delta increases. To keep the portfolio hedged, we should change the composition of the portfolio. Table 12.4 shows that δ passes from 0.67 to 0.78. This means that a δ-hedged portfolio would include about four long stocks and five short calls. The previous portfolio is no longer δ-hedged. Notably, the value of the portfolio also decreases when the spot price falls. If the spot price falls to 95 (Table 12.5), δ becomes 0.47.

A δ-hedged portfolio would include approximately one long stock and one short call. The convexity of the spot-price/option-price relationship causes the price of the call to fall less than expected. Therefore, the negative effect given by the spot-price fall prevails, and the value of the whole portfolio falls as well. We can make an analogy between the δ coefficient and duration examined in Chapter 10.

TABLE 12.3   Changes of the Value in the Portfolio for a $\Delta S = 0.5$

Strike	100 d1	0.481875
Spot	100.5 d2	0.401875
Volatility (year)	0.08 Price	5.81
Risk free (year)	0.04 Delta	0.69
Expiration (year)	1 Portfolio	183.5723

TABLE 12.4 Changes in the Value of the Portfolio for a ΔS = 3.6

Strike	100	d1	0.785671
Spot	103.6	d2	0.705671
Volatility (year)	0.08	Price	8.22
Risk free (year)	0.04	Delta	0.78
Expiration (year)	1	Portfolio	182.5456

Although the price-yield relationship is nonlinear (convex), duration provides a reasonable local approximation of the price change of a fixed-income security for small changes in the YTM. When changes in the YTM are large, duration tends to underestimate the price change of a fixed-income security and convexity becomes an important factor for adjusting our estimates. Like duration, δ has the great advantage of being additive. With a portfolio of options and other derivatives, where there is a single underlying asset, the delta of the whole portfolio is a weighted sum of the deltas of the individual derivatives in the portfolio. For a portfolio of derivatives with a single underlying asset, the δ of the portfolio is given by:

$$\delta_p = \Sigma_j w_j \delta_j \tag{12.14}$$

For example, an Italian bank has the following three positions in options to buy or sell USD:

1. 100,000 long calls to buy USD at 1,800 ITL/USD expiring in three months, with a $\delta = 0.55$.
2. 200,000 short calls with a strike price of 1,850 ITL/USD expiring in five months, with $\delta = 0.70$.
3. 50,000 short put with a strike price of 1,780 ITL/USD with a $\delta = -0.50$.

TABLE 12.5 Changes in the Value of the Portfolio for a ΔS = -5

Strike	100	d1	-0.08093
Spot	95	d2	-0.16093
Volatility (year)	0.08	Price	2.54
Risk free (year)	0.04	Delta	0.47
Expiration (year)	1	Portfolio	182.3843

The δ of the portfolio is given by

$$100,000 * 0.55 - 200,000 * 0.70 - 50,000 * (-0.50) = -60,000$$

The portfolio can be made δ neutral by being long on 60,000 USD, either in the cash market or with an equivalent position in the futures market.[8]

Notwithstanding its simplicity, δ-based approximations are often insufficient. This is particularly important in the context of VaR if the portfolio is highly optionalized. As for bonds, precise estimation of price changes due to changes in the interest rates can be obtained by fully repricing the security. For fixed-income securities, full repricing is obtained by discounting all cash flows at their appropriate zero-coupon rate. Alternatively, a quadratic approximation can be added to increase accuracy. With option pricing, we can either reprice the option by using the new spot price in the BS formula or add a quadratic term to the linear approximation provided by δ. This second-order coefficient, called γ, is aimed at capturing the nonlinearity in the relationship between spot price and option price. This term plays exactly the same role that convexity plays for fixed-income securities.

USING THE GREEKS: GAMMA

Gamma measures how δ changes with changes in the spot price. Gamma is the second derivative of the option price to spot price or

$$\gamma = \frac{\partial^2 C}{\partial S^2} = N'(d_1)\, S_t\, \sigma\sqrt{T-t} \tag{12.15}$$

Interestingly, $N'(d1)$ is the standard normal probability density function. Gamma is zero—or close to zero—when options are deep in-the-money or deep out-of-the-money. In these cases, in fact, the relationship between spot price and option price is almost linear, with δ close to—respectively—one and zero. On the other hand, γ reaches its maximum when the option is at-the-money. As described earlier, δ changes faster when the spot price is close to the strike price. Therefore, the sensitivity of a call option to changes in the spot price can be rewritten as:

$$\Delta C \approx \delta\, \Delta S + \tfrac{1}{2}\gamma\, \Delta S^2 \tag{12.16}$$

Gamma is always positive for long calls and puts, implying that the option price grows more, or declines less, than predicted by linear approximation. It is always negative for short calls and puts, implying that the option price declines more, and grows less, than predicted by linear approximation.

The marginal function of γ to the spot price and to the time-to-expiry is bell-shaped.[9]

DELTA AND GAMMA IN THE CONTEXT OF VaR

Significant levels of γ, as for convexity, invalidate linear VaR. In fact, since the relationship between spot price and option price is nonlinear, it is no longer possible to assume that normality of asset return will cause normality of return on options. The confidence level calculated using the normality assumption would be a poor predictor of true Value at Risk. One could always use a second-order approximation for the option price, assuming that the payoffs of the option (e.g., a call option) maintain an approximately normal distribution.

It can be demonstrated that,[10] if dS is normally distributed, the VaR for a call option can be calculated as

$$\text{VaR} = \alpha \sqrt{\delta^2 S^2 \sigma^2 \frac{ds}{S} + \frac{1}{2}\left(\gamma S^2 \sigma^2 \frac{ds}{S}\right)^2} \tag{12.17}$$

which shows the nonlinear relationship between the changes in the underlying asset and the option's VaR. When $\gamma = 0$, Equation 12.17 becomes the VaR of a linear contract. It must be stressed that Equation 12.17 provides an approximation of the true VaR. The exact VaR can be measured only from the actual distribution of option payoffs.

THE OTHER GREEKS: LAMBDA, RHO, AND THETA[11]

Although options are extremely sensitive to changes in the spot price, the importance of the other factors (volatility of returns of the underlying asset, risk-free interest rate, and time) cannot be neglected. The λ of a portfolio (also called vega or kappa) is the rate of change of the value of the portfolio with respect to the volatility of the underlying asset. If lambda is high, the portfolio's value is very sensitive to small changes in volatility. If lambda is small, volatility changes have relatively little impact on the value of the portfolio. As in the case of δ and γ, it is possible to make a portfolio λ neutral: if λ_p is the lambda of a portfolio and λ_T is the lambda of a traded option, a position of $-\lambda_p/\lambda_T$ makes the portfolio lambda neutral. A lambda-neutral portfolio is generally not a gamma-neutral portfolio, unless at least two traded derivatives are added.

For a European call or put option paying no dividend, lambda is equal to $S\sqrt{(T-t)}N'(d_1)$; so it is approximately bell-shaped with respect to the spot price. In fact, it is close to zero when the spot price is significantly higher or lower than the strike price and reaches its top when the spot price is equal to the strike price. This is intuitive since, when options are deep out-of-the-money or deep in-the-money, it is not likely that changes in volatility will lead the spot price to be higher (or lower) than the strike price at expiration.

The rho of a portfolio of derivatives is the rate of change of the value of the portfolio with respect to the interest rate. It measures the sensitivity of the value of a portfolio to interest rates. The rho for a European call option paying no dividend is equal to $X(T-t)e^{-r(T-t)}N(d_2)$; for a put option, it is equal to $-X(T-t)e^{-r(T-t)}N(-d_2)$.

If we abstract from time (which is not, strictly speaking, a risk factor), we can incorporate both lambda and rho in a δ-normal model to calculate the VaR for an option. VaR can be calculated with the standard formula $\alpha\sqrt{\delta'\Sigma\delta}$, where δ' is the vector (δ, λ, ρ) and Σ is the variance-covariance matrix of these three risk factors.

The relationships between the option price and interest rate and between the option price and volatility can be considered approximately linear, so that it is not unreasonable to use the δ-normal model. On the other hand, it is a very approximate formula, since it does not take into account the nonlinearity of the relationship between the option price and the spot price. This effect is illustrated in detail in the following section.

A COMPREHENSIVE EXAMPLE

In this section, we will provide a comprehensive example of the calculation of VaR for a call option on an asset paying no dividends. Therefore, the BS model will be used. We want to calculate the VaR for a call option on a stock paying no dividend, expiring in 51 days. The strike price was assumed to be 100, the risk-free rate 10% per year, and the annual volatility 20%.

We also assumed the spot price to be 100 at day 0. We assumed the stock price to be lognormally distributed. In a risk-neutral framework, $\ln(St/St-1)$ is normally distributed, with a mean equal to $(rf - \sigma2)^*(T-t)$ and a standard deviation equal to $\left(\sigma\sqrt{T-t}\right)$. We assumed an annual volatility of 20%, a risk-free rate (rf) equal to 10%. The price of the call option, according to the BS model, was 3.70. Using Microsoft Minitab 10.1™ we

TABLE 12.6   Statistics for Simulated ΔS and ΔC

	ΔS	ΔEC
Mean	−0.02	−0.03
Standard Deviation	1.04	0.62
Skewness	1.75	4.97
Kurtosis	−1.20	0.23

drew out 1,000 numbers from a normal distribution with a mean equal to 0.03% and a standard deviation equal to 1.05%. Then, we computed 1,000 simulated prices for day 1.

Using the Black-Scholes formula, with a maturity equal to 50 days, we computed the call prices corresponding to each of the 10,000 simulated prices at the end of day 1. We also computed the set of simulated 1-day ΔSs and ΔCs. The statistics for ΔS and ΔC are provided in Table 12.6.

The standardized skewness and kurtosis are the sample skewness and kurtosis divided by their asymptotic standard deviations, $\sqrt{6/N}$ and $\sqrt{24/N}$, respectively.

Figure 12.1 shows the distribution of ΔC as a consequence of ΔS. What emerges is a significant positive skewness of ΔC that results from the nonlinearity of option payoffs to the spot price. The asymmetry occurs because option prices react differently to changes in the spot price of signs that are different but of the same magnitude. We have also computed the Value at Risk of this call option, using two approaches: the δ-normal and the simulation model.

FIGURE 12.1   Simulated Distribution of Payoffs for a Call Option

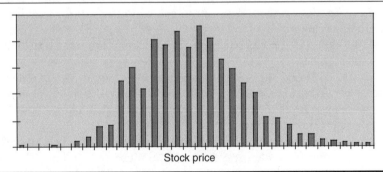

Stock price

TABLE 12.7   Comparison between δ-Normal VaR and Simulation VaR

	δS (%)	δEC	Error (%)
Delta VaR	95	−1.01	8
Simulation	95	−0.94	
Delta VaR	97.5	−1.20	9
Simulation	97.5	−1.10	
Delta VaR	99	−1.43	12
Simulation	99	−1.28	

Under the δ-normal approach, we assumed the distribution of ΔC to be normal, as a result of the assumed linear relationship with ΔS that, by construction, is normally distributed. Under the simulation model, we selected the value of ΔC that leaves 5%, 2.5%, and 1% of the simulated distribution at its left. We expect the VaR, computed using the δ-normal approach, to be higher than the VaR computed using a simulation approach, since the δ-normal approach does not take into account the nonlinearity of payoffs. We used the delta coefficient at day 0 equal to 0.5887. Table 12.7 summarizes the results.

The δ-normal model clearly overestimates the VaR for call options. The reverse is true for put options: the δ-normal model would underestimate the VaR, while the simulation model is able to fully capture the nonlinearity of ΔC. Obviously, the magnitude of the overestimation increases with the confidence level since higher confidence levels correspond to larger changes in the spot price.

ALTERNATIVE OPTION PRICING FORMULAS

The BS model holds for a European option on an underlying asset paying no dividends. Alternative formulas, based on the BS intuition, have been derived to account for assets paying dividends, for options on futures, and for options on foreign currencies. If the underlying asset pays a dividend, the BS formula cannot be applied. R. Merton has suggested an adjustment to the BS formula to account for dividends paid at a continuous rate. Essentially, the adjustment for continuous dividends treats the dividend rate as a negative rate. Merton's formula for a call option is

$$C_t = S_t e^{-\eta T} N\left(d^M{}_1\right) - X e^{-rT} N\left(d^M{}_2\right) \tag{12.18}$$

where η is the continuous dividend rate,

$$d\,d^M{}_1 = \frac{\left[\ln(S_t/X) + \left(r - \eta + .5\sigma^2\right)T\right]}{\sigma\sqrt{T},\ d^M{}_2} = d^M{}_1 - \sigma\sqrt{T}$$

and r is the risk-free rate. When $\eta = 0$, the Merton model collapses to the BS model.

The δ coefficient for Merton's model becomes $e^{-\eta T}N(d^M{}_1)$. When the option is on a future or forward contract, the basic BS model can be altered to adjust for the changed nature of the underlying asset. The following equation describes the price of a call option when a future contract is the underlying asset (this is known as Black's model).

$$C_t = e^{-rT}\left[F_t N(d_1) - X N(d_2)\right] \tag{12.19}$$

where F is the future price of the underlying asset and r is the risk-free rate. Garman and Kohlhagen have derived a modified formula for options on foreign currency.

The value of a call option on a foreign currency is defined by

$$C_t = S_t e^{-rfT}\left[N(d_1) - X e^{-rdT} N(d_2)\right] \tag{12.20}$$

where rf is the foreign risk-free rate and rd is the domestic risk-free rate.

EXOTIC OPTIONS[12]

In recent years, a variety of complex options, that are collectively known as "exotic options" have been created. The challenge in the context of VaR is that payoffs of exotic options are considerably diverse—and more complex—than the payoffs of plain-vanilla options, that still constitute a great challenge to the models assuming normality of payoffs.

Many exotic options are path-dependent; that is, their price depends on the path of the price of the underlying asset rather than on the current value. Some have a closed-form solution; others can be priced only by using simulation techniques. None of them have a linear relationship between the spot price and the option price. Linear VaR models perform poorly, and quadratic approximations are not always satisfactory. In many cases, simulation becomes the only way to accurately estimate the true VaR. A complete treatment of exotic options is far beyond our scope. We do, however, show how exotic options can be dealt with for calculating

VaR and review some common European exotic options for which a closed-form solution exists. As with plain-vanilla options, VaR is computed using both a δ-normal model and a simulation approach.

Forward-Start Options

In a forward-start option, the price of the option is paid at the present, but the life of the option starts at a future date. Typically, the strike price is specified to be the current price at the beginning of the option's life (this implies that the option is set to be in-the-money at the beginning of the option's life). For a forward-start option, there are three dates to consider:

1. The valuation date (t).
2. The date at which the option begins (the grant date—tg).
3. The date at which the option expires (T).

It means that $t \leq tg \leq T$ and that the option's life begins at $tg - t$, and the option's life is equal to $T - tg$.

The value of a forward-start option is simply the value of an option with the current stock price and a time-to-expiration of $T - tg$, with its value being discounted by the dividend rate of the underlying good over the period the option is granted (i.e., $tg - t$).

If the asset pays no dividend, the value of the forward-start option is equal to the value predicted by the BS model. If the underlying asset pays a dividend, then Merton's model should be used.

The basic idea is that the spot price and the strike price on the underlying asset will move proportionally. At the beginning of the option, these two prices usually coincide. Being discounted by the continuous-dividend rate for the time from the valuation date to the grant date, the price of a forward-start option is lower than the price of a plain-vanilla option.

Chooser Options

The owner of a "chooser" option has the right to determine whether that option will become a call or a put by a specified choice date. After the choice date, the option becomes a plain-vanilla call or put, depending on the owner's choice. Chooser options are called "as-you-like-it" options. As for forward-start options, there are three dates to consider:

1. The valuation date (t).
2. The choice date (tc).
3. The expiration date (T).

where $t \leq tc \leq T$. The problem is to evaluate the option at time t, before the choice date. After the choice date, the value of the option is the value of a plain-vanilla call or put, to be valued with the standard BS or Merton's models.

We assume that the call and the put have the same exercise price and expiration. When $t = tc$ (the choice must be made immediately), the value of the option is simply given by $MAX(Call, Put)$, where the maturity of both options is $T - t$. When $t = T$, the chooser is simply a straddle, so that its value is equal to $Call + Put$ with expiration $T - t$. These extreme values represent the upper and lower bounds for the value of a simple chooser:

$$MAX[Call(T - t), Put(T - t)] \leq Chooser \leq Call + Put \qquad (12.21)$$

At any day tc ($\geq t, \leq T$), there is no need to make the choice. The payoff of the chooser can be defined at tc. The value of the chooser is equal to:

$$Chooser = MAX(Call, Put) \qquad (12.22)$$

Using the put-call parity, we can rewrite Equation 12.21:

$$Chooser = MAX\left(Call, Call + Xe^{-r(T-tc)} - S\right)$$
$$Chooser = Call + MAX\left(0, Xe^{-r(T-tc)} - S\right) \qquad (12.23)$$

Viewed from time t, Equation 12.23 is equivalent to a call with strike price X expiring at T and a put with strike price equal to X and maturity tc.

For VaR purposes, a chooser option represents a tricky situation, since the option value is a U-shaped function of the spot price. It means that linear approximation, if spot price variations are not very small, can lead to large estimation error. A possible approach could be to decompose the chooser option into a plain-vanilla call and a plain-vanilla put with the same strike price and different maturities. The whole position would be simply the sum of the value of the call and the value of the put, since they both depend on the same market factor.

Asian Options

Asian options are path-dependent options where the payoff depends on the average spot prices. In particular, an average price call has at expiration a value equal to $MAX(0, S_{avg} - X)$ while an average price put has at expiration a value equal to $MAX(X - S_{avg}, 0)$ where S_{avg} is the average value of the underlying asset calculated over a predetermined averaging period. The value of the option at expiration depends on the price path of the underlying asset, on the averaging period and on the way the average is calculated.

If the underlying asset's spot price is lognormally distributed and S_{avg} is a geometric average of S, analytic formulas are available for valuing European average price options.[13] This is because the geometric average of a set of lognormally distributed variables is also lognormal. A geometric average price option can therefore be treated like a regular option with the volatility set equal to $\sigma/\sqrt{3}$ and the dividend yield equal to $\frac{1}{2}(r + \eta + \sigma^2/6)$. If the average is arithmetic, exact analytic formulas are not available since the distribution of an arithmetic average of lognormally distribution variables is not known. The standard approach—providing an approximation solution—is to calculate the first and the second moment of the distribution of the arithmetic average and then assuming the arithmetic average to be lognormally distributed with the same first two moments. The option can be treated like a regular option with dividend yield equal η_A to $r - \ln(M_1)/T$ and volatility equal to $\ln(M_2)/T - 2(r - \eta_A)$ where M_1 and M_2 are the calculated first two moments of the distribution.

The price of an Asian call (both arithmetic and geometric) is much more stable than that of its regular European call counterpart. In fact, it has lower delta values. The reason is intuitive: the effect of spot price changes is partially offset by averaging procedures.

Lookback Options

The payoff of lookback options depends on the maximum or minimum stock price reached during the life of the option. The payoff from a European lookback call is the amount by which the final stock price exceeds the minimum stock price achieved during the life of the option. The payoff from a European lookback put is the amount by which the maximum stock price achieved during the life of the option exceeds the final stock price. A lookback call is a way in which the holder can buy the underlying asset at the lowest price achieved during the life of the option. A lookback put is a way in which the holder can sell the underlying asset at the highest price during the life of the option. Closed form solutions—assuming that prices can be observed continuously—are available for European lookback options.

Binary Options

Binary options are options with discontinuous payoffs. A simple example is a *cash-or-nothing call*. This option pays off nothing if the stock price ends up below the strike price and pays a fixed amount K if it ends above the strike price. In a risk-neutral world, the probability of the stock price being above the strike price at expiration is given by $N(d_2)$. The value of a cash or nothing call is therefore $Ke^{-rT}N(d_2)$. This is the present value of the amount to be received at maturity if the spot price is higher than the strike price multiplied by $\text{Prob}(S_t > X) = N(d_2)$.

Another type of binary option is the *asset-or-nothing-call.* This pays off nothing if the underlying stock ends below the strike price and pays an amount equal to the stock price if it ends above the strike price. We recall that $N(d_1)$ in the BS formula is the expected value of S multiplied by the probability of S being greater than X at maturity. The value of an asset-or-nothing call is then equal to $SN(d_1)$.

A regular European option is equivalent to a long position in an *asset-or-nothing* call and a short position in a *cash-or-nothing* call where the payoff equals the strike price.

Barrier Options

Barrier options are options where the payoff depends on whether the underlying asset's price reaches a certain level during a certain period of time. A number of different barrier options regularly trade. These options can be classified as either *knock-out* or *knock-in.* A knock-out option is an option that ceases to exist when the underlying asset price reaches a certain barrier.

Usually four kinds of barrier options are defined:

1. *Down-and-out.* The option ceases to exist if the asset price reaches a certain barrier level H (below the initial stock asset price).
2. *Down-and-in.* The option comes into existence if the asset price reaches a certain barrier level H (below the initial stock asset price).
3. *Up-and-out.* The option ceases to exist if the asset price reaches a certain barrier level H (above the initial stock asset price).
4. *Up-and-in.* The option comes into existence if the asset price reaches a certain barrier level H (above the initial stock asset price).

Barrier options may be viewed as conditional plain-vanilla options. "In" barrier options become plain-vanilla options if the barrier is hit. "Out" barrier options are plain-vanilla options, with the condition that they may pass out of existence if the barrier is hit. These conditions make barrier options inferior to unconditional plain-vanilla options, so barrier options will be cheaper than otherwise identical plain-vanilla options. A portfolio manager can choose a down-and-in put with a strike price slightly below the spot price to protect its portfolio at a price significantly lower than the one of a plain-vanilla put.

For barrier options, an analytic formula—more complex than the simple BS formula—exist. For barrier options, too, the underlying assumption is that the probability distribution for the asset price at a future time is lognormal.

CORRELATION OPTIONS

A new group of derivatives involving a new form of risk—the correlation risk—has been created. This group is generally referred to multifactor derivatives. The value of a multifactor derivative is determined by the behavior of two or more financial prices. In this section, we review some of these new derivatives and show how calculation of VaR is affected by this new financial instrument.

Exchange Options

An exchange asset is the option to exchange an asset for another. Upon exercising, the owned asset is exchanged for the acquired asset. If we call the owned asset Asset 1 and the underlying asset Asset 2, an exchange option may be regarded as a call on Asset 2 with the exercise price being equal to the future price on Asset 1. A simple formula can be used to evaluate an exchange asset. If both the spot prices S_1 and S_2 follow a GBM with volatilities σ_1 and σ_2 and instantaneous correlation ρ, the value of the option at time zero is

$$S_2 e^{-\eta_2 T} N(d_1) - S_1 e^{-\eta_1 T} N(d_2) \tag{12.24}$$

where $d_1 = \left[\ln(S_2/S_1) + (\eta_1 - \eta_2 + \sigma^2)T \right]/\sigma T$ and $\sigma = \sqrt{\sigma_1^2 + \sigma_2^2 + 2\rho\sigma_1\sigma_2}$

Rainbow Options

The value of a rainbow option is determined by the relative performance of two or more underlying assets. The number of assets involved determines the "colors" of the rainbow. Rainbow options can differ on the basis of their payoff structure. The most common type of rainbow option allows the owner to choose among n-assets. For example, a 2-color rainbow option would allow the owner to choose among Asset 1 and Asset 2. In some cases, a third option—a fixed cash amount—is provided to the owner. Prior to exercise, the value of the option will equal the sum of the present values of the expected payoffs. The performance of the two assets will depend, at least partially, on their degree of correlation.

Quanto Options

Quanto options are options that eliminate the exchange rate risk inherent when a buyer buys an asset denominated in a currency other than its domestic currency. For example, suppose a U.S. portfolio manager wants to buy a call option on a DM-denominated asset (e.g., the DAX) but without incurring the foreign exchange risk. This is accomplished by fixing the exchange rate on the date the option is issued. Thus, the investor is not exposed to the risk that the currency in which the underlying asset is denominated will outperform the investor's home currency. The additional risk faced by the dealer offering a quanto option is correlation risk. It is necessary for the seller of the quanto option to make some assumption about the covariance between the value of the asset and the exchange rate and to hedge the portfolio against potential changes in this covariance.

Basket Options

A basket option pays off on the basis of the aggregate value of a specified "basket" of financial assets rather than on the value of individual assets. As long as the financial assets in the portfolio are not perfectly correlated, the option on the basket will be less expensive than buying individual options for each of the assets. Basket options are generally used for currency hedging. The basket option creates an index that represents the dollar or other home currency value of a portfolio of FX positions. The premium on such an option reflects the probability that the index will change in value rather than the individual currencies will change. Basket options make use of portfolio theory, since—provided the currencies are not perfectly correlated—the volatility of the whole index will be lower than the sum of the volatilities of single currencies. A basket option is able to protect a portfolio less than the package of standard options. As we have seen, the value of the option is positively correlated with the volatility of the underlying asset. Lower volatility also implies lower cost of hedging. The low correlation among different currencies constitutes per se a form of protection that reduces the cost of hedging. Depending on the composition of the portfolio, the cost of the basket option can be as much as 20% lower than the combined premiums of individual options.[14]

For VaR purposes, both exchange options and basket options add to the complexity of plain-vanilla options, since correlations among assets not only must be estimated but may also change over time. Although for short time horizons correlations can be considered constant, for longer time horizons this effect cannot be neglected, exposing the option to additional λ (or vega) risk.

CALCULATING VaR FOR NONLINEAR INSTRUMENTS: A SIMPLIFIED APPROACH[15]

Options create a great challenge for VaR models. The calculation of VaR when a portfolio includes a large portion of nonlinear instruments can become significantly more difficult. Traditional linear models provide only a poor approximation of the true VaR. The underlying contradiction of linear models is that they assume small changes of market factors (i.e., they are *local*, see Chapters 13 to 16) while VaR is intended to calculate the risk for an unusually large movement of market factors. Traditional models are based on two assumptions:

1. Instruments' payoffs are linearly related with merket factors.
2. Market factors' changes are normally distributed.

Hypotheses 1 and 2 jointly imply that the instrument's payoffs are normally distributed too because the linear transformation of a normally distributed random variable is a normally distributed random variable as well.

Simulation techniques, on the other hand, by exactly repricing a whole portfolio for thousands of simulated scenarios, are able to fully capture both nonlinearity of payoffs and non-normality of market factors' changes. Nevertheless full simulation is very expensive in computational terms.

We propose an extremely simple approach that is able to relax the hypothesis of linearity while keeping the hypothesis of normality of market factors' changes. We only require the monotonicity of the function relating the instrument's payoffs with market factors rather than linearity. Weak positive monotonicity means that instrument's payoffs must increase or remain constant as market factors increase. Weak negative monotonicity means that instrument's payoffs must decrease or remain constant if market factors increase. The hypothesis of monotonicity wipes out the possibility of U-shaped or twisted payoff functions, while it allows for any degree of convexity (positive or negative).

If market factor changes are normally distributed, the worst scenario at 95% probability level is given by -1.65σ where σ is the standard deviation market factors' changes. Based on this assumption, we can calculate the worst *level* of the market factor at 95% probability level and use this value to reprice the instrument.

If market factors' changes are normally distributed, this method provides the same results as full simulation. We will refer to this method as limited simulation. It has in common with the full simulation approach using closed forms to calculate the new price of the instruments rather than using linear or quadratic approximations. It is computational much easier since it requires the calculation of the new price of the instrument only for selected values of market factors instead of for the full spectrum of simulated changes. These values are chosen on the basis of a normal distribution for market factors' changes (i.e., in a parametric way). We can illustrate this approach with an example using the same call option described earlier ($S = 100$, $X = 100$, $rf = 0.1$, $\sigma = 0.2$, $T = 51$ days).

Table 12.8 describes the approach. Since simulated spot prices have a standard deviation of 1.04, the worst scenarios (assuming normality) for different probability levels are 97.58 (99%), 97.96 (97.5%), and 98.28 (95%). We used these prices to calculate the day 1 values of the call option (expiration = 50 days). These values are shown in the column labeled "LS VaR." The delta VaR approximation (for a $\delta = 0.5887$) and the full simulation results also are shown. The results are remarkable. The limited simulation approach allows to capture nonlinearity of payoffs providing an impressive improvement in accuracy. The difference from full simulation is due to the slight non-normality of randomly selected data (the standardized skewness is 1.75 close to the significance level of 1.96).

The two basic assumptions (normality of market factors' changes and monotonicity of the relation between payoffs and market factors' changes) are respected. Normality is respected by definition (we draw out 1,000 numbers from a normal distribution) while monotonicity (strict positive monotonicity for a call option) is satisfied because of the intrinsic properties of call options. For put options, we would have had strict negative monotonicity.

It is worthwhile to underline that limited simulation works also for any distribution provided its cumulative function is known. If market

TABLE 12.8 Limited Simulation Approach with a Plain-Vanilla European Call Option

	Black-Scholes		
Spot	Delta VaR	LS VaR	FS VaR
97.58	−1.43	−1.31	−1.28
97.96	−1.20	−1.13	−1.10
98.28	−1.01	−0.97	−0.94

**TABLE 12.9 Limited Simulation
Approach with a European Lookback
Call Option**

Spot	Lookback	
	Delta VaR pv	LS VaR
97.577	−1.48	−1.26
97.962	−1.24	−1.11
98.284	−1.05	−0.97

factors' changes were generated by a t-distribution with, say, 5 degrees of freedom, a scenario with 5% probability level would have occurred if spot price would have changed by 2.015σ (rather than 1.645σ). The corresponding spot price would have been 97.904 (instead of 98.28) and the VaR $3.7064 - 2.5485 = 1.1579$. The "full" simulation approach would have required 1,000 new randomly selected numbers from a t-distribution to be selected, the payoffs for each of this price recalculated, and the 5% lowest percentile observed.

The limited simulation approach is flexible enough to be adapted to almost any exotic option (see Table 12.9). We used limited simulation to calculate VaR for a lookback call option identical to the previous plain-vanilla call but with a minimum price (equivalent to the strike price) of 95 rather than 100. The δ of the lookback option has been calculated for a 1% change of the spot price and was equal to about 0.61 (see Table 12.9).

As shown, the limited simulation approach provides a fairly easy way to include nonlinearity of payoffs in the calculation of VaR, correcting (for call options positively) the intrinsic overestimation of linear approaches.

For portfolios made up of multiple assets, the LS approach can be used to calculate undiversified VaR for each asset or risk factors. Aggregation of risk across market factors and/or multiple assets is performed through the familiar approach of the variance-covariance matrix of market factors' changes (see also Chapter 4).

NOTES

1. The example is taken from S. Das, *Risk Management and Financial Derivatives,* New York: McGraw Hill, 1998, 575–585.

2. The forward price is given by $1.44(1 + 0.02)/(1 + 0.06) = 1.3857$. Since the U.S. domestic rate is higher than the Swiss rate, we expect an appreciation of the USD vis-à-vis the CHF.

3. S. Das, *Risk Management and Financial Derivatives,* 573.

4. *Ibid.,* 575.

5. Sometimes the Greek letter λ (lambda) is defined as the percentage change of option price in response to a 1% change in the spot price (elasticity of the option price to the spot price) is judicated. See S. Das, *ibid.,* 385.

6. For sake of simplicity, we will refer hereafter to a call option. The same line of reasoning can be applied to a put option but formulas need to be slightly modified.

7. This is true for a call option. For a put option, approximations based on delta coefficient will lead only to overestimation of the option price.

8. See J. Hull, *Options, Futures and other Derivatives,* Englewood Cliffs, NJ: Prentice Hall, 1997, 320.

9. A further measure of option price sensitivity to spot price is called *speed* and is the third derivative of the option price to the spot price; it measures the rate of change of gamma as the spot price changes.

10. See P. Jorion, *Value at Risk: The New Benchmark for Controlling Derivatives Risk,* New York: McGraw-Hill, 1997, 144.

11. In our analysis we have considered almost exclusively option sensitivity to risk factors such as the spot price, volatility, and interest rates. Option sensitivity can be measured with respect to time to expiry. For example, the *charme* measures the change of delta in response to a change in the time to expiry, and *colour* measures the change of gamma in response to a change in the time to expiry.

12. The following section is based extensively on R. Kolb, *Futures, Options and Swaps,* Blackwell, 1997, Chapter 18.

13. See J. Hull, *Options, Futures, and Other Derivatives,* Englewood Cliffs, NJ: Prentice Hall, 1997, 466.

14. See C. Smithson and C. Smith Jr., *Managing Financial Risk: A Guide to Derivative Products, Financial Engineering and Value Maximization,* Irwin, 1990, 399.

15. The calculations provided in this chapter for plain-vanilla and exotic options have been performed using the software *OPTION!*

13

Calculating VaR: An Overview

In Chapter 4, we provided a brief introduction to VaR, assuming that market-factor expected returns were normally distributed and that a linear relationship between each market-factor expected return and asset or portfolio return could be estimated. This approach is an overwhelming simplification, since, as we have seen in Chapters 10 to 12, the relationship between market-factor returns and asset returns (especially for bonds and options) is not linear. Furthermore, we know from Chapters 5 to 9 that asset returns rarely conform to the normal distribution, but are often leptokurtic—if not fractal indeed!

The method we used in Chapter 4 is the most intuitive for those who have a financial background, since it heavily relies on modern portfolio theory. Nevertheless there are other possible approaches that try to circumvent the implicit weaknesses of the model outlined (known as *delta-normal* model), even if at the cost of more complexity. In Chapters 13 to 16, we review models most used for calculating the VaR of a portfolio of assets, underlining the pros and cons of each model and analyzing the methodological and statistical assumptions implied in each model.

Chapter 13 is devoted to a general overlook on the issues implied in the calculation of the Value at Risk. Chapters 14 to 16 are devoted to the analysis of the three most common class of methods for calculating VaR: parametric "normal" models, historical simulation models, and Monte Carlo simulation models.

ISSUES FOR CALCULATING VALUE AT RISK

The calculation of the Value at Risk for a single asset or for a portfolio of assets is based on two critical steps:

1. Estimating the asset/portfolio sensitivity to market factors.
2. Estimating the (joint) probability distribution of market returns over the desired time horizon.

Once these estimations are obtained, the calculation of the VaR is possible and easily implemented. The standard RiskMetrics approach assumes linearity for Step 1 and normality for Step 2. If *both* these hypotheses hold, it is possible to have a closed-form formula for the VaR of a portfolio like the one used in Chapter 4:

$$\text{VaR} = \alpha\sqrt{x'\Sigma x}\ \sqrt{\Delta t} \tag{13.1}$$

where α is the constant that gives the appropriate one-tailed confidence interval for the standardized normal distribution, x is the Nx1 vector of undiversified VaR for each "position" in the portfolio, and Σ is the correlation matrix of market-factor returns.

The most common critiques to VaR models do not rely on its conceptual framework or on its practical usefulness, but rather on the joint assumptions (linearity and normality) that are implicit in the most common computational techniques. That is why we devoted such a large part of this work to the analysis of alternative statistical tools for modeling returns and risk of financial assets.

The three most common critiques rely on:

1. Assumptions about the sensitivity of portfolio return to market factors.
2. The probability distribution of expected returns.
3. Parameter assumptions.

PORTFOLIO SENSITIVITY ASSUMPTIONS

Assumptions about portfolio sensitivity to market returns are one of the basic ingredients for calculating the VaR. There is a certain degree of discretion in the choice of factors. The most obvious choice is to rely on financial theory, it is not assured that asset returns can be explained by state-of-the-art models. This is especially true for equity, where (see Chapter 11) standard models such as CAPM or APT have a relatively small explanatory power.

Risk Misspecification

In other words, standard models capture only some risk that can affect the value of a portfolio of assets. Specific risk factors, for example, can affect single equity returns and, hence, the return of a portfolio where this equity is included. Idiosyncratic (i.e., specific) volatility is a source of risk generally not accounted for in standard equity pricing models. We can refer to this problem, with an analogy with econometric model building, as *risk misspecification.*

Options and Fixed Income Securities

The problem of risk misspecification is even greater for options. Standard VaR approaches include only price risk (delta risk) in their calculations; sometimes gamma risk is included, but it is only a second-order approximation of the delta risk, much like convexity is a second-order approximation of fixed-income securities pricing. Standard methods fail to include the volatility or vega risk for options even if (particularly for trading portfolios) it can be a significant source of risk, especially if the portfolio is constrained to be delta-hedged (hedged against price risk). If we include volatility as another market factor, we can consider vega risk as a different form of delta risk and incorporate it into standard VaR calculation approaches.

For options and fixed-income securities, as shown in Chapters 10 to 12, second-order approximation is of crucial importance to assess price risk in response to changes of the price of market factors.

The size of the error increases with the size of the market movement; therefore, although linear approximation methods work well for small changes in market factors, they fail to capture price risk when market factors changes are significant. The use of a second-order approximation significantly reduces the size of the error.

Second-order approximation is needed not only to adjust linear approximation of price changes due to market-factor changes but also to capture important cross-gamma effects. An example[1] is an at-the-money foreign currency interest rate forward rate agreement (FRA). Profits and losses, and hence Value at Risk, is reported in the domestic currency. As long as the currency FRA is at-the-money, there will be no currency risk. However, if foreign interest rates were to move in an adverse manner, creating a foreign currency loss, their impact could be mitigated or exacerbated by foreign exchange rate movements when translating the losses into domestic currency. The net impact on risk capital depends on whether foreign interest rates are positively or negatively correlated with exchange rate movements. This cross-rate effect caused by P&Ls translation may be of substantial importance for all standard, first-generation products such as forward rate agreements, straight equity positions, FX forwards, interest rate and currency swaps. Second-order cross-rate effects become even more important for some second-generation correlation products (e.g., choosers, diff swaps, or quantos, etc.), which are expressly designed to play a view on correlation risks.

A delta-gamma approximation overcomes many of these problems by capturing the direct- and cross-gamma (or convexity) risks of the portfolio and incorporation them into the VaR calculation. This is the objective of the delta-gamma method, described in Chapter 14.

Local versus Full Valuation Methods

Methods relying on portfolio sensitivity to market factors for calculating VaR suffer from the remarkable drawback that they are often able to approximate price changes of a portfolio for small variations of market factors only. Standard "local" sensitivity measures, or "Greeks," such as deltas, gammas, and vegas are often used as the basis for representing the portfolio P&Ls profile when calculating VaR. To enhance accuracy, analysts sometimes construct a Taylor Series Expansion to represent the portfolio payoff profile, which greatly simplifies the calculations.

These representations of the portfolio P&Ls profile based on local measures may be insufficient to fully characterize the portfolio payoff for large market events. Although the delta-gamma method captures the portfolio's convexity or gamma risk, increasing accuracy, it still suffers from the fact that the approximation error most likely increases with extreme market rate movements. Thus, using local risk measures alone may be inadequate when calculating VaR in response to very large movements. The point is that sensitivity parameters themselves change so that even nonlinear approximation techniques become inadequate if market factors movements are large. The option delta, for example, changes as the price of the underlying asset changes. Large variations in the price of the underlying asset lead to a change in the value of delta that cannot be accounted for by local risk measures.

Large Market Movements and Liquidity

An implicit assumption of local methods is that liquidity does not change as a consequence of market-factor changes. While it may be true for very small variations, it is extremely likely that large market movements lead to a decrease of liquidity and hence to an underestimation of risk. The implicit assumption of constant liquidity is that it is always possible to rebalance portfolios as needed. In some situations, however, it is not possible, or is possible only at the expense of further losses.

DISTRIBUTIONAL ASSUMPTIONS

Leptokurtosis

In Chapter 8, we emphasized how actual time series of returns depart from the standard hypothesis of normality. In particular, these series are leptokurtic (i.e., they have a peak around the mean higher than the normal distribution and have fatter tails than the normal distribution). The consequence of fatter tails is straightforward. Large events are more likely to occur than predicted by a normal distribution. Using a normal distribution for calculating VaR while the actual distribution is leptokurtic leads to an underestimation of risk, simply because events larger than 2σ or smaller than -2σ are actually more likely to occur than 5% (provided σ is finite). Two possible approaches are possible to overcome these departures for normality:

1. Increase the distance from the mean when assessing risk for a given level of probability (looking at 3σ for 95% level of probability in a two-tailed test).
2. Use different distributions for market factors' variations, such as the Student-t distributions or Pareto stable distributions.

Stability of Relationships

Most methods of calculating risk capital rely on estimates of the volatilities and correlations of market-factor changes to aggregate diverse risky positions. These parameters are estimated based on specific statistical models, many of which require that the parameters be constant over the sample period (provided they exist).

The problem is that correlation may be highly unstable; in extreme situations, correlation between market-factor returns may dramatically change, as the European Monetary System (EMS) crisis of 1992 demonstrated. So, while the risk manager might believe he or she is entering into a relatively riskless position, the amount of VaR should actually be much higher since the relationship itself, although historically stable, might prove to be unstable in times of stress. Suppose, for example, to have an asset denominated in deutsche mark and a liability denominated in Dutch guilder.[2] The historical correlation between these two currencies is very high, close to one.

Based on historical correlation, the VaR for the combined position is very low since any gain (loss) on the DEM-denomiated asset would be offset by a loss (gain) on the NLG-denominated liability. Nevertheless, in an extreme situation, this correlation may dramatically change (e.g., falling to 0.75), thus increasing the VaR for the joint position.

These same qualitative statements can also be made regarding the stability of market-factor volatilities. As shown in Chapter 7, forecasting techniques for conditional heteroskedasticity have been developed to describe and forecast market rate dynamics. These techniques have been included to perform a better forecast of future market-factor changes and are used in simulation techniques such as Monte Carlo techniques. Nonetheless, these "next generation" methods are not immune to the criticisms of traditional methods assuming constant volatility. Although they may provide better forecasts in normal 2σ times, their prediction capability in 5σ times is highly questionable.

An important caveat when using models that incorporate sophisticated techniques is that although they increase prediction accuracy and have proven to be useful for assessing VaR as well as supporting front-office activities, these models (and *all* models) must be backtested continuously against actual market developments.

SUMMARY OF ISSUES REGARDING VaR CALCULATIONS

As noted when introducing VaR models in Chapter 4, a major source of criticism depends on the relative arbitrariness of some of the key parameters, especially confidence level and time horizon. Both the confidence level and the time horizon vary at different institutions. While J.P. Morgan uses a 95% confidence level and a daily time horizon, Bankers Trust uses a 99% confidence level and a 1-year time horizon. While the G-30 recommends a 95% confidence level and 1-day holding period, the Bank of International Settlements (BIS) Market Risk Guidelines recommends the use of 99% confidence level and a 10-day holding period.

This fact makes comparison among different models difficult. BZW sets its time horizon equal to an "orderly liquidation period." This approach has the advantage of allocating more capital to illiquid position but must be assessed on a case-to-case basis. In addition, the standard approach of scaling VaR using the square root of time to make measures of VaR comparable for different time horizons relies on the normality assumption, which is all but empirically tested (see Chapter 10 for the consequences of Pareo-stable distributions of returns for the process of scaling risk). Table 13.1 summarizes some of the most common criticisms of VaR calculation methods.

TABLE 13.1 Summary of Critiques of VaR Calculation Methods

Portfolio Sensitivity		Distributional Assumptions		Parameters Choice
Standard models	Critique	Standard models	Critique	Time horizon
Linearity of price changes (sometimes a quadratic approximation is added)	Delta ignores convexity or gamma risk	Normality of market factors' changes (or returns)	Leptokurtosis	Confidence level
	Delta + gamma do not provide good approximations for large market movements		Skewness	
			Unstable volatilities and correlations	
			Infinite variance and Pareto-stable distributions	
	Other risks (vega and rho) are often not included in standard models			
	Liquidity problems are not accounted for (it is always possible to rebalance a portfolio)			

NOTES

1. The example is provided by T. Wilson, "Calculating Risk Capital," in C. Alexander, *The Handbook of Risk Management and Analysis,* New York: John Wiley & Sons, 1996.

2. Obviously, before the introduction of the Euro in 1999!

14

Parametric Normal Models

P arametric models are the most common used model to calculate VaR. They assume normality of returns (the attribute "parametric" stems from the fact that they rely on a specific distribution assumption). In this chapter, we present four alternative approaches:

1. Portfolio normal.
2. Asset-normal (RiskMetrics).
3. Delta-normal.
4. Delta-gamma.

The first three models assume linearity of the portfolios' payoffs. The last model allows for nonlinearity of payoffs.

PORTFOLIO-NORMAL METHOD

This method calculates the VaR as a multiple of the standard deviation of the portfolio's returns:

$$\text{VaR} = \alpha \, \sigma_p \, \sqrt{t} \tag{14.1}$$

where α is the constant that gives the appropriate one-tailed confidence level interval for the standardized normal distribution while σ_p is the standard deviation of the portfolio over the chosen time horizon.

This approach is based on the assumption of normality of portfolio returns:

$$R_p \approx N\left(\mu_p, \, \sigma_p\right) \tag{14.2}$$

This approach can be justified:

- If the portfolio consists of even a small number of assets the returns of which are normally distributed.
- The portfolio is made of a large number of positions whose limiting distribution is the normal distribution.

Given these assumptions, all the limitations seen in Table 14.1 apply.

The portfolio-normal method is useful in two contexts. The first context involves well-diversified portfolios comprising a large quantity of independent positions whose limiting distribution is the normal distribution. Provided that the distributions of returns of any asset in the portfolio have a finite mean and variance, we can invoke the central limit theorem and hypothesize that portfolio returns are normally distributed. The second potential use of this method is to develop a fast approach to measuring the capital allocation for trading business units. If we could observe the past records of returns of any trading business units, it would be possible to calculate the mean and the standard deviation of returns (for example, quarterly or annual returns). It would be possible to set

TABLE 14.1   Comparison of Different Parametric Normal Methods

	Portfolio Normal	Asset/ Delta-Normal	Delta-Gamma
Description	Assumes that portfolio returns are normally distributed. $VaR = \alpha * \sigma$	Assumes that assets' returns (or market factors' returns) are jointly normal, implying linear assets, payoffs, and normally distributed portfolio returns.	Assumes that market rate innovations are normally distributed and that payoffs can be approximated by local, second-order terms.
Advantages	Simplicity	Simplicity	Captures some forms of nonlinearity of payoffs
Disadvantages	Ignores leptokurtosis, skewness	Ignores leptokurtosis, skewness Predictable and stable covariances Linearity of payoffs	Ignores leptokurtosis, skewness Predictable and stable covariances Does not capture risk of nonlocal movements

aside reserves to cover possible losses or to set trading limits for the whole units.

It cannot be considered a definitive solution for risk measurement and management, especially if portfolios include a large portion of highly nonlinear assets (e.g., options) or when evaluating a portfolio of businesses. Its main plus is its simplicity: compared with asset-normal and delta-normal methods, it does not require the estimation of a large correlation matrix.

ASSET-NORMAL (RISKMETRICS) APPROACH

Differently from the portfolio-normal method, this method calculates the standard deviation of the portfolio on the base of the weights of any single assets in the portfolio and the correlation among returns of different assets included in the portfolio.

$$\text{VaR} = \alpha \, \sigma_p \, \sqrt{t} \qquad\qquad (14.3)$$

The standard deviation of the portfolio, instead of being estimated on the basis of historical returns of the portfolio, is calculated using Equation 14.4:

$$\sigma_p = \sqrt{w' \, \Sigma \, w} \qquad\qquad (14.4)$$

where w in the $N \times 1$ of portfolio weighted undiversified VaRs and Σ is the correlation matrix of position returns.

The underlying assumptions are:

- Positions' returns are jointly normally distributed. What we assume is that *returns on single positions*[1] *included in the portfolio* (zero bonds—or coupon bonds mapped—equity index, equity options, etc.) are normally distributed.
- The normality of portfolio returns stems from the fact that each position in the portfolio has normally distributed returns. In fact, since the sum of n normally distributed random variables is a normally distributed random variable, the portfolio returns are normally distributed too.

The asset-normal approach has a particular appeal since it directly derives from modern portfolio theory (MPT) by Harry Markowitz. In fact, its basic assumptions (normality of assets' returns and that the standard deviation of the portfolio returns is the measure of risk) are the grounds on which both MPT and, lately, CAPM are founded.

The asset-normal method is the methodological basis of RiskMetrics, the famous software by J.P. Morgan (disclosed in the early 1990s even on the Internet) that has had a tremendous impact on the whole industry and has boosted the interest and researches about Value at Risk.

Nonetheless, the asset-normal approach suffers from the same drawbacks outlined in Chapter 13:

- It relies on normality of positions' returns.
- It is a local method (i.e., it works well only for infinitesimal changes of positions' returns).
- It is an exclusively linear method; it does not include any quadratic (or second-order) approximation for assets (namely options) with highly nonlinear payoff.
- It is computationally intensive, since it requires not only assets' decomposition and cash flows mapping but also the computation of a highly extended correlation matrix.

THE DELTA-NORMAL METHOD

The most obvious problem with the asset-normal method is that it is extremely computationally intensive, especially when the number of positions increases. For N positions it is in fact necessary to calculate N variances plus $N(N-1)/2$ covariances. The rationale of the delta-normal method is to reduce the computational burden imposed by the asset-normal method by identifying a limited set of risk factors and linking price changes (or returns) of single assets to price changes (or returns) of *market factors*. The use of a limited number of risk factors contains the number of correlations and facilitates efficient calculation of market risk even for large portfolios. This reduction of the dimensionality of the problem is accomplished by focusing on risk factors (market factors) rather than on risk positions. It does not wipe out the necessity of decomposition (the classic example is a currency FRA that must be decomposed into three fundamental positions reflecting its sources of risk—domestic money market rate, foreign money market rate, and exchange rate), but it greatly simplifies the calculations required. For fixed income securities, an alternative approach to cash flow mapping is to use modified duration as the coefficient linking market factor changes (market interest rate) to price changes of the asset.

Risk and Return on a Portfolio

Under this delta-normal model, single assets' variations are obtained multiplying estimated variations for each market factor by sensitivity parameters that measure the variation, for example, of the asset in response to variations of market factors j. These sensitivity parameters are called *delta factors*.

Formally, we assume that the market value of a portfolio is function of a set of M market factors S, for example, $MV_p = f(S_1, S_2, S_3, \ldots, S_M)$. The market value of the portfolio can be rewritten as

$$MV_p = \theta \Delta t + \Sigma_j \delta_j \Delta S_j X_j = \theta \Delta t + \delta' \Delta S \tag{14.5}$$

where X_j is the portfolio exposure to market factor j

$$\delta' \text{ is } \left[\partial MV / \partial S_1, \partial MV / \partial S_2, \ldots, \partial MV / \partial S_M \right]$$

For delta models, the change in price of a portfolio is given by Equation 14.6:

$$\Delta MV_p = \theta \Delta t + \delta' \Delta S \tag{14.6}$$

where $\theta \Delta t$ is the portfolio's value changes due to time (the portfolio's theta multiplied by the time interval).

The risk of the portfolio is given by Equation 14.7:

$$\sigma_p = \sqrt{\delta' \Sigma \delta} \tag{14.7}$$

The VaR can be calculated by Equation 14.8

$$\text{VaR} = \alpha \, \sigma_p \sqrt{t} \tag{14.8}$$

The Choice of Market Factors

The process of risk decomposition is intrinsically linked to the number of risk factors specified. The selection of risk factors is inevitably a compromise between the accurate and full capture of the market risk of the portfolio and the computational efficiency considerations identified. In practice, the following minimum risk factors have been nominated by the BIS in its Market Risk Guidelines:

- *Fixed income.* To be represented by cash flows allocated to a number of maturity points (a minimum of 6 vertices—RiskMetrics has 15 vertices) sufficient to capture exposure to changes in zero and forward rates as well as changes in yield curve shape. The credit risk of fixed income securities is captured through the use of a minimum of two yield curves, namely, a risk-free government curve and a credit-adjusted yield curve (usually the swap curve). The credit spread curve is required to be specified such that any specific credit risk is captured in the risk measures.
- *Currency.* Represented by relevant cash flows.
- *Equity.* At minimum, should be related to marketwide movements in the relevant equity market, based on the equity market index, with individual stock positions being captured by utilizing the beta of the stock.
- *Commodity.* Risk should encompass both the directional price risk and other aspects of the commodity risk including basis risks of change in convenience yields.

Assumptions of Delta-Normal

The delta-normal model is based on these assumptions:

- Market factors' changes have joint normal density functions: estimates of future volatility of market factors' changes and covariances between changes of market factors are based on this hypothesis.
- There is a *linear* relationship between market factors' changes and single asset's changes: this means that changes in a portfolio's values can be obtained by a linear transformation of market factors' changes.
- Since a linear combination of normal variables is a normal variable itself, the assumption of normality of market factors' changes implies that portfolio's changes density function is normal as well.

Use of the Delta-Normal Model

Delta-normal method is a reasonable compromise between accuracy and complexity. It is well suited for short time horizons (e.g., intraday variations) and for portfolios with few or no options included. Compared to asset-normal, it has the advantage that it can capture volatility risk (if volatility is considered one of the market factors) and reduce the dimensionality of the problem significantly.

DELTA-GAMMA METHODOLOGY

Delta-gamma models are a natural extension of delta-normal models. It is aimed at capturing convexity risk still using local measures rather than global measures. Compared to simulation models (see Chapter 15), delta-gamma methodology is easier to implement while providing increased accuracy in estimation.

In this section, we provide a closed-form approximation for calculating VaR with delta-gamma methodology although other approaches (quadratic optimization and numerical iteration) can be used.

Market Factors Assumptions

Delta-gamma methodology relies on a standard assumption regarding market factors' changes: that market factors' changes are jointly normally distributed with zero mean:

$$\Delta S \approx N(0, \Sigma \Delta t) \tag{14.9}$$

where Σ is the $M \times M$ covariance matrix of market factors' innovations, Δt is the elapsed time, and market factors' innovations are assumed to have zero mean. From a theoretical point of view, this assumption can be justified for all diffusion processes by using Ito's lemma if the time horizon is sufficiently short.

This assumption is also consistent with the idea that market factors are governed by a joint geometrical Brownian motion process. To incorporate vega risk into our analytical framework, we can consider implicit volatility of market factors itself as a market factor included in variance-covariance matrix Σ.

Price Sensitivity Assumptions

The assumptions about the change of value of our portfolio are standard. The price function of the portfolio can be considered a generalization of Equation 14.5 where a quadratic term is added. Equation 14.10 is a Taylor-series expansion of the current market value of the portfolio up to the second order in contrast with the first-order approximation of delta-normal models.

$$
\begin{aligned}
\Delta MV_p &= \theta \Delta t + \delta' \Delta S + \tfrac{1}{2} \Delta S' \gamma \Delta S' + o(3) \\
&\approx \theta \Delta t + \delta' \Delta S + \tfrac{1}{2} \Delta S' \gamma \Delta S'
\end{aligned}
\tag{14.10}
$$

where θ is the portfolios' theta or $\partial MV/\partial t$

δ is the $M \times 1$ vector of delta sensitivities to changes in market factors or $\partial MV/\partial S_j$

γ is an $M \times M$ gamma-cross gamma symmetric matrix with respect to various market factors or $\partial^2 MV/\partial S_i \partial S_i$

By treating interest rates and volatility as market factors, we can incorporate rho and vega into our framework considering them as two additional deltas.

The γ matrix is the Hessian of the market value function of the portfolio (the vector δ is the Jacobean). On the main diagonal, the gamma matrix shows the second derivatives of market value of the portfolio to any single market factor. They represent the rate of change of the respective delta coefficient with respect to the market factor. The off-diagonal elements represent the cross-second derivative of the market value of the portfolio with respect to two different market factors. Usually off-diagonal elements of the γ matrix are trivial and can be ignored.[2]

Calculation Rule

Following the standard definition, VaR is the maximum loss over a specified time horizon within a given confidence interval. In its essence, it is an optimization problem that can be solved by maximizing an objective function subject to one or more constraints. If we know in advance the boundaries of the confidence interval, there is no need of optimization (this is the case for previously illustrated methods). In this case, the problem is more complex since delta-gamma methodology involves a second-order transformation of market factors' innovations. So, even if Equation 14.9 holds, the outcomes of Equation 14.10 will not be normally distributed.

In general, the problem of calculating VaR is expressed by Equation 14.11:

$$\text{VaR} = Max\left[\delta'\Delta S + \tfrac{1}{2}\Delta S'\gamma\Delta S\right]$$

$$\text{subject to } \Delta S' \Sigma^{-1} \Delta S \le \alpha^2$$

(14.11)

where α is the number of standard deviations required to give the one-tailed confidence interval for the desired probability level. The form $\Delta S \Sigma^{-1} \Delta S$ defines an M-dimensional ellipsoid for the joint innovations of market factors.

Our objective is to find out the worst case (given by the combination of market factors' innovations that lies at the interior or at the boundaries of the ellipsoid) and then calculate the VaR for the given portfolio.

There are several possible approaches to solve Equation 14.11 that respect the given constraints. A formal demonstration is beyond the scope of this book. We provide the results of two possible approaches: (1) Quadratic optimization, and (2) Closed form solution.

Quadratic Optimization

A possible approach is to solve Equation 14.11 as a classic quadratic optimization problem. The Kuhn-Tucker condition is defined by the first derivative of the constrained function:

$$\frac{\partial\left[\delta'\Delta S + \frac{1}{2}\Delta S'\gamma\Delta S' + \lambda\left(\Delta S'\Sigma^{-1}\Delta S - \alpha^2\right)\right]}{\partial\Delta S} = 0$$

$$\delta' + \gamma\Delta S + \lambda\Sigma^{-1}\Delta S = 0$$

$$\delta' = \left(-\gamma - \lambda\Sigma^{-1}\right)\Delta S = A(\lambda)\Delta S$$

(14.12)

A possible solution consists of performing a numerical search over $\lambda \geq 0$, inverting $A(\lambda)$ for each λ and to solve for ΔS verifying that the constraint is satisfied. As long as the number of market factors—and hence the dimension of Σ—is not relevant, this process can be solved through functions normally available in spreadsheets such as Microsoft Excel.

Closed-Form Approximation[3]

To obtain a closed-form approximation for delta-gamma methodology, we need to make some transformations in original data. The objective is to make individual factors independent from one another and to isolate their first- and second-order influence on the portfolio's value. By isolating each risk factor, its influence is approximated via a linear function valid only when the worst scenario is likely to occur (at the boundaries of the M-dimensional ellipsoid). Having linearized the portfolio's sensitivities to the transformed risk factor at the extremes, we could use the properties of the normal distribution and apply the standard RiskMetrics formula to calculate Value at Risk.

The original market factors' innovations ΔS are transformed into ΔS^* so that $\Delta S^* \approx N(0, I)$. This can be obtained by multiplying the original ΔS by $T'P^{-1}$ where P is the nonsingular Cholesky decomposition of Σ (so that $P'P = \Sigma$) and T is the orthogonal matrix that satisfies the equation $T'(P'\gamma P)T = \gamma^*$ where γ^* is the diagonal matrix of the eigenvalues of $P'\gamma P$ and T is also the matrix of the eigenvectors of $P'\gamma P$.

It follows that Equation 14.11 can be rewritten as:

$$\text{VaR} = Max\left[\delta^{*\prime}\,\Delta S^* + \tfrac{1}{2}\Delta S^{*\prime}\,\gamma^*\Delta S^{*\prime}\right]$$

subject to $\Delta S^{*\prime}\,\Delta S \le \alpha^2$

(14.13)

where $\delta^* = T'P'\delta$. By construction, Equation 14.12 is equal to 14.11. The difference is that market factors are now independent from each other and their impact can be analyzed separately.

We can concentrate only on one factor i. The objective function is transformed into

$$\text{VaR}_i = Max\left[\delta_i^{*\prime}\,\Delta S_i^* + \tfrac{1}{2}\Delta S_i^{*\prime}\,\gamma_{ii}^*\,\Delta S_i^*\right]$$

(14.14)

To derive the worst possible scenario, we take the first-order condition that gives Equation 14.15:

$$\frac{\partial \text{VaR}_i}{\partial \Delta S_i^*} = \phi_i \Delta S_i^*$$

(14.15)

where $\phi_i = (\delta_i^* + \gamma_{ii}^*\,\alpha/2)$ since, at the extremes, $\Delta S_i^{\prime *}\,\Delta S_i^* = \alpha$.

The coefficient ϕ_i can be considered the delta of the portfolio for a change of the transformed market factor S_i^*. Substituting Equation 14.14 for Equation 14.13 linearizes (locally) the portfolio payoff. The approximate delta coefficient ϕ_i incorporates the effect of nonlinearity being dependent on γ.

We can now restate the classic delta-normal formula for calculating VaR:

$$\text{VaR} = \alpha\sigma_{\delta\gamma}\sqrt{\Delta t}$$

(14.16)

where $\sigma_{\delta\gamma} = \sqrt{\Sigma_i\,\phi^2_{\,i}} = \sqrt{\phi'\phi}$ where ϕ' is the vector of the approximate delta coefficients of the portfolio.

This approach has many advantages:

- It captures the portfolio's straight and cross-gamma risk and includes it into the calculation of VaR.
- It uses readily available portfolio information requiring less system integration and effort.

Notably, if the original payoff can be expressed only as a linear combination of market factors' changes ($\gamma = 0$), Equation 14.16 becomes:

$$\text{VaR} = \alpha\sqrt{\delta^{*'}\delta}\sqrt{\Delta t} = \alpha\sqrt{(T'P'\delta)'(T'P'\delta)}\sqrt{\Delta t}$$
$$= \alpha\sqrt{\delta PTT'P'\delta}\sqrt{\Delta t} = \alpha\sqrt{\delta PP'\delta}\sqrt{\Delta t} = \alpha\sqrt{\delta \Sigma^{-1}\delta}\sqrt{\Delta t} \qquad (14.17)$$

CONFIDENCE INTERVAL FOR PARAMETRIC VaR

The usefulness of any VaR estimate depends on its precision. How confident can management be in this estimate? VaR figures are nothing else than random variables, subject to estimation error that can be so large to make the calculated figure useless.

The most natural way to gauge the precision of a VaR estimate is to construct a confidence interval. Under the assumption of normality of portfolio returns, this task can be easily accomplished. The main difficulty is that the standard deviation of portfolio returns is unknown and must be estimated. The precision of the estimated VaR depends on the precision of the estimated standard deviation of the portfolio's returns. If we denote by s^2 the estimated standard deviation of portfolio returns and by σ^2 the true standard deviation, the variable $(n - 1)\,s^2/\sigma^2$ is distributed as a χ^2 with $n - 1$ degrees of freedom. Therefore, a 95% confidence interval for σ^2 is given by:

$$\frac{(n-1)s^2}{\chi^2_{0.975}} < \sigma^2 < \frac{(n-1)s^2}{\chi^2_{0.025}} \qquad (14.18)$$

and therefore

$$-1.65sP_0\sqrt{\left[\frac{(n-1)}{\chi^2_{0.975}}\right]} < \text{VaR} = -1.65\sigma P_0$$
$$< -1.65sP_0\sqrt{\left[\frac{(n-1)}{\chi^2_{0.025}}\right]} \qquad (14.19)$$

where P_0 is the initial portfolio value.

We can use this approach wherever we can assume that the distribution of the portfolio's P&Ls is stable and normal. Under delta-gamma approximation, normality of market factors' returns does not imply normality of portfolio's returns, so this approach can be used only in the context of parametric normal models.

CONCLUSION

The choice of the best method—among the class of parametric normal methods—is often related to the objective to be pursued. Sometimes a "quick and dirty" solution is more effective than a complex and sophisticated solution, since the increase in accuracy is not worth the effort needed. In Table 14.1, we present a synoptic comparison of the methods we have examined. The choice of the method is left to the financial analyst and the risk managers and depends on the specific context where these models are applied.

NOTES

1. We use the word *position* instead of asset to indicate the relevant cash flow after the asset has been decomposed into its fundamental components and its cash flows allocated to the proper vertices.

2. But it is not always the case. See the example of a currency FRA.

3. For more details see T. Wilson, "Calculating Risk Capital," in C. Alexander, *The Handbook of Risk Management and Analysis,* John Wiley & Sons, 1996, 205-210.

15

Historical
Simulation Models

I n Chapter 14, we examined the so-called parametric methods (i.e., methods that expressly rely on a given probability distribution of returns to calculate VaR). Simulation models provide an alternative approach. Simulation models, although computationally more intensive than parametric methods, overcome many of the weaknesses evidenced by parametric models. Simulation models can be divided into two groups:

1. Historical simulation models.
2. Monte Carlo models.

In this chapter, we review the historical simulation technique. Chapter 16 is devoted to analyzing Monte Carlo techniques.

SIMULATION VERSUS PARAMETRIC APPROACH:
AN OVERVIEW

Before analyzing in detail historical simulation techniques, we will briefly review the most important differences between the two approaches. This comparison will help us understand the pros and cons of both these approaches for calculating VaR.

The first characteristic of simulation models is that they are *full valuation* models (vs. parametric methods, which are *local*). It means that every time a change of market factors is simulated, all the assets in the portfolio are simultaneously repriced. There is no use of linear and (eventually) quadratic approximation as with parametric methods. Consequently, simulation models have as their output the true price change of the portfolio rather than an approximation. This characteristic is important especially when the relationship between market factors and single assets is not linear as with options. Simulation models can thus solve the methodological paradox between the rational underlying parametric models (yielding approximations for small changes of market factors) and the fact that VaR is calculated for relatively rare events that require significant changes of market factors since, even for a 95% confidence level, market factors are required to change for 1.65σ. The result is often an approximation error that may be significant.

A second distinctive feature of simulation models is about how VaR is computed. With parametric models, VaR is computed analytically by defining confidence intervals based on the assumption of normality of assets or market factors' changes. In simulation models (an example for a simulated time series is given in Chapter 4), VaR is calculated on the basis of actual percentiles. Out of, say, 1,000 P&Ls on a portfolio, VaR is computed by excluding the worst 50 outcomes for a 95% level of probability. This approach is by far more flexible than the parametric models because it allows the incorporation of situations where payoffs are not linearly— or even positively—correlated with market factors' changes. The payoff of a long straddle is a good example where losses are incurred for small or no variations of the underlying asset (and then of the appropriate market factor) while profits are incurred for large variations, regardless the direction of the changes.

When the relationship between a portfolio and market factors is not strictly increasing or strictly decreasing over the full range of values that the market factor can take, then any calculation based on confidence intervals drawn from the market factors' changes distribution will be misleading in terms of P&Ls of the portfolio. In this case (e.g., a straddle) only the use of percentiles on simulated P&Ls distribution can avoid this problem.

Last, simulation models are independent from the hypothesis of normality of assets' returns or market factors' returns. Parametric models rely on normality to define confidence intervals. With probability density functions (pdfs) other than the normal distribution, there would be serious problems in terms of analytical tractability. Although analysts recognize that empirical distributions have fatter tails, they often overcome the problem by artificially increasing the number of σ for a given level of probability for every level of probability chosen.

Simulation models overcome this problem, not being constrained to use the normal distribution for expected market factors' changes (or assets' changes).

Historical simulation models use the actual distribution of returns taken from the past. Monte Carlo techniques require choosing a pdf to generate simulations. Obviously, one could always generate simulations based on market factors' returns normally distributed, but this would be of limited benefit over parametric methods, while adding a high degree of complexity. On the other hand, Monte Carlo techniques allow the generation of scenarios based on distributions other than on the normal distribution, so adding a high degree of realism to generated scenarios.

DEFINING THE APPROACH

Historical simulation is a simple, atheoretical approach that requires relatively few assumptions about the standard distributions of the underlying market factors. This method, although difficult to implement in a cost-effective manner if even the simplest derivatives are included, is the one most often chosen by regulators to set the optimal parameters for the "Building Block" approach because it is considered more robust and intuitive than other parametric or simulation methods.

The method is based on a three-step simulation technique using historical rate movements and is therefore intuitive:

1. Take a suitably long historical time series of market factors returns, $[Fj(t)]$ for t = $-T$, $-T + 1$, . . . , 0, typically three to five years of daily data, where Fj, is the vector of market factor j.
2. Given the series obtained in Step 1, calculate a time series of the change in value of the (current) portfolio of interest over the assumed liquidation period; to price single instruments included in the portfolio, use the actual price functions (e.g., the Black-Scholes or Garman-Kohlhagen formulas for simple options, zero-coupon discount functions for cash flows), or use any approximation based on delta or delta-gamma parameters. Obviously, this payoff function approximation step is optional if all the portfolio's transactions can be accessed and evaluated directly in an efficient manner.
3. Finally, tabulate the empirical return distribution generated from these historical rates and determine the appropriate risk capital for the portfolio by examining the extreme values of that distribution at the chosen level of probability.

ASSUMPTIONS OF HISTORICAL SIMULATION MODELS

This method makes very few assumptions about the market price processes generating the portfolio's returns: it simply assumes that market price innovations in the future are drawn from the same empirical distribution as those market price innovations generated historically. Using a statistical jargon, the only implicit assumption is that market factors' returns are generated by a stationary process, so that the pdf does not change—or does not change significantly—over time. The historical period selected for obtaining the time series of factors' returns can be misleading since it could arbitrarily include or exclude extreme price fluctuations such as the stock crash of 1987 or the EMS crisis of 1992.

On the other hand, by using the empirical distribution, analysts would avoid many of the problems inherent in explicitly modeling the evolution of market prices, such as that market prices tend to have fatter tails and be slightly more skewed than predicted by the normal distribution, the instability of volatilities and correlations.

In addition, few or no assumptions are made about the price functions (how prices of single instruments vary because of changes in market factors). Whenever possible, the whole portfolio is repriced using actual price functions. This implies that the actual payoff profile of the portfolio is captured globally, instead of being based on local approximations. If, for computational reasons, an approximating payoff profile is used, an approximation error is introduced in the model.

ADVANTAGES AND DISADVANTAGES OF HISTORICAL SIMULATION

Historical simulation has three intuitive advantages over parametric models:

1. The model's substance is extremely simple. Most of the time no parameter needs to be estimated and market factors' series are just those observed.
2. Actual distribution of market factors is fully captured. All the moments of the distribution (even those of higher order than the second) and the whole set of correlations among market factors are preserved in the simulation.
3. It is extremely easy to explain to top management.

About item 2, we should emphasize that if market factors are not normally distributed but their distribution is fairly stable over time, then historical simulation will provide better results than parametric models.

The historical simulation model has many drawbacks and weaknesses. The first—and perhaps most important—is that if the future distribution of market factors differs substantially from the historical distribution, computed results can be very misleading.

The second weakness is that historical simulation, like all simulation models, can be computationally intensive especially for a bank. In fact, it requires that:

- *All* the institution's positions are accessible by the same system in some form or another or, equivalently, that the organization have an institutionwide, transaction-oriented database. This presents certain challenges in itself for institutions that have to integrate a wide variety of legacy systems, or whose operations are geographically dispersed or that innovate new products frequently.
- All these transactions can be priced centrally on the back of this transaction database. Again, this may be a difficult task if new product structures are being introduced frequently and there may be a lead time before the new structures are implemented centrally.
- Substantial computing power should be available for calculating the empirical return distribution, essentially entailing the marking-to-market of the portfolio every day over the three-to five-year historical period to calculate a single risk capital number.
- Construction of an adequate historical time series of market rates. This method may therefore be difficult to apply in emerging markets with no history or when attempting to capture market risk factors that are not directly observable such as for rate volatilities and correlation-dependent options.

The last point deserves particular attention. If the number of observations from which market factors' returns are drawn is too low, then it is possible that the tails of the distribution cannot be defined with sufficient accuracy. If the sample time horizon is too short, extreme variations can be underestimated or overestimated when compared with the true distribution. On the other hand, if the sample period is too long, it becomes difficult to hypothesize the stationarity of the factors' distribution. Because of its simplicity and its intuitive appeal, historical simulation is used by important institutions.

The main advantage of this method, therefore, is that one does not inadvertently introduce model risk into the calculation of risk capital, except to the extent to which models of the stochastic behavior of market rates are required to calculate nonobservable parameters.

16

Monte Carlo
Simulation Models

In Chapter 15 we examined a simulation method based on actual past observations of asset prices or market factors' prices. In this way, it is possible to obtain n possible outcomes of the P&Ls of the portfolio and calculate the VaR on the basis of the observed P&Ls' distribution.

Monte Carlo simulation models are based on a similar philosophy, with the remarkable difference that assets' returns or market factors or returns[1] are not taken from past observation but simulated through a computer application.

The objective is to simulate n (10,000 indeed!) scenarios to obtain 10,000 outcomes of the value of the portfolio and, then, based on the distribution of calculated P&Ls, determine the VaR by cutting off the worst 500 outcomes (for a probability level of 95%) or the worst 100 observations (for a probability level of 99%).

Monte Carlo techniques overcome most of the problem encountered with parametric methods and with historical simulation models. Its main drawback is that it is highly computational-intensive since it requires thousands of different scenarios. On the other hand, because of its high flexibility, it can potentially account for a wide range of risk, including volatility risk and credit risk: in other words it can account for the most subtle form of risk: the model risk (i.e., the risk that the model used is in some way inadequate).

Monte Carlo simulation has been used by institutions such as Bankers Trust and BZW and is gaining popularity thanks to the growing availability of computing power. The analysis of all the technical aspects, especially the underlying mathematical and statistical background, is far beyond our scope. In this chapter, we take a quick look at the rationale of this technique and how it can be implemented for calculating the VaR of a given portfolio. As outlined in Chapter 12, Monte Carlo techniques are almost the only way to price complex exotic options for which a closed form still does not exist.

SIMULATING A SINGLE PRICE

The basic concept of Monte Carlo is to simulate repeatedly a random process for the financial variable of interest covering a wide range of possible situations. Thus simulation re-creates the entire distribution of portfolio values. As with parametric models, we start by analyzing a portfolio of a single asset and then extend our analysis to a multiple assets' portfolio.

Suppose we want to simulate the price path of a single asset (e.g., a stock or an equity index) using a simulation technique. The first, and most important step, is to choose the stochastic process that generates the price under examination. The most common model is the Geometric Brownian Motion (GBM), the continuous form of the random walk model.

The model assumes that innovations are uncorrelated over time and that small movements in prices can be described by Equation 16.1:

$$dS = \mu_t S_t d_t + \sigma_t S_t dz \tag{16.1}$$

where dz is a random variable distributed normally with mean zero and variance dt. This variable drives random shocks and does not depend on past information. The variance of this process continuously decreases with time and this rules out jumps. The parameters μ_t and σ_t represent instantaneous drift and volatility. They are usually supposed to be constant, but the model can be accommodated to allow conditional heteroskedasticity (see Chapter 7).

In practice, it is easier to work with the discrete form of Equation 16.1:

$$\Delta S_t = S_{t-1}\left(\mu \Delta t + \sigma \varepsilon \sqrt{\Delta t}\right)$$
$$S_t = S_{t-1} + S_{t-1}\left(\mu \Delta t + \sigma \varepsilon \sqrt{\Delta t}\right) \tag{16.2}$$

Both the mean and the variance of this process grows with time, as for Equation 16.1. Suppose that a stock follows the process described in Equation 16.2 with a daily drift of 0.8% and a daily volatility of 1%. We want to simulate the daily price path for 20 days with an initial price $S_0 = 100$. The first step is to generate a sequence of ε_t, that we suppose to be Gaussian with zero mean and unit variance. Then, applying

FIGURE 16.1   Price Path for a Random Walk with Drift

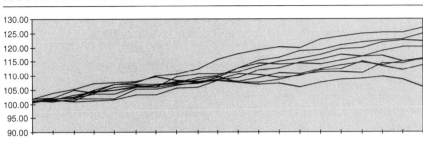

Equation 16.2 we must obtain a price path for 20 days. Replicating this simulation 10 times gives the outcomes represented in Figure 16.1.

Three caveats are at order:

1. Equation 16.2 is often expressed in log form, so that the ending price can never be negative.
2. The process described is only one of the possible processes that can describe the price path. A different process may produce different results. (See Appendix to Chapter 6.)
3. The probability distribution of the innovations has been chosen to be the standardized normal distribution. Monte Carlo simulation allows for different processes and distributions of the innovation terms, thus allowing for much more complex and interesting simulations.

SIMULATING ALTERNATIVE APPROACHES

We can now use different probability distributions and stochastic processes to analyze how the choice of these crucial variables can dramatically change the VaR for a single asset portfolio. Suppose we have a single stock in our portfolio with an initial price of 100 count unit. We want to calculate the 1-day VaR at 95% confidence level, assuming different probability distributions for the innovation term.

We are going to use the random walk with log returns (Equation 16.3)

$$\ln\left(P_t\right) = \ln\left(P_{t-1}\right) + \varepsilon_t \,(\text{random walk}) \qquad (16.3)$$

using three different probability distribution functions for the innovation term:

1. Normal distribution with zero mean and variance equal to 0.01.
2. Laplace (double exponential) distribution with location 0 and scale 0.01 (to allow for leptokurtosis).
3. Cauchy distribution with location 0 and scale 0.01.

The VaR has been calculated simulating 1,000 1-day innovations for the only stock in the portfolio. The results are illustrated in Table 16.1. The VaR has been computed by subtracting the price obtained for the 10th, 25th, and 50th worst observations from the original price. Transforming Equation 16.4, the price has been calculated as $100e^{\varepsilon}$.

The results are impressive. If innovations are generated by a normal process, the VaR is less than 50% than what it would be if the innovation term were generated by a fractal Cauchy distribution at a 95% level of probability. The loss would be underestimated by 10 times at a probability level of 99%, reflecting that larger events are more probable for fractal distributions. We find intermediate results for the finite variance leptokurtic Laplace distribution.

The power of Monte Carlo simulation stems from the ability to simulate different scenarios and incorporate features (such as fat tails) not encompassed by standard parametric models.

To better understand how the choice of a different stochastic process for modeling asset returns—and hence prices—may lead to different results, we tested three alternative models:

$$\ln\left(P_t\right) = \ln\left(P_{t-1}\right) + \varepsilon_t$$
$$r_t = +\varepsilon_t \quad \text{(random walk)} \tag{16.4}$$

$$r_t = 0.9 r_{t-1} + \varepsilon_t \quad [\text{AR(1)}] \tag{16.5}$$

$$r_t = 0.9 r_{t-1} + 0.02\, r_{t-1}\varepsilon_{t-1} + \varepsilon_t \quad [\text{BL(1,0,1,1)}] \tag{16.6}$$

TABLE 16.1   Comparison of VaR for a Single-Asset Portfolio with Different pdfs

Distribution	Normal	Laplace	Cauchy
VaR at 99%	2.21	4.06	23.31
VaR at 97.5%	1.99	2.96	9.78
VaR at 95%	1.71	2.26	4.26

TABLE 16.2 Comparison of VaR for a Single-Asset Portfolio with Different Stochastic Processes

Distribution	Random Walk	AR(1)	BL(1,0,1,1)
VaR at 99%	15.16	17.96	33.93
VaR at 97.5%	14.69	15.70	27.15
VaR at 95%	14.21	14.18	24.43

Using a popular spreadsheet, we drew out 100 innovation paths, each made up of 20 observations. The innovation term was drawn out from a normal distribution with zero mean and standard deviation equal to 0.02. For all the tested processes, the starting price was 100.

We computed 100 simulated paths for each model and we calculated the results at the end of day 20. The results are shown in Table 16.2. Notably, all the innovations were Gaussian, so the different results can be attributed only to the different stochastic process chosen. Compared with the RW, the AR(1) series shows up an higher VaR at the end of day 20. This may be because an autoregressive process—although mean reverting—shows longer swings around its unconditional mean (zero). The bilinear series looks more jagged than the random walk with higher jumps and bursts.

The conclusion is that simulation per se is not a panacea unless we have a good knowledge of the stochastic processes underlying, financial markets. Monte Carlo simulation techniques, although flexible, may be even more dangerous than historical simulation and may force unrealistic assumptions into the model.

CREATING A RANDOM SERIES OF INNOVATIONS

A common problem when dealing with Monte Carlo simulation is to draw out a random series of innovations from a given distribution. Usually the chosen distribution is the normal distribution, but that may not be the case. Nowadays, several packages allow the generation of long series of random numbers from a vast set of distributions. The results shown in Table 16.1 were obtained by drawing random numbers from three alternative distributions using Microsoft Minitab 10.1™ software. Although useful for our purposes, software never generates truly random numbers, but they incorporate deterministic algorithms with very long periods. Nevertheless, for our purposes we can consider these numbers as random.

An alternative approach can be applied when using spreadsheets. Every spreadsheet has a random function able to generate random numbers from 0 and 1. Using the inverse cumulative function, it is possible to draw out random numbers from any given distribution, provided it is included in the package.

For example, if a random number equal to 0.5 is drawn, the inverse functions for the standardized normal pdf will yield 0, since half of the pdf lies on the left of 0. If the random number was 0.95, the results of the inverse function would have been 1.645 and so on. This process can be applied to other distributions (beta, logistic, hypergeometric and so on) providing a great deal of flexibility during simulations.

Formally, once a random number x $(0,1)$ has been drawn, what is needed is to compute a corresponding number y $(-\infty; +\infty)$ such that $y = N^{-1}(x)$. This technique is also called the *transformation method*.

To avoid problems arising from pseudo-random algorithms one could draw—say—10 random number between 0 and 1 and then take the average. Although computationally expensive, this process should be able to wipe out any relic of determinism embedded in the algorithm.

SIMULATION WITH MULTIPLE VARIABLES

Rarely can we assume that a portfolio is made up of just one asset or that it is subject to only one source of financial risk. Most likely, the portfolio will have more correlated assets or will be subject to different risk factors (market factors) that, in general, will be correlated. In the simplest possible example, we can expect a purely domestic portfolio of equity, fixed-income securities and options to be subject to two market factors: interest rates and stock index returns. Generally, interest rates and stock index returns are negatively correlated, so it is highly unrealistic to simulate scenarios where the two series are uncorrelated (or independent).

If the two variables are uncorrelated, the randomization can be performed independently for each variable. If not, some form of adjustment must be performed. The most commonly used method is the *Cholesky decomposition*.

Suppose we have a vector of innovation $\{\varepsilon\}$ where $E(\varepsilon'\varepsilon) = \Sigma$. The Cholesky decomposition states that matrix Σ can be decomposed into PP' where P is a lower triangular matrix with zeros on the upper right corners. If we start with a vector of innovation $\{\eta\}$ where $\Sigma(\eta'\eta) = I$ (*white noise*), we can construct a vector of correlated innovation by multiplying the vector $\{\eta\}$ with the matrix P, so that $\varepsilon = P\eta$. Obviously $E(\varepsilon'\varepsilon) = E(P\eta\eta'P') = \Sigma$.

For two variables with two correlated variables Σ can be expressed as:

$$\varepsilon_1 = \eta_1 \tag{16.7}$$

$$\varepsilon_2 = \rho\eta_1 + \sqrt{\left(1-\rho^2\right)}\,\eta_2 \tag{16.8}$$

The formal procedure can be found in many finance textbooks.[2]

The procedure can be repeated as many times as needed. This explains how a multivariate set of random variables can be created from simple building blocks consisting of *iid* variables. Suppose, for example, we have an equally weighted portfolio consisting of two stocks. Each stock has an initial value of 100 count unit so the value of the portfolio is—at any point in time—just the sum of the values of the two stocks.

We tested three different "states of the world":

1. Correlation between the stocks equal to +0.5.
2. No correlation.
3. Correlation between the stocks equal to −0.8.

For each state of the world, we generated 100 scenarios consisting of the price path of each stock from day 0 to day +20. Our objective is to calculate VaR at 95% probability level.

We assume that the price of each stock follows Equation 16.3 so that $P_t = P_{t-1}e^{\eta}$.

We first generated 100 series of normally distributed uncorrelated random variables with zero mean and standard deviation equal to 0.02. Then, using Equations 16.8 and 16.9, we constructed two series of correlated innovations. This process was used for State 1 and State 3. For State 2, we simply used the original time series.

Using Equation 16.4, we generated 100 scenarios each with two price paths consisting of 20 observations and then we calculated the value of the portfolio after 20 days.[3] From the resulting empirical distribution, we cut off 5% of the outcomes and we found out VaR at 95% probability level.

According to financial theory, the lower the correlation the lower the risk and hence VaR. We expect that:

$$\text{VaR}(\rho = 0.5) > \text{VaR}(\rho = 0) > \text{VaR}(\rho = -0.8)$$

The results are shown in Table 16.3. The data provided conform to the financial theory confirming the validity of simulation models for modeling financial prices and returns.

TABLE 16.3   Comparison of VaR for Different Correlations

Distribution	$\rho = +0.5$	$\rho = 0$	$\rho = -0.8$
VaR at 95%	23.39	17.46	3.63

THE USE OF NON-NORMAL DISTRIBUTIONS IN MONTE CARLO SIMULATIONS

One of the most appealing features of the Monte Carlo technique is that it is possible to simulate data series (e.g., price paths) extracted from non-normal distributions. The problem for univariate distributions is easy, provided the desired distribution is known. In this case, it is possible to use the transformation method even with popular spreadsheets.

Nevertheless, actual probability distributions of returns rarely conform exactly to known distributions. Although unknown, actual distributions can be characterized by their sample moments. Usually only the first four moments (mean, standard deviation, skewness, and kurtosis) are taken into account. The final goal is to define a generalized probability density function that incorporates sample moments and that can be used for generating random data series.

An interesting approach was developed by Tuckey and later by other authors.[4] Tuckey starts by defining a random variable that depends on a given parameter λ and on a random number p ranging from 0 to 1.

The random variable is defined by what is known as *lambda function*. The lambda function is expressed by Equation 16.9:

$$R(p) = \frac{\left[p^\lambda - (1-p)^\lambda \right]}{\lambda} \tag{16.9}$$

The lambda function can be used in conjunction with a uniform random numbers generator, to simulate data series from almost any distribution.

A "generalized lambda function" has been provided:

$$R(p) = \lambda_1 + \frac{\left[p^{\lambda_3} - (1-p)^{\lambda_4} \right]}{\lambda_2} \tag{16.10}$$

where λ_1 is a location parameter, λ_2 is a scale parameter, and λ_3 and λ_4 are parameters for skewness and kurtosis. It is possible to define a vast variety of distributions just by varying the four lambda parameters. $R(p)$ represents a random variable depending on both the lambda parameters and p. Although a closed form for the cumulative distribution function does not exist, the probability density function for $R(p)$ is given by:

$$f[R(p)] = \frac{\lambda_2}{\left[\lambda_3 p^{\lambda_3 - 1} + \lambda_4 (1 - p)^{\lambda_4 - 1}\right]} \qquad (16.11)$$

The probability density function can be plotted by drawing a random number p and plugging this number into Equations 16.10 and 16.11 simultaneously.

Another interesting issue involves the generation of random numbers from multivariate non-normal distributions. In general, these distributions are not known and are estimated from actual data. For non-normal distributions, the Cholesky decomposition does not work, so a different approach is needed. BZW uses a methodology called *rank correlation*. The first step is to construct an $n \times d$ matrix with the n vectors of historical data of the variables to be simulated. The second step is to substitute the observations with their rank in every column.

Variables are then simulated according to their marginal distribution and a procedure based on rank correlation defines the relations among the simulated variables.

CALCULATING VaR

Monte Carlo technique differs from historical simulation about how data for simulation are generated. Historical simulation takes data from the past; this way it is able to capture all the existing relationships among instruments but at the same time requires the stationarity of the process generating actual data along time.

With Monte Carlo technique, we choose the stochastic process and the probability distribution that generate time series of interest and then we create an incredibly high number of scenarios to evaluate the P&Ls on the portfolio of interest. Once we can generate series with the desired correlations, the next choice is to decide how many series to generate. A possible choice would be to generate a series for each asset in the portfolio. From historical data, we can calculate the volatility of each instrument and the correlation with any other instrument in the portfolio. If we have N instruments, we should generate N correlated time series for say 10,000 times and obtain the payoff distribution for the portfolio of interest. In some ways, this approach resembles the asset-normal approach. A more common and by far more parsimonious approach is to generate the time series only for market factors. This allows reducing significantly the number of time series. In this case, the changes in value of any asset in the portfolio are usually evaluated through delta or delta-gamma approximation.

In simpler words, if we have a portfolio of N equities and bonds, we could generate only two time series (stock index and interest rate structure) and evaluate the portfolio using the techniques examined in Chapters 10 and 11. An even different approach would involve repricing the whole portfolio via direct price functions. This would mean, for example, using the Black-Scholes formula for options or the discounted cash flows for fixed income bonds. Direct repricing, nevertheless, substantially increases the computational burden required for performing the simulation since it must be performed for every generated scenario.

MODELING THE TERM STRUCTURE OF INTEREST RATES

One of the major weaknesses of the Monte Carlo simulation technique is its reliance on the stochastic process that generates the price path of the variable under exam. If the process is unrealistic, so will be the simulations. So far, we have examined stochastic processes aimed at describing the behavior of stock prices or stock indexes. We need to look more closely at the stochastic process generating the dynamics of interest rates.

Usually the term structure of interest rates is defined so that it involves only one source of uncertainty, the short-term interest rate i. These models are called "one-factor models" and are the most widely used in financial modeling of interest rates. They are aimed at deriving a process for the short-term risk-free rate i and then at exploring what the process implies for bonds and option pricing. The key underlying assumption is the hypothesis of risk neutrality. Once we have fully defined the process for i under this hypothesis, we have fully defined everything about the initial term structure and how it can evolve at all future times.

One of the first models of term structure of interest rate was the Rendleman-Bartter[5] defined by Equation 16.12:

$$di = \mu \, i \, di + \sigma \, r \, dz \tag{16.12}$$

This means that i follows a GBM with a drift equal to μ and a constant volatility equal to σ. The assumption that short-term interest rates behave like a stock price is less than satisfactory since it does not take into account the well-known phenomenon of mean reversion: interest rates appear to be pulled back to some long-run average level. When i is high, mean reversion tends to cause a negative drift; when i is low, mean reversion tends to cause a positive drift.

An alternative model that takes into account the mean reversion is the Vasicek model. The risk-neutral process for i is defined by Equation 16.13:

$$di = a(b - i)\, dt + \sigma\, dz \tag{16.13}$$

The short rate is pulled back to level b at rate a. Superimposed on this pull is a normally distributed stochastic term $\sigma\, dz$. The price at time t of a zero-coupon bond that pays 1 unit of count at time T is given by

$$P(t,T) = A(t,T)e^{-B(t,T)r(t)} \tag{16.14}$$

where $A(t,T)$ and $B(t,T)$ depend the parameters a,b and σ. What is interesting is that $R(t,T)$, the continuously compounded interest rate at time t for a term $T - t$, is given by

$$R(t,T) = \left(\frac{1}{T-t}\right)\ln A(t,T) + \left(\frac{1}{T-t}\right)B(t,T)\, i(t) \tag{16.15}$$

implying that the whole term structure is determined as a function of $i(t)$ once $a,b,$ and σ have been chosen. Depending on these parameters, the curve can be upward sloping, downward sloping, or humped. The value of $i(t)$ determines the level of the term structure at time t.

A further refining of the Vasicek model, prohibiting short-term rate to be negative, is the model proposed by Cox, Ingersoll, and Ross. The risk-neutral process for i in their model is

$$di = a(b - i)\, dt + \sigma\sqrt{i}\, dz \tag{16.16}$$

This model has the same mean reverting behavior of the Vasicek model, but it also has a standard deviation proportional to $\sqrt{i}$. This means that as the short-term interest rate increases, its standard deviation increases.

Bond prices have the same general form as in Vasicek's model (Equations 16.12–16.13) but the terms $A(t,T)$ and $B(t,T)$ are different. As in the case of Vasicek's model, upward sloping, downward sloping, and humped curve are possible.

Monte Carlo experiments consist of first simulating movements in short-term interest rates, then using the simulated term structure to price the securities at the target date. Remarkably, since the term structure is continuous over time, there is no need of cash flow mapping into predefined buckets, but cash flows can be discounted at their own maturity.

CONCLUSION

The Monte Carlo technique is by far the most powerful and flexible method for calculating VaR. Its main advantages are:

- The large number of scenarios generated provide a more reliable and comprehensive measure of risk than analytic models.
- It captures convexity of nonlinear instruments and changes in volatility and time.
- It can be used to simulate several alternative hypotheses about returns' behavior (white noise, autoregressive, bilinear, etc.) and distribution of returns/innovations.

Its main disadvantages are:

- Its reliance on the stochastic process specified or historical data selected to generate estimates of the final value of the portfolio and hence of the VaR.
- Its impressive requirement in terms of computing power that makes calculation often very time-consuming (several hours). This fact may lead to the use of alternative methods for calculating VaR for a trading portfolio.

NOTES

1. Monte Carlo simulation technique can be used to perform a simulation on either single-asset returns or market-factors returns.

2. For example, P. Jorion, *Value at Risk*, New York: McGraw-Hill, 1997, 243.

3. For further reference, see J.P. Morgan, *RiskMetrics Technical Documentation*, Chapter 7.

4. J. Ramberg, P. Tadikamalla, E. Dudewicz, and E. Mykyta, "A Probability Distribution and Its Uses in Fitting Data," *Technometrics*, 1979, vol. 21, 201–214.

5. For a review of these models, see J. Hull, *Options, Futures and Other Derivatives*, Englewood Cliffs, NJ: Prentice-Hall, 1997.

17

Final Remarks:
Limits of VaR

VaR is not a panacea, nor can it be considered the final solution for measuring and controlling market risk, although it represents a quantum leap compared with previously used market risk measures. The greatest advantage is that it provides a single, easily understandable number in a unified and consistent framework measuring market risk for a whole portfolio made up of many complex instruments.

This chapter is devoted to analyzing the limits of VaR. Drawbacks of VaR can be divided into two main groups:

1. Limits intrinsic to the concept of VaR.
2. Limits due to the statistical methodology used to implement VaR.

VaR is a statistical measure of market risk. Conceptually, the only limitations it has are related to its purpose. Problems arise when we pass from the statistical concept to the practical implementation of the concept through specific methodologies. We review the limitations VaR has for managing banking risk and the main problems arising when translating this concept into a number.

LIMITS OF VaR

VaR Is Only for Traded Assets or Liabilities

Although VaR is gaining increasing popularity in financial institutions, its main drawback is that it covers only a limited set of risks. In particular, it covers market risk that, by definition, is limited to traded assets and liabilities. Only traded instruments have a continuously recorded market price that can be statistically measured and modeled. This is not the case for nontraded assets/liabilities, such as deposits or loans. The process of securitization will most likely reduce the nontraded assets to a total assets ratio but nontraded assets will remain an important portion of a bank's balance sheet. When facing interest rate risk, banks are often more concerned with the impact of interest rate changes on the margin of interest than on the price impact on traded instruments. In many respects, techniques like A&LM, examined in Chapter 2, provide much more useful information for top management than VaR. This is not true for institutions whose main business is to manage traded assets, such as mutual funds, hedge funds, and pension funds. Market risk is the main risk they face, and VaR is a comprehensive measure of their core-business risk.

VaR Measures Only Market Risk and Not Credit Risk

What banks need is an integrated instrument for measuring and managing all kinds of risk or, at least, their core business risks. Banks core business risks are *both credit risk and market risk*. They need to manage both the price risk they can incur on their portfolio of traded assets due to market factors' changes and the risk of default on nonsecuritized lines of credit. Consulting firms and investment banks are getting more and more aware of this need; J.P. Morgan has recently developed CreditMetrics™, a model aimed at managing credit risk. It is also most likely that some, if not many, market risk factors are also credit risk factors. For example, interest rate is both a market factor and a credit risk factor, especially for rolling lines of credit or indexed loans. Although credit risk models replicating RiskMetrics' methodology are under development, a unique measure of risk is needed incorporating both the probable loss on traded instruments and the probable loss (unpaid interest or principal) on nontraded loans. This is one of the most interesting fields of research toward a really integrated risk management system.

VaR Does Not Take into Account Liquidity Risk

One of VaR's greatest limitations is that it does not take into account liquidity risk. More appropriately, we should say that current methodologies are not able to fully incorporate liquidity risk. The problem can be particularly important for instruments traded in thin markets, where the buying or sales of relatively small quantities of a single instrument can cause large price variations. So, although the estimated loss, based on historical data, can be assessed ex ante, the ex-post loss may be much greater since it can be difficult to find a buyer, or large discounts may be needed to place the sale. A possible approach is to use the "orderly liquidation time horizon" for calculating the undiversified VaR for each instrument. VaR is calculated with the same time horizon for all instruments in the portfolio, so undiversified VaR can be underestimated when the time horizon is shortened and the variance scaled down using the standard square root rule.

This is particularly important because instruments traded in emerging markets can experience significant losses when sold. A possible approach is to use highly leptokurtic expected distribution of returns, based on real historic data. But, as discussed, departure from the hypothesis of normality leads to computational difficulties difficult to overcome. An arbitrarily chosen penalty factor can be included to artificially increase the estimated VaR using the standard asset-normal or delta-normal approach. Nevertheless, it seems to be far from the optimal solution.

VaR Only Measures Risk for Unusual but Normal Events

VaR cannot be used for measuring the expected loss for extremely unlikely market factors' changes. VaR is designed to measure risk for unusual but normal market fluctuations. Although a 2σ event is unusual, it cannot be considered rare. In a year, daily returns are expected to exceed 2σ about seven to eight times. These can still be considered a normal condition, where financial theory and statistical tools still work fairly well. Nevertheless, we do not know exactly what happens in extreme situations, for example, a 5σ or a 9σ event. In these cases, the rules we know simply break down. We enter into a world of unstable relationships where the framework we were used to does not exist. We can draw a parallel with physics: there is some point where theory breaks down. These points are called singularities. For example the Big Bang is such a singularity. At the exact moment of the Big Bang, physical laws break down and we cannot explain the event. There are some moments where market crashes resemble singularities: the structure of correlations collapses, relationships break down, and market behavior becomes totally unpredictable. Anyway, this is not a limit of VaR models. It is a consequence of our imperfect knowledge of capital markets.

LIMITS OF VaR METHODOLOGIES

An old adage says that there are lies, damned lies, and statistics. This is partially true. Statistics is the science (I prefer to say the "art") of approximation. A poet who lived in Rome in the nineteenth century defined statistics as that strange science which states, "If you have eaten two chickens and I am starving, we both have eaten one chicken each." The point at hand is that VaR is based on statistical assumptions and methodologies. If these assumptions are unrealistic or the methodologies are not able to capture the complexity of real-world financial markets, this is not a limit of VaR as a conceptual approach for measuring and controlling VaR but a failure of the statistical methods used. This point sometimes generates misunderstandings. For example, it is sometimes claimed that VaR is unrealistic because of the assumption of normality of market factors returns. Again, this is not a limit of VaR but a limit of our statistical capability to deal with distributions other than the normal distribution even when it is clear that normality "is not the norm!" In this section, we briefly summarize the most important statistical weaknesses of common VaR methodologies. Many of them have been outlined in previous chapters but here we take a closer look at some of them.

Seductive but Dangerous

In an article in the *Financial Analyst Journal*[1] entitled "VaR: Seductive but Dangerous," T. Beder analyzed three portfolios and calculated VaR using eight different methodologies (in particular historical simulation and Structured Monte Carlo with different structures of correlations and holding periods). She found out the eight methodologies provided eight different results. It should not sound strange; on the contrary, it is definitively normal. The statistical assumptions on which each of these models is based are so different that different results are perfectly normal. That's why we devoted Chapter 5 to the analysis of the statistical foundations of financial modeling for VaR purposes. From a managerial standpoint, CEOs can doubt the reliance of VaR numbers provided by their staff if different models provide different results. We must keep in mind that VaR numbers are only *estimates.* Financial markets—but we can say the whole world—are regulated by stochastic patterns that are still basically unknown. VaR models are aimed at reducing this uncertainty providing a scientifically based model to derive our predictions. It is not, and it could not, provide perfect forecasts, simply because the future is unknown for all people except magicians and witches. This does not mean that research has reached a point where no further efforts are required. On the contrary, we can do much to better our forecasting capabilities, but we have to realize that, in any case, we are moving in a stochastic rather than in a deterministic world.

Linear Models: Local Approximation for Large Variations

Some weaknesses of VaR models have been already encountered. The first and most important limitation of nonsimulation models is that they rely on local measures of price risk to estimate VaR for large variations.

For example, the δ of an option provides a reasonable approximation of option price changes due to very small price changes of the underlying asset. VaR is calculated for price changes equal to 1.65σ (at 95% probability level) or 2.57σ (at 99% probability level). We use a local measure, by definition valid only locally, to estimate price changes due to large although not exceptional price changes (i.e., price changes that take place 5 times out of 100 or 1 time out of 100). There is an evident inconsistency between the premises on which local measures are constructed and the use analysts make of them. Quadratic approximations do not provide any conceptual benefit because they only reduce the prediction error, but they still are local measures. In addition, the larger the variations of market factors, the larger the prediction error just when good risk management systems gain a fundamental importance.

There is an obvious trade-off between simplicity and accuracy. The simpler a model the less accurate predictions it provides. When choosing a particular methodology, one must always be aware of the limitations and drawbacks of that methodology. For example, J.P. Morgan suggests not to use RiskMetrics (asset-normal methodology) if the portfolio is highly optionalized. It does not mean that the VaR approach is not valid for options: it only means that asset-normal methodology is not satisfactory when dealing with highly nonlinear payoffs' profiles such as those of options. Simulation techniques, on the other hand, work exceptionally well even with nonlinear payoffs' profiles.

The problem is that targets can be reached only when appropriate tools are available. If the target is to have a quick and dirty assessment of VaR, linear models are valid also for options. If we want a precise measure, we must add quadratic terms or simulation techniques.

Normality

The most common, almost exclusive, assumption about the distribution of log returns is that they follow a normal distribution. Empirical evidence from at least 30 years has shown that stock returns are not normally distributed. Large events are more likely to occur than predicted by the normal distribution. Returns' distributions have fatter tails than the normal distribution. Some (even Mandelbrot and Fama) have assumed that returns follow Pareto-stable (fractal) distributions which have the "interesting feature" of having an infinite variance. The point is, we either still rely on the assumption of normality, and hence must accept significant approximation errors and underestimation of the probability of large events to occur or we choose a different distribution to model financial returns. Some timid efforts have been made to introduce finite-variance leptokurtic distribution such as the t-distribution into financial models, but we are still at the sunset of this approach. There are two main problems when we relax the hypothesis of normality:

1. From a statistical point of view, we do not know how to deal with non-normal distributions in an acceptable easy way.
2. From a financial point of view, we should consider most of the financial theory as slightly more than garbage.

From a statistical point of view, the normal distribution is, at the same time, a limit and a stable factor. In addition, manipulation of normally distributed random variables is incredibly easy and convenient. It is a limit distribution since the linear combination of non-normally distributed random variables (provided they have finite mean and variance) is (asymptotically) a normally distributed variable. It is stable since the sum of any number of normally distributed random variables is a normally distributed random variable. As discussed in Chapter 9, the normal distribution is a threshold fractal distribution, since it is a stable distribution with finite variance.

The central limit theorem has generated the strange conviction that natural and social phenomena should be normally distributed as if it were a law from God! Not only is this obviously not true, but that the normal distribution is the norm is also false. The normal distribution seems to be, at least in financial economics, the exception rather than the norm, it is the "exceptional" rather than the "normal" distribution.

Finally, one of the most appealing features is that two moments are able to fully characterize the distribution. If a distribution is assumed to be normal, knowing just the mean and the variance is enough to fully characterize the whole distribution. No other parameters are needed, and notably if two normally distributed random variables are uncorrelated, they are also statistically independent. All these features have made the normal distribution popular among academicians and analysts. It is often claimed that, even if returns are not normally distributed, the normal distribution constitutes a reasonable approximation. But the normal distribution is not able to account for large variations. For example, for a normal distribution, an event larger than 4σ has a probability to occur equal to 0.003%. For a t-distribution with 10 degrees of freedom the probability of the same event is 0.126% (42 times larger) as can be seen from Table 17.1.

Again, one could well wonder if these limitations threaten the validity of VaR. The answer is no; the assumption of normality can invalidate some models used for calculating VaR, but not the utility of a measure of market risk such as VaR.

TABLE 17.1   Probability of a 4σ+ Event for a t Distribution

1	7.798%
2	2.860
3	1.400
4	0.807
5	0.516
10	0.126
15	0.058
20	0.035
50	0.010
100	0.006
1,000	0.003
Normal	0.003

Why SMC with Normal Distributions?

The problem of the distribution of returns becomes particularly intriguing when we refer to the Monte Carlo technique. Monte Carlo technique is flexible enough to incorporate any kind of distribution of assets' returns. Almost invariably, the normal distribution is used. It is quite incredible that a technique that would allow the use of different and more realistic distributions is used assuming normality of returns. There is a specific reason for that. While it is relatively easy to generate normal correlated series using the Cholesky decomposition of the correlation matrix, this is much more difficult if the distribution is not normal. Since there is no consensus about the distribution of assets' returns, the normal distribution remains the standard. Nevertheless, the increase in accuracy obtained using Monte Carlo simulation techniques—often used as a benchmark for other methodologies—shows that the accuracy of VaR calculation is a statistical, not a conceptual problem.

Conclusion: Never Forget Common Sense

Forecasting is the science (or art) of predicting the future. It shares the final goals with divination. VaR is a product of this divination. Our final remark is a word of caution. We have examined the statistical and financial background of VaR methodologies because it was a necessary step for understanding the pros and cons of such an approach for measuring and managing market risk. Judgment becomes a key issue since it can incorporate the intuition and experience that models cannot. Our final caveat is taken from the preface to *RiskMetrics Technical Documentation:* "We remind our readers that no amount of sophisticated analytics will replace experience and professional judgment in managing risk." Although it may seem a discouraging conclusion, it shows that there is still a long way to go and a huge amount of research to perform. Risk managers, financial analysts, and researchers can remain calm: their jobs are still relatively safe!

NOTE

1. Tanya Beder, "VaR: Seductive but Dangerous," *Financial Analyst Journal,* 1995, 12-24.

Index